NO SILVER SPOON

NO SILVER SPOON

by

FRANK LEONARD BUNN

O.B.E., K.P.M.

In gratitude to
my old Chief, the late
A. R. Ellerington
Ex-Chief Constable of St. Helens
A Leader by Example

Published by F. L. Bunn.
Printed in England by J. Brock Ltd., Stoke-on-Trent.

Contents

Introduction

This book embraces some of the personal experiences of my life, as well as reminiscences and opinions interwoven with those of other people, friends, acquaintances, companions and advisers whom I met during childhood and up to the time when it became necessary, for obvious and various reasons, that I should think and act on my own initiative.

Like the great majority of boys, I got into unnecessary mischief. When my parents heard of my trespasses against my elders by my 'playful' ways, they asked me a question or two and judged me from the colour of my face, and were never wrong. They were never too strict with me, but they seemed to know when I had qualified for a 'tanning' which they proceeded to award before they forgot its necessity.

I deserved all I received.

My father talked to me occasionally, and taught me to love my country. He tried to teach me to love music, but I 'let him down', and have been sorry for my mistake. My hope is that any boy given the chance to learn something for his own good - outside politics - will take it.

When I was ten years of age circumstances of my own making, provided me a timely deterrent rightfully inflicted by a man who had been to the Klondike. It was good for me.

That same year, a war broke out, and a good many of my schoolboy friends had brothers serving in various regiments. All of us at once became 'soldiers' and had much fun not enjoyed by real soldiers and sailors.

At the age of 14, I became a 'Number-catcher'. In my spare time, I learned the rudiments of Soldiering in the Volunteer battalion of the Norfolk Regiment quartered in my home town. My attestation-papers recorded me a 'man'.

When 16, a few months on the Marine Society's training ship "Warspite" did me good. Among other things I learned that 'the best boxers' were not allowed to be outside the ring.

INTRODUCTION

I tell how I became a real soldier, some of my experiences, all enjoyable, under good officers, at home and abroad without anything to brag about.

My career as a policeman commenced just before Christmas 1911, when, on my transfer to the Army Reserve, I became a constable in the Great Eastern Railway Police at Liverpool-street, London, and I tell of my 'arrest' on the first day of duty.

I make mention of some of my experiences as a railway policeman in London and at Cambridge, with hope that they will be found of interest.

From October, 1912, when I joined the Norfolk Constabulary, until 1955, circumstances - of my own choosing - caused me to serve in six other and separate police forces, eight in all. It was in my last police appointment that I experienced difficulties which are described and were overcome. These difficulties are mentioned because I believe them to have been unique.

I

My Early Days

When I was old enough to understand what was being said to me I found that I had five brothers and two sisters. Later, two more brothers, three years apart, joined the family.

The eldest brother, Charles Frederick, who was sixteen years my senior held positions in the railway service during the whole of his working life.

The second eldest, Arthur, whom we didn't see very often, was an apprentice in the Mercantile Marine and sailed in those magnificent square-sailed Clipper ships to and from Australia and China.

Another brother, George Victor, who had been a boy clerk in a solicitor's office, died from typhoid when I was five. In his spare time he rode a penny-farthing bicycle, and was a gunner in the Artillery Volunteers.

Ernest was the only one of us with a wish to become an engine driver, though I had sometimes thought about becoming one, but only because such a man was able to get a lot of free rides. In those days railway engines were kept clean!

Brother Bill, was a bit of a lad who became a baker and confectioner. When seventeen years of age he joined the Rifle Volunteers and wanted to fight the Boers, but he was disappointed. I liked all my brothers, but Bill, three years my senior, was the only one I fought with. He always won.

Gordon Septimus, younger than me, and Oscar Valentine, the baby brother, and I, were the ones who caused mother the most trouble, though I suppose the others had been nuisances to her in their infancy.

Now what can a lad say about his sisters? Mine were all right! But there were occasions on which they thought that I had qualified for a clip on the ear; they didn't care which ear it was.

Mother was fairly tall, had beautiful blue eyes and was

1

of soft and healthy complexion, and distinguished, dignified bearing.

She was the youngest of a very large family, and had married at the age of seventeen.

A good cook, she fed her family as well as circumstances permitted, on the wages handed to her by father who, often being out of work, seldom earned more than thirty shillings per week, though as a teacher of music he had a number of pupils whose parents paid him half-a-guinea a quarter. But though mother was aware of the small fee father received as Organist and Choir-master, no part of it came her way nor did she expect it to.

According to mother, father was akin to Mister Micawber, whose constant expectations seldom materialised.

That father was a patient man was plain to me, he tried to teach me the rudiments of music. When father was out and I was practising those excercises which he had set me, I was disobedient and in a one-finger composition of my own played 'God Save the Queen', and stuck at it until mother came to warn me that while I was proving myself a very loyal subject of Her Majesty, my father would expect me to get on with his instructions, or else.

For some reason - probably a very sill one - I didn't take to music, and, my father's patience becoming exhausted, he decided that I was not an apt pupil.

My parents had known better days, and were of good education.

My grandfather, on the distaff side, had been a ship-owner in a small way, and was a wealthy man until he lost most of his money in a Bank failure, before I was born.

In those days, thirteen thousand pounds amounted to a large fortune, which, being lost in one fell stroke, must have been a catastrophe.

*   *   *

At the age of nine, of my own volition, I commenced to earn a shilling on Saturdays, by acting as a caddie on the local golf-links, and it was with a feeling of pride that I handed my earnings to mother.

My contribution to the family exchequer, though meagre, was most welcome.

Sixpence per round of eighteen holes which took about three hours to complete, was recognised and accepted as the rate for the job for boys of school age, and I saw no ground for complaint.

It is fair, however, to acknowledge the fact that players employing boys of tender age used to reduce the number of clubs for such lads to carry, and that there was a chance of receiving a threepenny tip at the end of the day. But a caddie would require to be a super-optimist to expect such a gratuity on all occasions.

Like most other lads, I got into unnecessary mischief. But when I was ten, a splendid deterrent came my way, quite unexpectedly and deservedly.

The person responsible for inflicting the deserved deterrent was an unfortunate individual who was reputed to have been to the Klondike, where with thousands of others he had searched for gold with little success to reward his efforts; the lack of success being described as 'fanny adams'.

The unfortunate man of whom I write, was known by two nicknames, Odd 'un and Odd leg.

He was certainly odd in appearance. Not a robust man, he was bent and round-shouldered. And on most occasions when seen in public, he was pushing a handcart laden with baskets of laundry, which he was delivering to their owners on behalf of his wife, a hardworking woman who took in washing for a livelihood.

Odd 'un, when in the streets, attracted to himself the attention of playful boys by continually chanting: "I don't eat more than old cock-sparrer, yet the old lady grumbles". And after a slight pause, he would continue: "She says I'm 'oggish".

On an occasion which I couldn't possibly forget, I was assaulted by Mister Odd 'un and thoroughly deserved the punishment, the effects of which I felt for some minutes.

I had rudely called out his nickname, and having taken cover at the corner of a low wall, I imagined that he wouldn't discover my hiding-place. But I was mistaken! The wall was the only bit of cover in the vicinity, so naturally, it was there that Mister Odd 'un came to find his tormentor.

As I peeped round the corner to make another call of derision, Mister Odd 'un and I came face to face, and in a flash I received a powerful short-armed jab on my chest, causing me some alarm as I fell back on my bottom, with a gasp.

This incident was a distinct lesson to me and did me quite a lot of good. It brought me down to size and was a deterrent of the right kind, received at an opportune time.

Mister Odd 'un had no more rudeness or trouble from me; in fact, though I say it myself, I became a well-behaved lad, and, from then on, was able to prevent other boys annoying him.

On looking back to this occurrence, I have excused myself by remembering that I was then only ten years of age and that in those days boys were compelled to find their own fun and play their games in the streets to a much greater extent than is the case today, though it was much safer to be in the streets in the 'old days' because the internal-combustion engine hadn't come into general use to add risks on the roads to pedestrians and others as those existing nowadays.   But I feel that at the beginning of the twentieth century there was greater temptation to juveniles - especially boys - to become delinquents than exists today; yet more excuses are being urged as reasons for juvenile delinquency than were ever made before when temptations were greater and educational facilities were much less.

I am sure that my encounter with Mister Odd 'un and the lesson he gave me, was the actual deterrent that brought about a change in my general conduct.   My mother thought so too, for I heard her say that to her it seemed that I was developing a conscience, a fact which gave her pleasure.

However, it must not be thought that I had suddenly become angelic.

About that period I was accepted as a chorister at the church where my father had previously been organist and choir-master.

The vicar, a kindly man, was also a disciplinarian. This was, I think, an essential trait in one having supervision of boys who are likely to get up to mischief whenever an opportunity presents itself.

One Sunday evening I was a minute late in my arrival at church and found the vicar and choir in formation.   My 'punishment' consisted of a frown from the vicar accompanied by an order to assist in pumping air to the organ.

The boy manning the pump was Walter Fenton, a school pal of mine.   Walter was proud of his job for he knew of its importance.   It was clear to me that he resented my presence, for when I asked him to let me 'have a go' at the pump, he refused.   A scuffle ensued, the organ developed a kind of cough and the organist got into difficulties for a moment or so.

When the service had ended and Walter and I were in the vestry preparing for home, the vicar gave us a sermon which indicated, very clearly to both of us, what was likely to happen in certain circumstances.   I explained the cause of the bother, and Walter was exonerated.   Walter became a soldier, served in India and paid the extreme sacrifice in the first World War.

4

NO SILVER SPOON

When I was ten years of age the South African War broke out, and many of my schoolboy friends had brothers who had 'gone to the front'. And there was great excitement.

The yarns told by my young friends about the marvellous and daring exploits of their brethren were extraordinary feats of imagination, and there was tremendous rivalry among the tale-tellers for supremacy, and it seemed that the news was coming each morning straight from the battlefields.

We all pretended to be soldiers, did our drill, put up earthworks, manned trenches and threw stones at the gang who had taken up their position opposite our own, until casualties caused a howl or two and a white - or nearly white handkerchief was displayed.

In those days, all boys were told that it was the duty of every man to defend his country when called upon. Many lads couldn't wait to be called, and as soon as it was possible they enlisted as buglers, trumpeters or drummers in the various arms of the fighting services, on reaching the age of fourteen.

I remember reading of Bugler Dunne of the Royal Dublin Fusiliers, who lost his bugle in action.

Queen Victoria called him home and commanded him to visit her. When Her Majesty asked him if he had a particular wish, Bugler Dunn said: "I would like to find my bugle! Her Majesty told him there was no need for him to go back to South Africa; and she presented him with a new one. It bore a silver plate, suitably inscribed. I had the pleasure of seeing it a year or so later, when I was sixteen.

*   *   *

My working life commenced when I attained the age of fourteen. My first job was that of a boy-clerk and 'number catcher' on the Great Eastern Railway, at Southtown, Great Yarmouth, at a wage of six shillings a week. Money was money in those days, and with my spending allowance of sixpence per week, I was happy and contented.

I spent one-third of my allowance in the purchase of 'The Union Jack' which told of the skill shown by a private detective named Sexton Blake, a man who never made a mistake. His powers of deduction were almost supernatural; and all the slow-witted, slow gaited and sluggish police were required to do was to place a hand on the shoulder of the world's worst criminals of all types whom he had run to earth, and handed over to them.

5

It seemed that if Sexton Blake expressed his opinion that alleged offenders were guilty, it _was_ so. And no evidence was required.

It went without saying, of course, that this brilliant investigator, whose services were in great demand by Governments and kings, was almost perpetually in extreme danger. And though adept at disguising himself, particularly clever miscreants had ability to suspect his presence in the most isolated and remote places in the world.

Perhaps it was because he had a particular kind of smell about his clothing or the odour from a special brand of tobacco he used; but only international criminals knew of such clues. But their fear of him was so great that they made themselves scarce in the hope of escaping his clutches, only to find themselves in the net so cleverly set for them in consequence of having left at the scene of their crime, a clue of such a nature that nobody except Sexton could have recognised as one leading to their identity.

I think that it was the reading of these sensational stories of hazardous adventure, skill and endurance, that engendered in me the desire to become a police officer; and, like most aspirants to the police service, I wished to be a detective thinking, no doubt, that I would turn out to be a brilliant one. At any rate, I made up my mind, that if fortunate enough to become a member of any Criminal Investigation Department, my aim would be to show that as a body of individuals, the police could not possibly be as dumb, daft and clumsy as depicted in fiction.

I didn't expect a detective's life to be easy or that all would be plain sailing. But Blake's alleged exploits made me think.

I began to wonder whether a boy of my age could be apprenticed to criminal investigation; but upon making inquiries as to the possibility, I learned that first of all - when old enough I would have to start as an ordinary uniformed constable. This fact was a set-back to my wishes, but my informant, the father of a boyfriend who was a detective inspector explained why such an arrangement was absolutely necessary, for there was much to learn before a police officer was called into a witness-box, to give evidence. For before a criminal can be brought to justice there must be evidence sufficient to substantiate the charge and which must be given in accordance with the Rules of Evidence as laid down by law.

And I have since learned how important it is to work one's

Beat with a view to the prevention of crime.

As I was then only fourteen years of age, many years were to pass before I could realise my ambition.

For two years I followed my employment with the Great Eastern Railway Company at Great Yarmouth, and at the age of sixteen, owing to the fact that several of my friends had joined the Royal Navy, while others had enlisted as boys in various branches of the Army, I was becoming restless and lonely, so much so, that I desired to follow their example one way or another.

It was, I think, the ultra-smart uniform worn by the boy-soldiers as Trumpeters in the Cavalry and Royal Horse Artillery together with the added attraction of their jingling spurs, plus the exciting yarns they told of their feats of 'rough riding' without saddles or stirrups, that made me think first of becoming a soldier, but my parents had other views, however, and, as a compromise, persuaded me to join the local Rifle Volunteers, in which they thought I would be able to obtain some kind of idea of what Army-life was like.

They were right, of course, but some time later a friend of mine advised me to do as he had done. So, with the consent of my parents, I applied for admission to the Training Ship "Warspite" then available to boys of good character who aspired to a career at sea.

The formalities completed, I was ready for my first indeterminate trip from home. The conditions which had been accepted for me were that I should undertake training for a year to fit me for service in the mercantile marine, but if during that period I wanted to join the Royal Navy, my wish would be gratified.

When the day of my departure from home arrived, my mother acted as I feared she would. Amid her tears, she asked me to excuse her inability to come to the station with me, and encouraged me to make the best efforts to learn and succeed.

My father saw me off, but not before giving me advice which I have found useful during the whole of my working-life.

"Now, boy", he said, "it is very certain that there will be occasions on which you will wonder whether or not you were wise in taking this step". I hoped that father would not have the time to continue talking, for a kind of a sinking feeling was coming over me. But there was more to come.

He reminded me that I wouldn't draw any wages, and among other matters he touched upon he expressed the opinion that on "Warspite" I would be required to do tasks

which I had never had to perform at home. Just as the
guard unfurled his flag, my father said: "Lest I forget,
judging from my own experience in life, it is worthwhile
listening to advice, since you can reject any part which
doesn't meet your approval". In a hurried manner, he said:
"Keep a stiff upper lip". It was then that my own - as
well as his - began to quiver.

ON THE TRAINING SHIP 'WARSPITE'

Arriving in London, I made my way to the office of The
Marine Society, to whom the training ship belonged. There
I joined a number of youths from various parts of the
country; all intent upon becoming sailors. Each of us was
ushered into a large room in which sat some elderly gentlemen with weather-beaten faces, who asked us several questions
the principal one being: "Why do you wish to go to sea?".
When the interviews were over, we were placed in charge
of an officer from the ship, and marched to Cannon-street,
where we entrained for a journey of about twenty miles to
Northfleet, Kent, where our ship lay at anchor, about a
quarter of a mile from shore. We were first taken to a
shore establishment on the side of the river, where each of
us was issued a full kit of uniform similar to that worn by
ratings of the Royal Navy. But before changing into it we
had to take a cold bath - a large swimming bath - in the
presence of the officer in charge of us. It was rather a
dull day and chilly. While we were undressing, the officer
disappeared for a moment or so. He returned carrying a
bucket of hot water. In a sharp voice he asked for our
attention. He then threw the hot water into the swimming-
bath, and said: "It's not as cold as it was". And in proof
of his statement he pointed to the spot at which his
contribution had struck the surface, where for a moment
vapour was to be seen.
Here, I thought, is one officer who has a sense of humour;
but as I was not assigned to his particular instruction-class
I saw no further evidence of it.
Now dressed as sailors, the party of boys was marched
down the quay, and in response to a semaphore message sent
by the officer, a large boat - known as a Cutter - manned by
a smart and healthy-looking crew came to take us, the
"Rankuns", aboard.
As we boarded the Cutter I looked at the ship which was
to be my home, and wondered what was in store for me.
The journey from the shore to the ship occupied a few
minutes, but the time taken was sufficient to indicate that

the training received by the boys, was of the best.

The orders of the coxwain were carried out with the utmost precision; but none of us new-hands understood any of the nautical terms used and acted upon in order to bring the cutter alongside the gangway of the high and mighty training ship. Casting my eyes up the vessel's side, I realised why she and other "Ships of the Line" were known as "The Wooden Walls" of old England. And I tried to imagine what a picture this grand old ship would make when in full sail, or as she attacked an enemy vessel to engage it in battle.

Looking up as we climbed the gangway, we could see a number of boys looking down on us from the upper deck watching us coming aboard. They were singing with gusto, a song with which I was familiar. The words were clearly pronounced as if following a rehearsal, for the purpose, no doubt, of informing us without undue delay, that from that particular moment we would have to fend for ourselves.

> "There'll come a time some day,
> When you are far away,
> There'll be no mother to guide you,
> From day to day".

There had, however, been no rehearsal. It had just occurred to one boy to put the song across to the new-comers, as appropriate to the occasion; and others had more or less automatically joined in. All the same, it was a timely warning; and I have had cause to remember it on several occasions.

It soon became obvious that cleanliness was next to Godliness aboard the "Warspite", for everything was as spick and span as it possibly could be. The first thing done each morning was the neat stowing of hammocks. And this was followed by a cold bath taken under the supervision of petty-officer boys, who took steps to see that no boy succeeded in taking evasive action.

The officers of the "Warspite", most of whom had served in the Royal Navy, were very smart and set a splendid example to the boys in their charge. And everything nautical a sailor was expected to know, was taught in a manner all could understand. Hard work and plenty of it was the order of the day.

I found knot-tying and navigation very interesting, but it was cutlass-drill, that first gave me a thrill; fancying myself as one of a boarding-party sent by Lord

Nelson to capture an enemy ship.   At first, the cutlass seemed very heavy, but seemed to get lighter as drill followed drill.   Our instructor was an ex-Royal Marine and a good swordsman.   He would keep his class going in the performance of the various practices and appeared to know the moment when I was likely to take an unauthor-ised rest by leaning on my sword, for he detected me on every occasion I took a chance.   His corrective treatment was a tap on one's stern with the flat blade of his own weapon when one's bottom was taut and in correct posture for the next exercise.   Discipline was good for one.

Taking the soundings - finding the depth of water in which a ship is sailing was called - appeared a little frightening to me at first.   With the leadline - a rope to which a piece of lead was attached and bearing tallow on the bottom to pick up evidence telling the nature of what was at the bottom of the sea; such as gravel, etc., for comparison with the ship's chart.   For in order to "swing the lead" one had to step into "the chains" as that part of the ship's side was called; lean over the side of the ship in what one would at first feel a precarious position.   But there was in fact little danger of falling overboard.   In the case of us boys undergoing training, however, there was always an instructor present.

Climbing the rigging for various purposes provided the boys with excellent training in which they gained confidence and courage.   I found that some boys would take risks that I would feel not to be necessary.

Each evening was spent in gymnastics and marching round the upper deck to martial and patriotic tunes played by the ship's fife and drum band, which was a particularly good one.   Favourite marching tunes included "Rule Britannia" and "Hearts of Oak are our ships, Jolly tars are our men". And the songs "Goodbye Dolly Gray" and "Farewell My Little Yousan; Farewell my Sweetheart true; Over the mighty ocean I've a duty there to do", were sung very feelingly by the boys led by an officer acting as Drum Major.   What more could lads want as a relief to feelings of nostalgia?   I never heard any complaint of home-sickness.

As one can well imagine, there were times when boys quarrelled among themselves.   But whenever two were found in ill-tempered altercation, any officer coming on the scene - and one was seldom out of earshot - would issue a set of boxing-gloves and would act as referee to the contest which usually took place on a part of the upper deck roped off for the purpose.   No sooner was it apparent that a boxing match was in the offing, a shout of 'Fight

10

chapsies' would go up, and in a jiffy, most of the boys
would become spectators.

As is usual in boxing matches, wherever held outside
The National Sporting Club, there are critics, and judging
from the advice shouted to the contestants, one would
imagine that the best boxers are always outside the ring.

On the "Warspite", a keen watch was kept for boys who
remarked upon the lack of skill displayed by the boxers;
and each one discovered was found an opponent for the next
bout on the programme, to give him an opportunity to
demonstrate exactly what he meant by his criticism.   I
had been so selected on one or two occasions before
discovering the reason.   And in consequence of speaking
out of my turn had carried bruises more painful than
dangerous.   This experience was good for me;   I was
learning that discretion is the better part of valour.

Each night, before turning in, the boys formed up their
watches, said prayers, and paraded past the Captain,
giving as they passed a salute, details including their
identity number; the instruction-class being attended; and
the watch to which they belonged.   My own details were:
147, second instruction,star watch-a-main top, sir.

Whenever the Captain noticed a bruised face or dis-
coloured optic, he would ask for the cause.   "I've been
boxing, sir" was the inevitable answer.   "Learn more about
defensive methods, and keep your chin in" was often the
advice tendered by the 'Skipper'.

Education, outside that necessary to the sailorman, was
not neglected.   This was a good thing and essential, for
many of the boys had been brought up in humble circumstances,
poverty and strife; and had left school without having
absorbed much knowledge.   Yet among them were some -
including myself - who considered they knew sufficient for
their needs in life.   These particular boys were unwise
enough to believe that their education ended at school.
Within a very short time of joining the ship, however, the
teaching staff of two officers, made it clear to these same
boys, that one's education continued through life.

These two officers did much good by telling us of their
own experiences and informing their pupils that they would
find - as they themselves had - that the more one learned
the more one realised how little one knows.   I, for one,
have learned the truth of this statement; and that much
knowledge can be gained by listening as well as by study.

As my training continued, I was, as my father predicted,
called upon to perform tasks which had not been demanded of
me at home; no fresh and different job caused me surprise.

Some tasks were more difficult than others, but all were
necessary in the training of those who have chosen to go
down to the sea in ships.

At hand-scrubbing with icy cold water and sand, I had
become expert.   Scrubbing the decks; manning the pumps;
ascending and descending the rigging with naked feet in
all kinds of weather, made me hard as nails, and made me
feel that I could withstand any kind of hard work.   It
made me realise, too, how much more dangerous and
hazardous the life of a sailorman must have been on a
sailing vessel in storm and tempest; no wonder we are
asked to pray for those in peril on the sea.

*   *   *

Being one of the bigger boys, I was fortunate enough
to be selected with others of similar stature to take part
in the Lord Mayor's Show in London.   This was in 1905.
On the morning of the great day we entrained for the City,
where, after a breakfast at Lockharts, we marched away to
take our place in the procession; how proud we were.   Our
band was in great form.   "The Guards' Band was now't to
ours" said a delighted fifer from Yorkshire later, when
narrating the events of that marvellous day to those
unfortunates who had been left aboard.

A week or so later I went to Chatham with intent to join
the Royal Navy, but failed to pass the medical test applied.

At Christmas, 1905, I returned home and later went into
hospital for a minor surgical operation; but I did not
return to the ship.   My short apprenticeship on "The
Warspite" had been distinctly beneficial to me in many ways.
Firm discipline and an occasional 'thick ear' from other
boys, had served further to teach me that success, which
really means worthwhile achievement, is not attained
without a few 'fights' against competitors, ourselves, or
both.

*   *   *

Within a short time my thoughts turned towards the
possibility of entering the Army; and after a parade or two
with the Volunteers from which I had not resigned, I went
to the barracks at Great Yarmouth to enlist.   I wished to
join the Norfolk Regiment, but both battalions were abroad;
so on advice given by the recruiting-sergeant, I joined
the Prince of Wales's Own Royal Artillery Militia, which was
then doing it's annual month's training at Great Yarmouth.
"You can live at home if you wish" the sergeant said, "and

12

in the meantime you could make use of the gymnasium" he
continued; so I was to learn the work of a Gunner, but I
had made up my mind to become a regular soldier as soon as
possible.

The battery-sergeant-major was a large and powerful man,
and to him I must have appeared to be a bit of a 'whipper-
snapper', because he too advised me to use the gymnasium.
Perhaps they thought that my chest required some development.   Anyhow, I thought gymnastics would do me no harm;
so I acted as they advised me, and benefitted by it.

My first parade as a gunner seemed to amuse the sergeant-
major.   The gun in use was an old muzzle-loading eighty
pounder, somewhat like the artillery used in the Crimean
war.   My particular duty was to 'sponge' the gun after
each round had been fired.   The battery was on high ground
and faced out to sea.   I picked up the 'sponge' - a very
heavy implement - inserted it in the muzzle, gave it the
required twist down the barrel, and in withdrawing it I
let it slip out of my fingers; down the slope it went
somersaulting continuously until it reached the bottom.
Battery-sergeant-major Tomlinson, found no difficulty in
expressing his opinion of me.   Among other words
describing me, I heard him say: "Anyone could tell that
you were a bloody militiaman".   I explained that the
utensil was too heavy for me.   "Yes, lad, I know", he
said as he patted my back.   "The same thing happened to
me, years ago".

In July, 1906, seven months after leaving the good ship
"Warspite", I presented myself for enlistment into the
Regular Army.   And found that the two battalions of the
Norfolks were still abroad, one at Gibralter and the other
at Bermuda, I think.   Making inquiries, I was told that
some local men had recently joined the Northamptonshire
Regiment, known as the 'Steelbacks'.   Later the recruiter
told me that the nickname was given because during the
Peninsula War the men of that Regiment, then the 48th
Foot, were said to be able to take corporal punishment
without moaning.   So I became a steelback.

I was now seventeen years of age, and I told the
recruiting-sergeant so.   "That won't do", said he, "from
today you're eighteen and one month".   He explained that
if I gave my age as seventeen, I would receive the pay of
a bugler-boy - two bob a week, but being eighteen I would
draw that of a 'man' seven bob a week.   "All right" I
said, "I'll be eighteen".   My attestation papers thus
bore 'a declaration false in a material particular.'

II

In the Army of Yesteryear

It was a good thing for me that my object in joining
His Majesty's Army was not to take part in a search for
wealth. So I did not feel it incumbent upon me to demand
an Inquiry to ascertain the reason why my first week's pay
was less than I had anticipated.

In fact, as time went on, there was never a week on
which my pay came up to expectations. However, I saw
nothing to complain about, for all soldiers were treated
alike, and it appeared that the 'conditions of service',
such as they were, were accepted by all as O.K. and never
did I hear a grumble. Though every member of the services
had the right to grumble, they seldom asserted it. I found
that soldiers - young and old - had a very good reason for
refraining to grouse.

There were stoppages for this and stoppages for that, all
coming within the category of 'barrack damages'.

In those days, so far as Infantry regiments were concerned
the Company Accountant was the colour-sergeant who was
compelled to balance his accounts; and the simplest method
to be adopted was one in which no questions would be asked.

So far as I was concerned, however, everything in the
garden was lovely.

Quite at home with my surroundings, I had found contentment; but it soon became apparent to me that punctuality
was absolutely essential for one's bodily comfort, in more
ways than one.

The food was plain and sufficient to sustain one; that
is to say, if one was at the mess-table in time to get it.
Being one minute late in sitting down was quite enough to
indicate that the absent one didn't require it.

Punctuality taught in this way was good for one. My
first lesson in this subject was sufficient for me. I
needed no second!

Hunger, though paradoxically providing food for thought,
is not conducive to marching discipline; nor is an empty
stomach to endurance or military precision.

15

Army life suited me.   It was just as well, for I had
enlisted for nine years with the Colours and three in the
Reserve.   I was anxious to serve beyond the seas, but
being a mere rookie, I had first to spend three months at
the depot, before being posted to the battalion then serving
in the Aldershot Command.

When I had been at the depot for a few weeks a fresh
drill-sergeant suspected me of being a deserter from another
Regiment.   "What mob have you done down before coming
here?" he asked.   I told him of my having been in the
Volunteers.   He said no more.   It was not unusual for a
soldier to describe his Regiment as a 'mob', but he
always took umbrage whenever any other person so described
it.

Being considered forward at rifle drill, I was placed
on fatigue duties earlier than should have been the case.
The first job in this category assigned to me was the
rather unpleasant one of cleansing the latrines and tidying
the barrack square under the supervision of the corporal of
pioneers.   This non-commissioned officer was an elderly
soldier, who, after many years experience, had become
extremely well versed in this particular and very necessary
work.   He was so wrapped up in his daily task that had he
been deprived of it or had been transferred to another, he
would have put in a request to see the Colonel to ascertain
the reason.

Smart by name, but not by nature, the pioneer corporal
was short in stature and almost globular in shape.   Such
was his figure, that whenever he fired his annual course of
musketry, he found it necessary to dig a hole - about eight
inches deep - and of suitable area to accommodate his belly
before he could fire from the 'prone' position.   He was
short-sighted too.   "Titch the Blowhard", was his nickname, and none more appropriate could have been given or
earned; for he was blowing incessantly during the whole
time that he was engaged in the latrines, and no wonder!

My work as an assistant to Titch was not to his
satisfaction; I was not too pleased with it myself.   "You're
no ruddy use to me", quoth he with some heat.   "Why didn't
they send me the man I had yesterday?" he continued.
"What's his name corporal?" I asked.   "Hammond", said he,
"blimey, he knew the job, he did", Titch went on.   I was
hoping that Private Hammond would be chosen on the morrow to
be Blowhard's assistant.   But no such luck; I found that it
was to be my job again.

Immediately after reveille next day, I reported to the
corporal of pioneers for the second time.   It was then that
I discovered that he was short-sighted.   "What's your name?"

he asked. "Hammond", said I. "I'm glad to hear that",
said he, "the man they sent me yesterday was a proper
Mutt, he had no idea how to clean a pan". In the guise
of Private Hammond I could do no wrong for the dear old
non-com. Blowhard was so taken with my work that day,
that he asked for Hammond to be his assistant during that
recruit's stay at the depot; the request was granted.
    Private Hammond was also considered good at rifle-drill;
he had served in a militia battalion of the King's Royal
Rifles in the London area. Both Hammond and myself would
rather have been engaged in Infantry drill, instead of
performing the tasks set us by Pioneer Corporal 'Titch the
Blowhard' Smart. The training he gave us, however, did us
no harm. We were learning the ways of men. I had, and
have since come to the conclusion - almost amounting to
certainty - that discipline coupled with compulsion to
perform humble and unpleasant tasks occasionally is good
for the building of character. It is, I think, a
dependable remedy for conceit, which is never an attribute.

* * *

    Every Sunday morning the troops at the depot paraded
for Divine service and marched to church about a mile away.
In the barrack room in which I was quartered there were
about a score of bandsmen, most of whom were old soldiers.
One of these was a flutist who was invariably the last
musician to fall-in though actually never late. This
individual always polished his instrument and laid it upon
his bedstead just inside the door. On the 'Fall-in'
sounding, he would seize his flute on his way out to the
square. One particular Sunday, when the instrument was
lying in its customary place, someone hid it and sub-
stituted an ebony ruler. There was no time for questions;
the flautist took the ruler and rushed on parade. The
officer inspecting the band passed by without detecting
the unusual 'instrument' in the possession of the flautist
who gave a sigh of relief. During the march to church
the musician concerned went through the motions, placed
the ruler to his lips, and played to the best of his ability.
That Bandsman's leg was pulled for a considerable period;
and he often told the story against himself.

* * *

The adjutant at the depot was a captain who had served through the South African War of 1899-1902. Tall and slim in build, he was of very smart appearance. Captain 'Jimmy M' as he was popularly known, had been wounded, and there were times when the effects of the wound troubled him somewhat. And in consequence there were occasions when his actions - especially when a kit inspection was being conducted - suggested that he had 'got out of bed the wrong way'. He was keen on paying close attention to the red tunics to see that they bore no stains; everything had to be in perfect condition to give satisfaction to him. 'Smart and soldierlike' were words he liked to use for the benefit of recruits. On one occasion he discovered a mark on a tunic which had escaped the notice of its owner. Displaying irritability, the captain took hold of the garment and ripped it from bottom to top. A look of dismay appeared on the face of its owner who gloomily imagined himself drawing little pay for the next month or so. But he needn't have worried. The officer immediately regained his equilibrium, and seeing the sorrowful facial expression of the young soldier, turned to the colour-sergeant accompanying him, and said: "See that he gets a new tunic at once and ask the quartermaster to put it down to me".

As the adjutant and the colour-sergeant left the barrack room in which the tragedy to the tunic had occurred, the recruit gave vent to his feelings and said: "There'll be no squarepushing for me tonight". For the benefit of the uninitiated I must explain the expression 'squarepushing' meant - in those days - 'going out with the girl'.

Like other young soldiers, I had an eye for the girls and liked their company.

In the days of which I write, however, the wearing of uniform was compulsory for the rank and file, and although those who enlisted had done so voluntarily, it became obvious to me that there were people who, in times of peace, regarded soldiers as the lowest form of life outside prison. But I was not disturbed.

The South African War had come to an end four years previously, so the value or need of soldiers and sailors could be forgotten until the next war.

Girls not ashamed of being seen with soldiers were mostly those engaged in domestic service; and good girls they were too. These hardworking members of the community had little leisure; an evening off once a week and a half-day about twice each month, was small reward, but they seemed satisfied with their lot; even though their remuneration in terms of cash was extremely low. Casting

my mind back to those days - when I had the good
fortune to meet and keep company with a girl engaged in
domestic service.   Whenever on short leave or furlough -
I have a feeling of pride when remembering that my
finances did not permit me to give her anything but love.
There were occasions, however, when I was able to regale
her with a bag of sweets, a quarter of a pound of choc-
olate almonds to wit, at a cost of threepence ha-penny.

To find favour with girls in domestic service, a
soldier had to be meticulous in dress and precise in gait.
Such being the case, a soldier soon discovered that the
wearing of the clumsy and heavy iron-clad boots issued
for marching, was not conducive to success in attracting
the attention of the fair sex.   So the obvious step for
a soldier to take without undue delay was the purchase of
lighter and smarter footwear; which could be acquired at
the cost of a fortnight's pay.   Yes! "square-pushing
boots" were essential.

Smartness in dress was also imperative in order to get
out of barracks; it being compulsory to report to and pass
the eagle eye of the sergeant of the guard, whose business
it was to see that every soldier and his uniform and
accoutrements was impeccable concerning dress discipline.

No good soldier ever grumbled at having to appear
smart on all occasions.   Much of his spare time was spent
in cleaning his kit; self-discipline being very necessary
for one's self respect.

Life at the depot was reasonable for those, who, in their
childhood, had not been pampered.   And I was happy in the
thought that with others I would soon be posted to the
battalion of the Regiment then serving in the Aldershot
Command, to be moulded into the shape of a really hard-
boiled soldier.

Bordon Camp, in Hampshire, consisted mostly of tin huts,
and was miles from a town of any size.   It certainly was
not one of the best military stations in England.

All of us who had just joined the battalion soon found
that all we had been taught at the depot had to be
forgotten.

On the very first drill parade we were informed that we
were no longer 'in the nursery'.   "You're real soldiers
now", barked the sergeant instructor, and he lost no time
in making us believe him; for within one short hour with
this particular sergeant we were made to realise that so
far as drill was concerned, nothing short of perfection
would ever be good enough for his satisfaction.

The number of 'as you weres' he made us comply with

gave us a distinct clue as to his requirements. But apart from losing an extraordinary amount of perspiration, we suffered little.

From this first lesson we learned that submission to lawful authority without asking the reason why, would, from now on, be required of us to keep our records clean.

On all sides one heard that 'jankers' a minor form of punishment as confinement to barracks was called, had been experienced a number of times, one was not considered to be a real soldier. Such a statement, however, was pure nonsense; for many a good soldier had never been 'crimed', but it must be admitted that there was always an element of luck on the side of anyone who had not been detected in committing an offence, imaginary or otherwise, of one kind or another, alleged to be an act or omission contrary to good order and military discipline.

Mere confinement to barracks was not all that a defaulting soldier had to bear. There was pack-drill in full marching order, and many tedious jobs for him to perform. Pack-drill consisted of rapid marching; doubling at controlled speed; bayonet fighting exercises; turning about and about until the defaulter became dizzy. This reformative treatment lasted for an hour or so each day. Just to bring hope for 'a stand-at-ease' the command 'Order Arms' would ring out from the tonsils of the drill-sergeant; but as soon as the command had been complied with, it was immediately cancelled with one of 'shun!' And the drill went on.

All jankers did not consist of pack-drill, however; as is well known by soldiers and other humans, weeds have a habit of growing and making a nuisance of themselves in all kinds of places. But whenever they occupied spots on or around a barrack square or between cobble stones defaulters were mobilised to remove them. Armed with their own knives and forks, they would set to work under remote supervision to accomplish a task which gave them little satisfaction. Housemaids knees were common in the ranks of defaulters, but apart from the utterance of a few profane words of blame to himself for being caught out resulting in his becoming a defaulter, no further thought was paid to the matter, except that he would avoid being detected in the future. Being able to take punishment without complaining of its nature was regarded as a soldierly quality.

The bugle call summoning defaulters to the guard-room where they were required to answer the roll-call to prove that they were still confined to barracks, was known as 'the Angel's Whisper'; and it rent the air every thirty minutes during leisure hours, from just after Reveille until ten o'clock at night.

Every time the call sounded, the naughty lads had to gallop to comply with it; some of them became good sprinters, but no prize was awarded to the one 'first home'.

Set to music, the words of the call were said to be:

> "You can be a defaulter as long as you like;
> So long as you answer your name".

It was not long before I qualified to listen for this urgent call. I had arranged with a chum of mine to take a stroll with a view to doing a spot of courting girls of our acquaintance; but just before the time arrived for us to leave barracks, my chum was placed under 'open arrest' by a lance-corporal who alleged that my chum had made a remark amounting to insubordination. In the result, I was compelled to go alone; for my friend had to remain in barracks until the charge made against him had been disposed of. In the Army of those days - though I presume the position is the same today - a soldier was regarded guilty immediately he was placed 'on report'; there being no such thing as 'the presumption of innocence'.

I remonstrated with my comrade for agitating the non-com to wrath, and made known to him that I had not yet been called upon to answer the Angel's Whisper, and had no intention of doing so. Just then, a sergeant passed so close to us that he must have heard my little speech of admonition, which, unfortunately for me, he misinterpreted. Next day I was detailed for fatigue duty, whilst so engaged, the sergeant referred to took the action necessary to ensure my becoming a defaulter without undue delay.

Upon returning to my barrack room I found that my name was written on one of the windows with soap, a material which required quite a lot of rubbing to remove it. I had no objection to cleaning the window - it would have been the same if I had - but having had no knowledge of the task awaiting me, I was taken aback when the sergeant, who seemed to have been waiting for my return, asked: "Why haven't you cleaned that window?" before I could reply, he informed me that I was under open arrest for 'not complying with an order'. The morning following I was awarded three days confinement to barracks.

I had been 'framed' - there could be no doubt - but anger on my part would have served no useful purpose. In fact, the expression of it would have resulted in a much longer dose of jankers than I had already started. And there was no Court of Appeal.

Upon reflection, I realised that the sergeant, who had been responsible for putting me on jankers, was desirous of teaching me a lesson. In this he succeeded. Once again I had spoken out of my turn as it were; and once again I was required to pay for my imprudence. It served me right. I resolved that in future - if I could remember in good time - I wouldn't be so talkative.

Within a few minutes of receiving sentence, I was at a canter and was compelled to break into a gallop in order to answer my first defaulter call. My chum, with whom I had remonstrated on the previous day, made room for me to fall-in beside himself. He refrained from uttering a whisper of welcome; but on his face there was a smiling smirk sufficient to convey to me exactly what was in his mind. No doubt he was thinking as I was, that I wasn't as clever as I would have had him believe.

We did our pack-drill, etc., together, and became more chummy in consequence.

Because of our detention in barracks we had been unable to keep an appointment with our girl friends, so it became incumbent upon us to give them an explanation. The tale we had agreed to tell them was duly put over but dubiously accepted. We told them the truth, but not all the truth. We had been on a kind of special duty for which we had been specially selected.

*　　*　　*

The instructional staff at the garrison gymnasium was composed of trained gymnasts who were extremely fond of displaying evidence of their muscular development, and all members of it lost no time in letting recruits under their charge know that it was their intention to inspire all those under instruction with the desire to acquire a similar physique and figure in as short a period as possible.

With this laudable object in view, they did their utmost to instil in every young soldier the necessity for absolute bodily fitness to give them confidence and ability to overcome obstacles and difficulties with which they were bound to be confronted from time to time.

To most of the recruits, obstacles appeared quite early and too frequently. In fact, many difficulties presented themselves by way of the exercises set in the gymnasium itself.

·The instructors were always most precise in explaining what was required to be done, and, because they had

undergone an intensive course of training before
becoming qualified, they were expert in demonstrating
to their pupils how simple of performance were the
various exercises laid down for the express purpose of
providing an incentive to soldiers to become athletes.
That athletics were good for soldiers there could be no
doubt, but not all soldiers appreciated the necessity,
especially by some of those being put through their
paces.   As could be expected a number of recruits soon
became proficient, but there were others who took quite
a time to overcome their awkwardness and clumsiness
which was so obvious that it suggested to the fertile
minds of the instructors a picture which they usually
found no difficulty in describing, in a second or so of
time, and in a manner and in language incapable of being
misunderstood by anyone but an Eskimo.

And although the remarks made in such circumstances
were sharp, inflammatory, sarcastic and rude, they were
taken philosophically by a young soldier as mere
vituperation to be forgotten by all before the next
session of gym, when, no doubt, awkwardness on the part
of any pupil - perhaps one or more who had not been
eulogised or ridiculed on previous occasions - who had
earned for himself and his perambulations a description
he'll never forget, if, at any time in the future he
has the courage to tell a story against himself.

From time immemorial, recruits in the British Army
have thrived on descriptions given them and their
activities when undergoing gymnastic training.

Good instructors of all kinds are, I consider, too
easily forgotten.   A thought given occasionally to
those who by their teachings made others great in all
lawful undertakings and professions, are worthy of
appreciation.   Only too many people are apt to say and
imagine: "Alone, I did it".

*   *   *

In 1906, on November 21st, the regiment moved to
Colchester, and came part of the 11th Infantry Brigade.

Soldiering in this well know Military station was
much more pleasant than at Bordon.   The living quarters
were good; facilities for sport were excellent and all
ranks were encouraged to take full advantage of these.

Route marches through the picturesque countryside
were frequent and enjoyable to young soldiers like
myself, but among the old warriors were some who didn't
relish long marches.   They had done their share in

23

peace and war in various parts of the world, and could
be excused for not appearing enthusiastic whenever a
march seemed imminent.   There were times when their
moans and groans touching the subject of foot-slogging
were descriptive, amusing and somewhat colourful.

Our C.O., Brevet-Colonel A.C. Bolton, a fine
upstanding officer of distinction who had served in
three campaigns, including the Zulu War of 1879, was
extremely keen on physical training of all kinds.

During the Winter, one afternoon each week was taken
up for a cross-country run, and though the taking part
in it was said to be purely voluntary, all except those
on duty were expected to parade for it.   Some old
soldiers who were not particularly anxious to run or
didn't feel equal to it, took a chance and absented
themselves.   On being discovered, however, they were
found a spot of work to do, and it was of such a
nature that they decided against 'dodging the column'
in future.

It was a picture to see upwards of six hundred men
in running-kit waiting for the start.

Some of the older soldiers - especially those who
had just returned from abroad, were seldom successful
in completing the course in the time laid down as
reasonable.   They found it better for their health to
dash into a village inn, a mile or so from barracks,
and partake of reasonable refreshment, but they always
returned breathing heavily as if near collapse; they
were dramatic, but had been 'rumbled'.

These scrimshankers didn't get away with their
manoeuvres for very long.   There came an afternoon when
on trotting into barracks from such a run and
perspiring freely, a couple of lance-corporals were
there to greet them and ask them to produce evidence of
having covered the course.   This, the artful dodgers
were unable to do.   So justice was done, and what's
more it was seen to be done.

As a recruit I learned quite a lot of things from
soldiers old and young.   As time passed one was able
to pick the wheat from the chaff, and benefit accordingly.

*   *   *

Someone in the not too distant past expressed the
opinion 'that one volunteer was worth ten pressed men'.
This statement had probably been true in time of war, but
many soldiers including myself would find no difficulty
in proving its falsity in peace time.   Those who

succumbed to the call for volunteers in barracks or camp were led up the garden path by an offer appearing to result in the getting of something for nothing; an opportunity not to be missed.

One afternoon, when the troops were resting, a corporal - not an unpopular chap by any means - entered the barrack room and asked, in a manner suggesting urgency: "Is there anyone here who understands shorthand?" Quick on the uptake, and scenting a possibility of an office-job, I sat up, rubbed my eyes and said "Yes corporal, I do". And he ordered me to report to the cookhouse at once. "They're shorthanded there", he said.

No sooner had the corporal passed out of sight than there was quite an amount of muffled laughter indicating, I thought, that the other occupants of the room were not quite so foolish as I had proved myself to be. Later, I discovered that the corporal had been informed of the possibility that I would be the only one in that particular room likely to respond to a call of that nature.

Cleaning dixies, so that tea should not taste like soup, was my task that afternoon; but consolation came to me in the form of food of a variety not available to those who had chaffed and tittered when the corporal had taken advantage of my innocence.

My experience in this episode taught me that one's display of alertness and zeal should not occur on a sudden impulse without a moment's thought respecting the motives lying behind another's request for them.

A week or so later, the same corporal became a lance-sergeant, and it was shortly after he put up his third chevron that I believed he had provided me with an opportunity to take retaliatory action against him without great risk to my own comfort. Just before mid-day meal one day, a message came through to the effect that the Brigade Commander was about to pay a surprise visit in order to see for himself the kind and quality of the food being served to the troops. Acting upon instructions of the colour-sergeant of the company, the newly promoted sergeant detailed some men - of whom I was one - to visit the dry-canteen, pick up some large jars of pickles, bring them to the messroom and place one jar on each mess table. They were to be in plain view; and the instructions regarding what was to happen to them were made particularly clear also. The jars of pickles were not to be opened. And the men who had fetched them were told to return them to the canteen in perfect condition.

The main idea behind this well-planned little scheme was,

of course, to 'wipe the eye' of the General by giving
him the wrong impression that all was right.

Placing the jar of pickles with which I had been
entrusted, upon the table for which I was responsible,
I prised it open and signalled to my messmates to find
homes for its contents. They did so with alacrity, and
with such completeness, that nobody imagined that I
would desire a share.

There was the usual calling of the troops to
attention, and the accompanying thunderous crash of knives
and forks as they smote the table tops. The General was
most polite. "Get on with your meal", he said, and,
satisfying himself that the soldiers under his command
had something of a nourishing nature before them, he and
the numerous officers with him, passed on to the officers'
mess.

It was then that the sergeant ordered the return of the
pickles. "Sorry, sergeant", I reported, "Ours have been
eaten". The sergeant went pale. He seemed ready to say
something to me, but remained silent. As he turned away
I smiled at the thought that he would be required to pay
for the delicacy my messmates had enjoyed. Next pay day,
however, I found that the 'pleasure' was mine. Many are
the ways they have in the Army, but the value of lessons
learned therein are incalculable.

*   *   *

For soldiers to be deficient in their kit was a very
serious matter. It was, in fact, a Court Martial crime,
yet many a man took the risk of being so arraigned by
'flogging' or selling part of it when his finances were
particularly low. The garment most usually disposed of
was the grey-back shirt; but seldom it was that the
vendor, or purchaser either for that matter, was detected,
for though the vendor was deficient of a shirt, he was able
to show what appeared to be a full and complete kit
by the simple expedient of borrowing from a chum who
belonged to a company not showing kit on the same day.

Every non-commissioned-officer serving in the British
Army must have known the manner in which soldiers were
able to show a complete kit whenever asked to do so; for
they themselves had followed the same modus operandi
before gaining promotion. And they were aware of the
way in which fictitious regimental numbers of the borrowers
were applied to articles and removed as soon as they had
served their deceitful purpose, and were ready to be
restored to their rightful owners. So it can be said with

little fear of genuine contradiction that every private
soldier had qualified for trial by Regimental Court
Martial at one time or another. Were I asked to give
a reason for the lack of courts martial arraignments for
this particular military 'offence' I would have no hesitation in suggesting that 'sleight of hand' tricks by
which articles of all kinds were won and lost were so
numerous and so cleverly carried out, as to be beyond
trace. Have we not all been told more than once, that
'necessity is the mother of invention?'

One very particular kit-inspection stands out in my
memory for all time. The inspecting officer on this
occasion was a major, the second-in-command of the
battalion. He was not wearing his sword as was usual
on such occasions, but was carrying an ash walking-stick
with which he tapped each article of clothing and equipment as it was checked with the inventory carried by the
colour-sergeant. As the major approached me I began to
dither; my conscience was pricking me. Relief came when
he passed me without finding fault. All went well until
he reached the kit of the soldier standing two beds away.
Again the stick came into use, and as it came into
contact with what had previously been declared the neatest
rolled-shirt on view, a sharp metallic sound of 'ding'
rang out. The major almost sprang to attention with
surprise, and, perhaps because he was a lover of music,
he struck again. Again the flannel 'shirt' answered
'ding!. "Unroll that shirt", the major said. The
soldier stooped to obey, turned his head and spluttered,
"I know what you mean, sir, but this isn't a shirt, sir".
The major apologised for his false description and said:
"Let me see what you have there!" The soldier lifted
the musical flannel and out rolled two empty salmon tins
which had been placed end to end. How can one explain
what prevented the major giving vent to mirth. Just pure
and strict discipline, I imagine; exactly the same reason
for failure on the part of the other inmates of the room
to bend their faces.

"Put this man in the guardroom" the colour-sergeant
said, but there wasn't the expected 'snap' in his voice.
I was one of the escort.

Later the same morning, the major caused the soldier
in detention to be brought before him. Complimenting the
man on his ingenuity, the officer told him that he
possessed the attributes of a good soldier and had proved
that he had initiative. "Your clever little scheme", he
said,"went awry by accident, it deserved a better fate.
You're not a defaulter, you may dismiss. The colour-

sergeant will tell me when you have drawn a new shirt".

Possessed of a sense of humour, the major, a companion of The Distinguished Service Order, won in the South African War of a few years before, was an officer held in high regard by all ranks. He was known as 'good old Teddy' but his Christian name was Charles.

Not yet eighteen, I was learning how necessary it is in most cases, to temper justice with mercy.

* * *

Before being regarded as a fully-trained soldier, I was chosen to take a course of signalling. And while under-going instruction in this important phase of soldiering, I became a competitor at a rifle meeting and won a small fortune of thirty shillings. As soon as it was known by my room-mates that the prize money was in my possession, somebody suggested that an air-rifle would provide some fun in the barrack room, and I, as the only man of means, was asked to buy one. Thinking only of possible fun, I did so. It was known as a Daisy, and cost three shillings and sixpence.

Trouble was soon a 'brewing'. When used under cover, it was almost noiseless, and to youthful soldiers this fact suggested mischief in variety. Within a very short time Sniping was being exercised with success in dislodging a few sparrows and starlings which had made nuisances of themselves by creating fatigue-work for the troops. But the sniping did not end there; human beings were bigger and better to aim at. Somehow, lance-corporals became good targets, but why they were so attractive I only had a rough idea. Perhaps shots in their direction were made to test the truth or otherwise of the statement that they had an optic at the back of their necks. Anyhow, it was agreed that wisdom dictated there should be near-misses only.

The room across the passage and opposite ours was in use as a company store-room in which the colour-sergeant and a private soldier of long service did some work at times, checking items of equipment. On one such occasion, the storeman had his back turned towards the door and was leaning over a table facing the colour-sergeant. The storeman's posterior presented a target at which a near miss would have been too much to expect of any man in possession of the airgun at the moment. Fired through the keyhole, the slug-bullet reached its billet. The target - Private Oby Dussell - fell forward over the table and yelped. "What the hell's up with you" gasped the colour-sergeant. "Don't know, Flag" Oby replied, something struck me on the gongapooch, it was sudden like".

In those days, a colour-sergeant was often addressed as 'Flag'. This was a term of respect, and came about because he wore a badge depicting two flags crossed representing the King's and Regimental Colours respectively, above his chevrons.

*   *   *

When out of use, the airgun was hidden under a mattress; and the lance-corporal in charge of the room knew nothing of its existence or presence. One night, the aforementioned corporal came into the room a bit squiffy. He was not a popular individual by any means, for he had the habit of borrowing small sums from soldiers quartered in his room, and his memory wasn't as good as it ought to have been; but perhaps he wasn't entirely to blame for this particular failing of his, for his creditors considered it tactful on their part to show that they too were somewhat forgetful; so they refrained from reminding him of the day and date on which they came to his financial assistance.

All the other occupants of the room were in bed when the corporal entered. Undressing himself, and breathing stertorously, the while, he managed to clamber into bed and was soon snoring loudly. The noise so created aroused two or three young soldiers, who, by the light of the moon, saw that part of the corporal's rear was open to view. Instantly, I thought of the gun and imagined the possibility of its being brought into use against that part of the corporal's anatomy offering itself as a target. There was no time to lose. Jumping out of bed with great speed, I just managed to get the gun just as another hand reached for it. What a bit of luck for me! As the owner of the weapon, I would have been in dire trouble had I failed to prevent its use that night.

Shooting at a superior officer, even with such a toy-like weapon as a weak springed airgun aimed at an inviting target such as a non-coms bare bottom, couldn't possibly be tolerated in a disciplined force. And such an act would have qualified the culprit for a court martial, plus detention in the 'glass house' for a considerable period.

On looking back at this episode, I have thought of the amusement that would have arisen for the adjutant taking 'a summary of evidence' prior to a court martial, convened to try a soldier for the offence of shooting a lance-corporal in the arse.

To prevent further bother I disposed of the airgun.

*   *   *

In course of time I became a fully fledged soldier and regimental signaller. About this time, there came to command the company of which I was a member, a captain who had just returned to England after service with one of the African Frontier forces. He was a dapper little gentleman, about five feet five inches in height, who took his soldiering very seriously. A good sport, he took part in all games in which one of his age could be expected to participate; and he showed concern regarding the welfare and comfort of his men. But it soon became apparent that he was a strict disciplinarian; for any soldier whom he considered guilty of a charge brought against him, was fortunate indeed if he left the company office with less than the maximum seven days of confinement to barracks which a company commander had power to inflict; but somehow or other the offender felt satisfied and seldom returned for a second dose of corrective medicine.

"Blimey", said a cockney defaulter on leaving the company office after an interview with the captain and the usual award of jankers, "can't the little skipper talk?" He told me what I could get from every kind of court martial, and scared me stiff. Then he asked me if I'd take his punishment. You know the rest.

Whenever the Company was in his charge on battalion training or manoeuvres, Captain Billy B., as he was popularly and unofficially referred to, always made those under his command feel that they were engaged in actual hostilities, and made each particular operation appear realistic.

Acting as signaller to the captain one day, I was in close attendance upon him. Suddenly, as the company was advancing in extended order towards its objective, it came 'under fire' of the opposing force which was holding a position on higher ground. I was at least six inches taller than the captain, and the enemy troops were a thousand yards away. "Get behind me, signaller", whispered the captain, "signallers musn't be shot".

The rifle-fire from the enemy caused us to get down on our bellies, and, after a reasonable pause, we resumed our advance by crawling through furze and bramble bushes, which provided us with cover and numerous painful scratches which brought forth many a damn and blast, or both, from the sufferers. "Silence, men" hissed the captain, "pass the order along, quietly". The captain's injunction was obeyed, but profane remarks, though muffled, continued incessantly until the last line of offending bushes was reached.

Emerging from cover, we charged the enemy, sustained and caused some 'casualties', and were acclaimed victorious.

After congratulating his troops and those of the enemy force, the captain gave us all to understand that what we had been through that day was of very little use as an indication of what a real battle is like. We were all attention, for the captain had served in two campaigns with distinction, and was worth listening to. "You have had nothing to cause you fright today" he said, "yet I heard some, if not all of you, grumbling because of the bushes through which we had to wend our way. Just try to imagine how you would have felt if live ammunition had been used against us. In such circumstances you would have thanked God for those bushes".

After this admonition - which we thoroughly deserved - we consoled ourselves with the thought that, as soldiers, we had one privilege, and that was the right to grouse, with the proviso, however, that it could not - if overheard - be construed as amounting to insubordination.

Most of the grumbles audible to me had reference to certain non-commissioned officers well-known to me, and, though all were slanderous, they appeared appropriate and deserved.

The chief grouse, however, in which incidentally, all ranks participated and gave expression to, was brought about by the atrocious weather regularly encountered whenever the troops were under canvas during the period chosen for brigade training and manoeuvres. Time after time, directly the camp had been firmly established, rain clouds assembled directly overhead as if keeping a specially and purposeful appointment in order to demonstrate what the elements were capable of in the way of causing misery to humans who had the temerity to challenge them with a mere textile habitation.

Satisfied with having proved their power to transform a peaceful and well organised encampment into a disgusting quagmire in a matter of moments, the clouds, not so angry now condescended to split up, and, as was alleged by a disgruntled defaulter, sent their smaller components ahead with instructions to search out similar targets for attention as soon as they themselves had replenished their supply of wretchedness with which to drop in their desire to treat all camps alike.

The last such drenching I remember in England was at Ringwood in Hampshire, where for two days the troops were compelled to discard uniform and move about dressed in blankets, wearing one as a skirt and another as a cape; but our grotesqueness was so evident that our feelings of misery and distress gave place to merriment and laughter. And many were the rude remarks and comparisons made regarding the appearance of soldiers short and tall, when some in fun walked about arm in arm, like lovers whispering sweet nothings to each other. These and other antics helped to keep up our morale.

It was at this camp that 'Good old Teddy' displayed resource and kindliness by arranging entertainment for the troops. He made it known that it would take the form of a competition in which talent would win prizes. There would be songs both comic and sentimental; monologues and recitations, and of course other items calculated by the artistes to bring happiness to the jaded.

There were numerous entries and much talent was shown by the contestants. The 'social evening' had been going splendidly for a reasonable time when a diversion was provided by the manner in which the audience reacted to a particularly doleful song sung by a soldier whose facial expression suggested that happiness and he were perfect strangers; but as the song did not call for glee, his face was appropriately sad. Shouts many and loud and sometimes rude and derisive came from all sides of the huge marquee and the artiste was enthusiastically invited to chew a sock. It seemed that there was nothing he could do but comply with the request; and this he did with great dignity, bowing most politely and feelingly to his audience. This act of his was received with approbation; and a new-comer to the marquee could be excused for coming to the conclusion that the soldier just leaving the rostrum had deservedly attained Stardom and that he would assuredly be popular for many a year.

Quite naturally, many eyes were turned upon the much applauded singer as he made his way from the stage; but if the audience expected him to make a hurried exit, they were in error; for he was intent upon proving himself competent in providing entertainment of a different kind. It started just as the next item in the programme was being announced, and before the pianist touched the keyboard. The melancholy one had singled out one of the most effusive of his critics, and lost no time in getting to him.

"Stand up!" he barked, as he adopted a defensive attitude, "I'm going to knock you down". And with a well-executed 'left hook' demonstrated his ability to carry out his promise. It was more than a knockdown, in fact, its recipient fell asleep. But there seemed little point in what the donor had done when he immediately resorted to applying artificial respiration to his victim.

As a result of the blow on his right ear the victim became somewhat deaf in it, and was much embarrassed in consequence. He was always a fraction of a second late in obeying orders when at rifle-drill. And after having withstood numerous stentorian and staccato commands to 'put a jerk into it', he decided to absent himself without leave.

When an inventory of the goods and chattels of the absent soldier was taken, and his kit-box was searched, the first thing to catch the eye was a model of a gravestone neatly carved in wood, and bearing an epitaph, which, having regard to all the circumstances, seemed appropriate:-

In Memory Of ----- who deserted this life on -----

"I'm going from this vale of woes,
Of long fatigues and sentry goes,
I'm going out to seek repose,
In another world and in other clothes".

At the right-hand bottom corner of the 'stone' was a word not as legible as it might have been. From a short distance, however, it seemed to be F R O L O X.

His freedom was of short duration. A few weeks after he had bidden farewell to Colchester and the regiment, he came back to stand his trial by District Court Martial and to take the medicine usually prescribed for the purpose of proving beyond reasonable doubt, that absence does not, in every case, make the heart grow fonder.

Although not aware of the fact, my friend undergoing detention, had been included in a draft to reinforce the battalion of the regiment serving in the East, and steps were taken to make certain that he could catch the troopship. He went aboard under escort, and was kept in custody until the vessel was well out to sea. It was in the Bay of Biscay that I welcomed him back to liberty.

"So you're a corporal now", he said, and seemed unduly surprised. "What's been going wrong with the British Army since I went to clink?" I explained that my substantive rank was still that given me on enlistment, but that I had been made a 'salt-water corporal' for the voyage. He seemed quite relieved when I told him that my temporary high and mighty rank would make no difference to our friendship.

My chum and I kept together as much as circumstances permitted, and our conversation aboard ship was mainly about India and what was in store for us there.

By information received from old soldiers we heard that

discipline in regiments serving abroad was not so strictly enforced as it was in the United Kingdom.

Discipline had never been a worry of mine, but I was rather anxious for my friend, whose disability had brought about a distinct change in his temperament. He was not so calm as he had been before receiving that clip on the ear in the marquee in which that not-to-be-forgotten social evening was being celebrated.

I was hopeful, however, that India and his service therein would be pleasing to him. He was a patriot and proud of his nationality as any other good soldier is. He had been a very happy and contented man until that unfortunate and damaging blow struck his right ear, changing his whole life in a second. But my hopes for his welfare and his behaviour when not in my company were rather dubious. For there were times when he saw soldiers apparently in earnest conversation and gesticulating that he thought they were 'taking the micky' out of him; when present, I had no trouble in explaining the cause of his rude remarks, but it was a bit more difficult when a soldier wearing one or more chevrons seemed to imagine that my friend had insulted him.

III

Tales of India

They voyage to Bombay had taken three weeks, and apart
from the effects of vaccinations and innoculations administered at intervals during that time in ideal weather, it
had been enjoyable, having regard to all the circumstances.
This was my first experience of a troopship. Our draft
consisted of a Sergeant and about a hundred men, but the
majority of the troops on board were N.C.O's and others
returning to India after leave in the United Kingdom.
Troopships are usually crowded, I believe, and this
particular vessel was no exception. For there was so
little vacant space on the upper deck, that it was a case
of 'after you for a walk'.

Our first day in India was a very pleasant one, the
sun was brilliant and seemed to fill us with vigour; what
a change from what we had been used to in England. And
what a thrill we felt when detraining at our destination,
we found our arrival awaited by the full regimental band
and drums of our new battalion.

I had often wished to see India, a country in which so
many historical events had taken place, and now my ambition
in this respect had been realised. My first impression of
this great country was so good as to be Utopian. And I
felt that I could soldier on for ever in these climatic
conditions; but perhaps my mind had been made up too quickly.
I hoped not.

On arrival in barracks we were met and inspected by the
Colonel who, in his speech of welcome told us that we should
consider it a great honour to serve our King and Country
in one of the outposts of the Empire; that we would soon
learn how different soldiering in India was from serving at
home; that the heat of the sun would inconvenience us in
various ways, and that we would soon respect its powers.
"Go in for all kinds of sport", he said, "and keep fit",
he continued. And he warned us to be on guard against
disease, telling us exactly what he meant.

As was usual, our draft was segregated under canvas for the purpose of finding out if any contagious disease had been contracted during the voyage, or since; and when the camp was declared to be free, the men were divided up and posted to the various companies.

I was still in my teens, and had been permitted to retain one of my temporary stripes, so from then on became a lance-corporal without pay. As a non-commissioned-officer please excuse the description, I was placed in charge of a barrack room in which were quartered several men with battle experience who were old enough to have been my father.

Just after Reveille each morning, it was customary for the troops to be regaled with very strong tea - without milk or sugar - known as 'gunfire'. And after a reasonably short interval to allow for attention to probable calls of nature, a run around barracks - just to serve as an appetiser - followed.

On the first occasion on which I led my squad on this morning sprint, an old soldier burst into song, and not-withstanding that the words of it were tenderly and feelingly warbled I distinctly heard - as no doubt the singer intended - "And a little child shall lead them, lead them gently on their way".

Was the singer putting me on 'test' I wondered? Was he intending to see whether or not I could take a 'leg pull'? But whatever his intention was, it was a matter inviting a smile; not one to get-out-of-step about. I kept my position in the lead, and enjoyed the crisp morning air.

I derived pleasure in listening to the stories told by those who eleven years before, had been engaged in active service on the North West Frontier during the Tirah campaign of 1897-98, in which the battalion I had recently joined had suffered heavy casualties. But there was no bragging on the part of those speaking of their experiences, a listener couldn't fail to appreciate the soldiering in India-especially in time of war - was real soldiering, and one wondered how one would behave if war came again. Certain it was, however, that there were great traditions to be kept up.

Much could be learned from soldiers who had been serving abroad for long periods; and from one particular 'old sweat' I received some good advice.

In northern India there had been trouble with various tribes at irregular intervals since the middle of the nineteenth century. Agitators who resented the presence of the British troops in India, roused the tribesmen to make nuisances of themselves whenever there was a chance of

success.   Some of the raids made by the tribesmen were
more serious than others, but troops had always to be on
the alert to prevent surprise.

Many of the raids made by the tribesmen consisted of
those in which a small number of them crept down from the
hills under cover of darkness for the purpose of stealing
rifles or any arms or ammunition they could lay their hands
on.   So the greatest possible care to prevent such thefts
was imperative, even when in barracks.

When on training in the open, or when under canvas and
resting, each soldier would have to sleep with his rifle
attached to one of his legs by means of its sling, and
the bolt - most important part of the rifle - was taken
special care of away from the rifle itself.   All soldiers
were warned that if they felt the slightest pull on the
sling while resting, they should remain perfectly still as
if fast asleep, to avoid the possible effects of a stab
wound and in order to enable an alarm to be raised when
safe to act if such an emergency arose.

Knowing that British troops in barracks were
encouraged to keep dogs and that dogs could thwart their
actions during a raid, the tribesmen were known to smear
their bodies with animal fat of the Cheetah, the scent of
which caused dogs to become terrified and useless.

'Safety first' precautions had always been necessary for
the protection of British soldiers in India.   Whenever on
the march, or even attending church parades or going to
hospital they carried live ammunition and firearms.   These
precautions had been taken ever since The Indian Mutiny.

*   *   *

The first piece of good advice given by the 'old sweat'
referred to was a warning, a warning which I must have
regarded as a leg-pull, for I took no heed of it.   And got
a severe shock in consequence.

"Should you have to attend to a call of nature during the
night" the old soldier said, "wake me or one of the others
to go with you", and explained why it was necessary that I
should do so.

For health reasons, the conveniences in all barracks in
India were as well ventilated as convention would allow, and
at the rear of such buildings was a passage or small yard,
and from each seat downwards there was an open space to
enable the native scavanger to change the pans when
necessary.

I was told that it was on record, that over the years
there had been occasions on which soldiers using the

lavatories at night had been attacked from the rear and seriously injured.

On the first occasion at night when it was necessary for me to make such a visit, I did so unaccompanied and noiselessly; and an awful shock awaited me.   No sooner had I taken my seat than something happened to make me fear the worst.   Jumping up with alacrity and in alarm, I yelled with fright; and with fearful thoughts felt around the appropriate region of my body.   I was intact. What a great relief it was to find that I was still a man!

Having seen my exit from the barrack-room, my adviser had hurried after me and by taking a slightly shorter route had overtaken me.   He was the cause of my fright.   A short sharp nip from him, and the noise made by myself had been sufficient to satisfy the old soldier that a good lesson had been taught and learned.

I soon regained my equilibrium, and when I had thanked my 'teacher' and expressed my regret at my failure to follow his advice, he said "Nobody else need know of this". He was a good fellow.

*   *   *

The loss of ammunition, whether live or blank, had always been regarded in India as a very serious matter, and every soldier was instructed to report a loss immediately he knew of it; and upon receipt of such a report a search had to be instituted without delay, no matter the circumstances. And it was imperative that a report of its recovery or otherwise be made.

In the company in which I was serving an elderly sergeant known as 'Windy' because of his conscientiousness.

One afternoon, when the company was marching back to barracks after several hours training, the sergeant referred to was in a happy frame of mind; wiping the dust from his mouth and nostrils in the customary manner, he told the rank and file of his section exactly what he intended to do to a quantity of a certain kind of beer on reaching the sergeants' mess.

Why, oh why, did the careless action of a private soldier have to be reported so as to cause a weary sergeant's disappointment at the postponement of his most earnest desire.

Private Slasher Wills had dropped a packet of live ammunition, and reported it as a loss.   Without hesitation, the sergeant dashed to the company commander and reported the 'loss'.   And the compulsory search began, but not before

'Windy' had uttered a few words of unforgetable and
unprintable language. Several other soldiers made use
of similar words, suggesting, I thought, they had been
educated at the same establishment.

Slasher knew where he had dropped what they were
searching for, and after covering about one hundred and
fifty yards it was recovered. But the practical joker
was told with a little heat, that on arrival in the
barracks he would be placed in 'The Mush' a fancy name
for the guard-room.

However, Private Wills was a man of initiative. And
having expressed his sorrow to the sergeant, he asked to
be allowed to make amends by playing the troops back home
on his mouth-organ. To the tune of "To be a farmer's
boy" and other popular songs he did so, fully earning
his reprieve from the guard-room and a large dose of
jankers.

$$* \quad * \quad *$$

Private Slasher Wills was a rather persistent offender
against military discipline, but in the aggregate, his
'crimes' wouldn't have been regarded as an infringement
of Civil law.

Against regimental rules and regulations he had set
himself up in business within barracks, as a 'universal
provider for soldiers'. And his transport consisted of
Shanks's pony and a large dressing-case. He worked to a
time-table and an off-duty schedule as it were; and would
visit all the bungalows with his stock-in-trade of everything
a soldier required to keep himself clean and wholesome,
and, so far as outside appearances were concerned, free
from bother or trouble of any kind possibly likely to attract
attention to himself by an inquisitive non.com. 'looking for
crime', be it ever so unlikely.

It seemed that every regiment - be it Artillery, Cavalry,
or Infantry, had its soldier-salesman who was popularly
known as a Box Wallah. By buying toilet requisites from
a box wallah, roughly an anna (equal to a penny) was saved
on each article, quite a consideration to the soldier whose
pay was unlikely to exceed eighteen pence a day.

The profits on the sale of goods bought at the regimental
institutes were spent in the provision of sports requisites
such as cricket and football gear, boxing gloves, etc., with
which the troops were well supplied. And that was why
troops were expected to buy their requirements from the
institutes.

I got to know Slasher very well indeed. He had been in

India for some years, and could make himself understood to
the natives in a somewhat spurious kind of Hindustani or
Erdu, and he was particularly good at shopping in the
bazaars, having great skill in bartering. He was a real
Knight of the Barter, and really earned the title.

I made it my business to get a knowledge of the characteristics of my comrades - especially those of my own company
quatered in the room of which I was in charge - before
paying regard to more serious matters, such as the
topography of the surrounding country, the location of
bazaars and a study of the manner in which the common
people lived and behaved.

It was chiefly the common people of India with whom the
British common soldier came to know, but as far as one could
see, there was no fraternisation. It was most obvious,
however, that natives working at menial tasks in barracks
were in far better physical condition than those of the
same caste who got their living - such as it was - by other
means; the explanation being that those working in and
around military establishments had the same substantial
food as the troops had during daytime, though it was not
available until the troops had fed.

We, the newcomers, did not have long to wait before becoming acquainted with the physical features of the country,
and realised - very quickly - how much more difficult to
negotiate and overcome they were than those we had been used
to in England. But we were not disappointed, for we had
been warned. In fact, most of us were conceited enough to
wish to look as if we had been in the tropics for a long
time, by getting sun-tanned as quickly as possible, though
as expected, the sun made us sore in places. It was our
white knees that gave us away, however. To old soldiers,
we were described as 'draftees' or 'squeekers'.

I was enthralled with a soldier's life in India. The
climate suited me, and there was great comradeship within
the rank and file. Petty offences against discipline went
unnoticed - or so it seemed to me - more so than in the
United Kingdom.

There were, of course, certain hardships to endure, but
what would real soldiering be without them? Hardships
aren't always harmful.

*   *   *

At the time of which I am writing there were no
mechanically-propelled vehicles available as transport to
the British troops in India; in fact, owing to the nature
and state of the country, its physical features, etc.

motorised transport would have been particularly troublesome in most parts of the country where troops were
stationed.

The sole form of wheeled transport was the bullock-
wagon, which, being without springs, often broke down and
required much manhandling, for they had to be pushed uphill
and held back going downhill.   And, having regard to all
the circumstances - many of which could be expected - no
time of arrival at any destination was ever correctly
estimated.   I could - if I desired - tell of times on
which troops anxiously awaiting arrival of food and
blankets, etc., expressed their feelings and said how
annoyed they felt.

At this period, the Commander-in-Chief in India was
Lord Kitchener, of Khartoum, that great but later much
criticised soldier, who by victory at Omdurman, in 1898,
over the Soudanese dervishes, avenged General Gordon.

The Endurance Tests for Infantry in India in the days
of my acquaintance with that country, included a long
march which had to be completed within a specified time
and under difficult conditions as near as possible as those
likely to be endured in war.   Time lost by infrequent
stops made necessary by calls of nature had to be made up
by steady doubling.   To march and run under India's sun
for hours when wearing battle equipment was a man's job.

At the end of the test-march, many weary miles from
barracks, the troops were formed up for inspection by the
brigade commander.   In response to whispers from our
officers we threw out our chests, and tried to make it
appear that we could have marched twice as far.   But I
don't think we deceived the brigadier-general, though he
said a few kind words to us.   He had been saying the same
words to tired soldiers for years.

The inspection over, the troops were given a brief rest,
and, unofficially, a bottle of mineral water which came
from our regimental factory in a mysterious manner.   Now
a further test awaited us, a test of stamina and powers of
endurance under battle conditions, except that live
ammunition - though carried by British soldiers - was not
used in the preliminary phase of the battle.

Our opponents were native troops, whom we discovered to
be most agile and better able than we were to move about
on the rough and rocky terrain, which they knew so well,
and, of course, they could withstand 'Jimmy the Sun' better
too.   But our task was to wear them down - a particularly
difficult job - which some kind officers, known as Umpires,
declared we had done.

The last phase of the exercise was an attack against a

range of hills, at the foot of which a number of old
helmets were stuck on poles as targets, for us - the
British troops - to fire at.   The native troops used
blank ammunition, of which they were well supplied.
And while they possessed a round of blank, it was very
difficult getting them to obey 'the Cease-fire'.

These tests, to which I have referred so briefly,
were conducted most realistically, and it was seldom that
a man fell out; for everyone was keen to show that he
could 'do it on his head'.   That this attitude was the
correct one, there could be no doubt, but in reality it
was a good example of 'playing the old soldier'; a
harmless game of deceit, as it were, that deceived
nobody.   So far as I personally was concerned, this
kind of training was imperative, but it was a good
thing, I thought, that it was not necessary to apply
such tests weekly or even monthly.

To tired footsore, dirty and dusty troops, a rinse
from the contents of a water-bottle is freshening; and
how cheering it is, when arriving at the nearest road,
to find the regimental band formed up and ready to make
the march back to barracks as pleasant as possible.   In
such circumstances, the band of any regiment is the best
in the Army.

*   *   *

During my service in India, I found all the commissioned officers of the 1st battalion from the Colonel
down to the junior subaltern, were gentlemen in all res-
pects; they understood their men and were ready to do everything possible for their welfare.

It was very noticeable that the senior officers were
keen on seeing that young officers - new arrivals from
England - didn't inflict too much march discipline unnecessarily on soldiers who carried more and heavier equipment
than themselves.   Experienced officers resented the
injunction: 'Left right, left right, left' on route marches,
when they and the rank and file were foot weary.   The
young officers soon appreciated the necessity for tact and
discretion, and became better leaders.

With cheery officers in command of them, men are usually
happy, and happy men, whether soldiers or civilians, are
appreciative.   A few words of encouragement, uttered
when most necessary, have seemed to me to work wonders,
and I have had cause to give them on numerous occasions,
chiefly in civilian life.

As a very junior non.com., I was anxious to gain

promotion though it was not my intention to make a career as a soldier, for my mind was on becoming a policeman and detective if possible.

In my battalion there were ninety-six lance corporals, but only half that number could be paid as such. Supernumeries were necessary in India because there were extra duties of various kinds to be performed than was the case in the U.K. In order to become a paid lance-corporal and receive the remuneration of three-pence a day, one was required to qualify for the full rank of corporal, under the supervision of a commissioned officer who witnessed one's qualities as a leader, drill-instructor in troop movements, bayonet-fighting etc. And in addition to qualifying, one had to wait for a vacancy which in peacetime was a long time coming. In my case, it took ten months.

Before the qualifying examination took place, the candidates were addressed by sergeant Smocky Smith of my company. He was a soldier of war experience, and a great guy as the Yanks say.

Each morning after 'gunfire' - that rather noxious concoction of strong tea without milk or sugar had been made available - but before breakfast, Sergeant Smocky Smith, a cockney, took us in hand and gave us some valuable tips. "I want all of you to pass", he said fairly regularly, "so don't let me dahn. You have got to satisfy the young supervising officer that you know your stuff; blimey, you've been doing company drill and bayonet fighting long enough to blind him with science". Standing us at ease and then at attention alternately three or four times rather rapidly, he told us not to be afraid to use a 'bit of swank' occasionally. It always goes dahn all right, and makes the officer think that you are really what you are supposed to be - 'a superior officer'. "In the next ten minutes" he warned us, "I'm going to make you and the squad sweat a bit by putting all of you through some balsam orders as an example of what I mean by swank". And he kept his promise. Among other things he caused us to fix bayonets and unfix them too, three or four times, by using a sharper and snappier tone of voice as if to show and express his annoyance at our slackness. He put us 'On guard' several times in very quick succession with alternate 'as you weres' and a similar number of advances, retires, first, second and third parries, until we were almost ready to drop with exhaustion. We learned much from the sergeant's patter and actions, and, when standing at-ease, told him so, but with little hope.

Sergeant Smith had more to tell us. "When the officer comes, and you see him pull out his pencil and paper and make copious notes" he said, "don't rush to the hasty conclusion that all of you have failed, he could be writing to his sweetheart in Blighty".

We all passed, I think; but as there were no deaths nor courts martial to create vacancies, the reward of threepence per diem was not immediately forthcoming. But, like silence, patience is a virtue.

I thought quite a lot of Sergeant Smocky Smith, he taught me much, not only how to do things, but what is of much greater importance, how to encourage others to do them, and do them well. Smock's little 'lectures' were put over in a manner guaranteeing undivided attention by his audience, and he always had the guts to invite questions, even if he recognised the fact that the object of them was to test his knowledge of the subject on which he had been speaking. And if questions were hypothetical, or upon a subject of which he had no knowledge, he would declare the fact. Yes, he could 'swank' when he thought it safe to do so, but on no occasion did he pretend to 'know it all'.

There was one particular occasion, however, when a question was so unusual and unexpected, that we all - including the questioner - thought that the sergeant would be beaten to a frazzle.

Having asked permission and been granted it, the questioner - with what appeared excessive politeness, probably brought about by excessive confidence or optimism - asked "what chance do you think sergeant, an infantryman, standing alone, with only his rifle and fixed bayonet but minus ammunition, would have against a mounted soldier with poised lance charging upon him with great speed, and,assuming that you yourself were that infantryman, how would you act in the circumstances?"

Sergeant Smith coughed and cleared his throat. "Two very good questions", he said, "but you must first understand that the time taken to answer them will be much longer than that taken by the horseman to reach that poor .... sergeant of infantry. In the first place, my chance of success would depend upon how far the cavalryman was away from me when he commenced to charge, and upon my own presence of mind. On the assumption that the distance was a reasonable one, giving me an opportunity of doing <u>anything</u> at all; that the cavalryman carried his lance in his right hand, and had no loaded firearm in his left hand, any infantryman of resource, even if he were a sergeant, would have a fair chance of getting the better of the matter", he said, and continued: "Now I must show you how!"

Fixing a bayonet on his Lee-Metford rifle, the sergeant took up a position sideways on to his audience, in the open air, of course, telling us to watch him and his movements, and in a sharper voice, he said "and use your imagination". Opening and closing the bolt of his rifle, he aimed it as if at a target slightly to his left side and just above his own height; then he came down smartly to the 'on guard' position for bayonet-fighting. "You see what I'm doing", he snapped. "The horseman was fifty yards away when I first saw him coming. He wouldn't know that I had no ammo, so I had to make him think I had. My action in aiming at him would tend to make him unsteady, even if it didn't cause him to fall off in fright; but this particular cavalry-man didn't get the wind up, he came on, so I had to deal with him. I stood my ground until he was nearly on me, then, as you saw, I took a short sharp step to my half-right in the hope of dodging his lance, then I turned abruptly left and poked him in the belly. Go and see if he's dead".

After a short interval to get his breath back, the sergeant asked if his explanation and demonstration satisfied his questioner. "Yes, sergeant", came the reply, "I ought to have known that you can't be caught groggy".

Sergeant Smocky Smith, though thoroughly smart and a good scout in many ways, had - as every man in his section had cause to remember - one weakness. He would volunteer for all manner of extra work and difficult jobs, especially those that cropped up during battalion train-ing or manoeuvres. So far as his men were concerned, it wouldn't have mattered a jot if his volunteering involved himself only, but it invariably involved them all without exception; that was the snag. I have cause to remember a particular occasion on which our company commander asked for a section to volunteer to take the part of a skeleton enemy. Feeling certain that I knew what would be forthcoming, my mind flashed back to my schooldays and the words: "then up spake brave Horatius, the captain of the gate". Sure enough, up spake Sergeant Smocky Smith: "Number three section would like to be allowed to be it, sir". And we got the job without testimonials.

The position to be taken up by us was pointed out. It was miles away, and the sun was at its meridian. "Very good, sir", said our sergeant, though no other soldier of

the section could envisage anything delightful in
nature arising from the task ahead.

As the loading of two bullock carts was in progress,
it became obvious to all of us that - judging from the
kind of materials our sergeant thought necessary for the
operation - he intended to provide all of us, with the
possible exception of himself, with full employment for
the next twenty-four hours; and many low-toned remarks
uncomplimentary to Smocky, were made in consequence.

"Stop moaning, soldiers", the sergeant said in a voice
all of us could hear. "I'll be like a mother to you, and
I'll bring you back mounted".

From two or three older soldiers than myself I heard
that similar promises made by Smocky had never materialised, but for one reason only, i.e., the only means of
transport available being shanks's pony. The older
acquaintances of our sergeant knew from practical and
previous experience, that when his section did eventually
reach camp on returning from any of his voluntary
expeditions, every member of it would be in a state
bordering upon collapse, rendering their morale so low,
that they would not appreciate the chaff and leg-pulling
of their chums of other sections, who always made a point
of forming a reception committee to welcome Smocky's
'volunteers'.

On this particularly solemn occasion I espied Private
Slasher Wills, with baton in hand, conducting the
committee's choir, whose members burst into song with the
queries: "Art thou weary, art thou languid, art thou
sore distressed?" at a speed of about thirty paces per
minute, which was most considerate of them. It would
have been impossible for number three section to stagger
any faster.

This was an occasion on which we would have had great
difficulty in throwing out our chests in an endeavour to
show our ability or to show our contempt for distance;
or to swank according to Sergeant Smith's formula. We
were beaten to the wide. Instead of giving us the order
to dis-miss, Sergeant Smocky Smith said, in a very tired
voice, "Go, you soldiers of number three, and rest in
peace".

Refreshing sleep worked wonders within us, and forgiveness of Smocky was unanimous; but we knew for certain
that further 'voluntary' exploits would be ours, though
there was consolation to be derived from lack of knowledge
of their nature. We felt, however, that it would be a
task that 'only number three' could perform.

*   *   *

The second-in-command of our battalion was known as Major Cakey. This name was given him by the Band Boys, in appreciation of his kindly weekly action as the donor of a large sugar-coated cake to the boy parading with the instrument adjudged to be the cleanest on the Sunday church parade. The cake also had a nickname. It was called 'a char-anna duster' because it cost four pence. The boys, however, regarded it as a prize worth winning, and competition was keen; so much so, that the major found great difficulty in picking out the winner. It was seldom that the same youngster won it a second time in succession.

Major Cakey Parker, a big man of very smart appearance, was a popular officer who always looked for the best in his men. He was loath to believe that any one of them would wilfully commit an offence against discipline. Always merciful, he was regarded as a religious and christian gentleman. But his faith in the belief that his men could do no wrong was occasionally shaken, of course.

I remember the day on which he took command of the battalion. We were stationed at Poona, in the Deccan, at that time. One of the first steps he took for the welfare of his men was the inauguration of a special evening picket to patrol the environs of barracks, a distance of miles, for the laudable purpose of preventing - if possible - soldiers coming in contact with native females and contracting venereal disease. A malady not only detrimental to health, but, so far as a soldier was concerned, one which caused him heavy financial loss, for, having become a patient, he was deemed to be inefficient for a period of twelve months, and though he performed full duty from the day he left hospital, he forfeited 6d. per day for the whole period of a year, i.e. at least one-third of his pay. But he was aware of what his compulsory loss would be in such circumstances, so there was nothing unfair about it.

In India at that time there existed in each military station licensed brothels which were usually situated in one particular street or district, and the women in them were of various nationalities, but none was British, though the majority were white. The others being orientals.

The women in the brothels were regularly medically examined, and scrupulously clean. And they took great care that their clients were free from disease. It was not from these women that soldiers contracted disease, but from young Indian women and girls of low class and of low caste, who wandered around the environs of military stations

accompanied by a native man, who actually did the solic-
iting for them.   These loose native women and girls were
described by soldiers as 'sand rats'.

The price charged soldiers at the licensed brothels
was one rupee, at that time valued at one shilling and
fourpence.   The usual price of a 'sand rat' was four
annas (4d.).

All soldiers up to and including the rank of full
corporal - married or otherwise - were liable to picket
duty, and each picket consisted of six pr[i]vates and two
non.coms., but in order to have a better chance of success
in this preventive work the picket was divided, three
privates with each non.com., working in opposite directions and agreeing to meet each hour to report.

The first time I was required to perform this kind of
picket duty, my senior corporal, Tim Pearl, was in charge.
He had just returned from furlough in England, during wh
which he had taken unto himself a wife.

Corporal Pearl, though not a jewel, was a rather chubby
man and was a good man to get on with.   He told me that
he didn't think it right for a married man to be put in
charge of a squad of what appeared to him to be nothing
less than contraceptives.   Corporal Pearl gave me instructions.   "Take your three men" he said,"and patrol the
roadway and the area by the side of the racecourse, keep
a sharp lookout for bibbies, and do what the C.O. wants
doing".

As I marched my men away, the corporal shouted: "Meet
me here two hours from now unless prevented".

The term 'Bibby' was used by soldiers to describe any
young native girl.

Set back from the roadway which formed one boundary of
the area I had been instructed to cover, were several
bungalows at irregular intervals apart, with well-kept and
pretty gardens and flowering trees of various kinds and
colours.

The first hour of our patrol was uneventful so far as
picket-duty was concerned, but it was then that we were
provided with a pleasant diversion from our monotonous task.

From a bungalow we were approaching there came the strains
of music played on a phonograph, and the tune was a popular
one indicating that the person working it was not averse
to comedy.   I caused the men to halt, and within a moment
the four of us had removed our accoutrements, and were
sitting 'at ease' on a low wall surrounding a disused well,
listening to songs old and new, forgetting for the time
being, the special duty assigned to us.

Within a matter of minutes we were to receive a further

pleasant surprise by meeting our entertainer. He was an Australian jockey. His conversation was bright and breezy, and in his expressed opinion Australia was the finest country in the universe; but he told us that his most earnest wish was to visit England, which every good Australian regarded as Home.

Having done his utmost to persuade us to emigrate to the Antipodes at the first available opportunity, this jolly little man lost no time in offering us hospitality which was gratefully accepted and enjoyed in his company by moonlight, and without leaving our 'beat'.

No sooner had evidence of the repast been removed, and the jockey had returned to his bungalow, two natives - one of each sex - appeared before us. The male bowed, touched his forehead in salute and asked: "Do you want bibby, sahib?" The question being quite sufficient proof of the purpose of their visit, we buckled on our belts and side-arms and by language and gestures, put them to flight.

The bibby was small and couldn't have been more than twelve years old, whilst the man - a lean emaciated individual - was probably a relative of hers.

Almost immediately after the natives had been scared off, the sound of running feet came to our ears, and a soldier came to a halt before us "Look out you chaps" he gasped, "there's a picket about here to-night". Taking a pace towards us, he saw we were wearing belts and bayonets signifying that we were on duty. "Lummy", he panted and almost fell, "you're the pp picket, too"; and fled like a sprinter. Actually, he needn't have done, for we hadn't seen him do anything wrong. Perhaps he wasn't so sure.

I took my party to meet Corporal Tim Pearl and reported 'all correct'. I didn't think it necessary to tell him that my party and I had been advised to emigrate to Australia.

In the battalion a strict record of venereal cases was kept, and our new colonel had ordered that a 'League Table' comprising the eight companies - as each battalion had in those days - and showing the position held by each according to the number of patients undergoing treatment, should be displayed in the regimental institutes for all to see. As one point was deducted for each patient, the company having the greatest deficit was placed at the top. The weekly publication of the league table caused so much banter, chaff and ridicule, that it acted as a remedy resulting in the cessation of the evening picket; the weekly bulletin; as well as providing beneficial psychological treatment of the 'risktakers' and a clean bill of health.

*   *   *

Poona was an important military station in Southern India, and a soldier's life was most pleasant.   One of the chief cities in that part of the country, it was the headquarters of the 6th (Poona) Division, and it was here that I spent two of the best and happiest years of my life.   The country in and around the city was picturesque and inviting for long walks in which I indulged at every opportunity.

Although in those days soldiers serving abroad had by force of circumstances to provide their own forms of amusement and entertainment, they made a good job of it, for there were no obstacles in the way.   All kinds of ball-games were available for all ranks, whenever circumstances permitted.

In 1909, Poona was selected as the venue for the Annual Boxing Championships of the British Army in India, and it was then Bombardier Billy Wells became the Heavyweight Champion by defeating Private Jarvis of my regiment, the 1st Battalion Northamptonshires.   The contests had been going on from Monday to Friday evenings inclusive. And all contests were in accordance with amateur rules, and each-at the various weights-consisted of three rounds. Since then I have attended many amateur and professional programmes, but I have never attended one which was conducted better than this military one.

Billy Wells was an acting-bombardier (one chevron), in No. 6 Mountain Battery, stationed at Jutogh in the Punjaub.   He was a grand boxer and gentleman.   I believe this was his last appearance as an amateur, and that he obtained his discharge from the service by purchase shortly after this Poona episode, for he returned to England and became a professional boxer.   The British Army was distinctly proud of him; and it was said that no boxer would ever beat him 'on points'.   He died in 1967.

*   *   *

PRIVATE RODDY

All telegraph stations in India - when the British Army was in occupation - were manned by white soldiers who had qualified as Army Telegraphists.   Such men belonged to regiments in all branches of the service, and were likely to be away from their unit for years.

NO SILVER SPOON

It was in January, 1909, that I first met Private Roddy. He had been acting as a telegraphist in a remote station for some years, and his return to regimental duties had come about by what he described as a mere indiscretion on his part.

A public schoolboy, Roddy could have been a commissioned officer but he, like two of his brothers, preferred to join the ranks. His father had been a colonel in the Indian Army and had earned high honours.

A day or so before Christmas Roddy was alone in his telegraph office feeling rather miserable, when he received a pleasant surprise in the form of a visit from an old friend whom he hadn't seen for a long time. And they resolved that the occasion called for a reasonable kind of celebration which shouldn't be delayed.

Roddy's chum was soon under the table, and when he regained consciousness there was no sign of Roddy. Thinking that his friend's absence was probably caused by response to a call of nature, he dozed off. In fact, however, he saw no more of Roddy that day; what could the explanation be?

Next day, some obvious clues were found at intervals over the countryside in the form of articles of a soldier's uniform and clothing. No clever detective work was necessary to conclude that Roddy had stripped himself to nudity; that he had been taken to the guard-room of a unit some miles away, and then to the station hospital.

It transpired that after the first bottle had been disposed of, Roddy had gone to the cupboard for a further supply, and, finding a bottle bearing a label similar to that on the 'dead one' he sat down and continued to imbibe. The contents of the second bottle, or rather the portion absorbed by Roddy, had an unusual effect upon him. In a stuperous state he left his office, knowing not whither he was going nor what he was doing. Discarding his garments as he went, he wandered on. At midnight, a young sentry was so astonished at being suddenly confronted by a naked white man staggering before him that he lost consciousness, and in falling his Snyder rifle went off. The guard turned out, and from the sight that met their gaze, feared the worst. But neither the sentry nor the naked man was hurt. Both men were carried to the guard-room, and Roddy - for the nude man was he - was later taken to hospital. After spending fourteen days in dock, Roddy was sent back to his regiment.

I ought to explain that the Snyder rifle was really an

obsolete weapon, but a very useful one.   A single
loader, its breech was opened by depressing a lever;
and the cartridge used contained three balls which
spread out when fired.   The Snyder had a kick like a
mule.   It was issued to white troops on sentry duty
from sunset (Retreat) to Reveille.   Roddy was indeed
lucky to escape death.

In those days it was customary in India for a soldier -
on discharge from hospital - to appear before his
Commanding Officer, who would ask him whether he had
any complaint to make as to the treatment given him, and
no exception was made in this case.

The C.O., knew why Roddy had been returned to his unit,
but was unaware of what had happened before that soldier
was admitted to hospital.   So Roddy was asked the usual
question.   "On the contrary, sir," Roddy answered,
"I had a marvellous time" and when asked to explain, he
said, "you see, sir, my good treatment came about by
water.   When I came round in hospital, I asked for a
drink.   When I drank it, a feeling of inebriation
came over me, and as water had never before had such an
effect upon me, I drank much of it".   The colonel smiled,
"that will do Roddy" he said.

The liquid causing Roddy's discomfort and great pleasure
in turn was for cleansing purposes; its chief constituent
was methylated spirit.

*   *   *

I got to know Roddy very well indeed as did many other
young soldiers.   On his return to regimental duties he
didn't show the greatest respect for discipline, and in
consequence was frequently in trouble.   But at making
excuses for his alleged offences he was supreme.   He
seemed able to explain to the officers before whom he
appeared as a defaulter, that he had been incited to
commit the offence with which he was charged, by the
conduct of the non.com giving evidence against him.   And
in this regard his superior education stood him in good
stead.   "I am well aware, sir", he would say, "that
all lawful orders should be punctually obeyed, and that
any complaint accruing from them should be made and
investigated later, but I am of the opinion that you will
agree with me when I say that such orders ought never be
accompanied by insults".   He would then urge in his
defence the nature of the insult which had caused him to
be hesitant in obeying the particular order or to make
use of the language complained of.   Roddy's allegations

were always denied, but there were occasions when they were believed to be true or thought to have created - in the mind of a tender-hearted officer - the slightest doubt of which he could, by a stretch of his imagination, regard as reasonable.

Private Roddy had a good knowledge of Military Law. As a telegraphist stationed away from his unit, he had devoted much of his spare time to studying it. And he was often consulted by soldiers who had kicked over the traces, and asked for his advice in their defence. On deciding to give advice, Roddy would ask to be given the full facts, and would emphasise that the story must be true. If satisfied that a possible Defence existed, he would give his advice 'without prejudice'.

I heard that there were occasiions when he gave his 'clients' a short lecture on the need for courtesy to N.C.O's, and of a case when reminded that he had been put upon a 'fizzer' for having been discourteous to them, he admitted the fact, and replied that circumstances altered cases.

There were occasions too, when defences recommended by this barrack-room-lawyer were acted upon and so well put across, as to bring forth from the officer hearing the case, the question: "Have you by any chance, consulted Private Roddy?"

*　　*　　*

ANOTHER TITCH

It was in the Autumn of 1909 - during which the battalion soccer championship was being contested - that I had what was to me, an interesting, amusing, instructive and unique experience, which was to be helpful to me in later years.

In order that my company could put its strongest team in the field, I volunteered to take the place of a fellow lance-corporal doing duty with the Garrison Police.

Reporting to the sergeant in charge, I was deputed to join Corporal 'Titch' Smart in patrolling Main-street and its environs within a reasonable distance of the brothels in Love Lane.

This particular "Titch" was a Londoner of no relation to the lance-corporal Titch 'Blowhard' Smart with whom I had performed important drill at the regimental depot described in Chapter 2. This corporal was a tall man of proportionate build, always spick and span when in uniform, really Smart in fact. Dedicated to his work as

a military policeman, he told me some amusing stories
of his experiences in dealing with soldiers whose conduct
out of barracks was calculated - by garrison policemen -
to be prejudicial to good order and military discipline;
a definition covering every kind of conduct absolute and
unassailable almost.

It was rather late in the evening of my first and only
day as a garrison policeman, when our attention was
attracted to a woman who was running towards us and scream-
ing in terror for help. "Come to Poona Poll's", she
gasped, "some bad soldiers won't go home". She was from
one of the brothels in Love Lane, probably the best known
one, its manageress had a good record in military rank and
file circles. She was popularly known as "Fat Poll of
Poona".

"Come on, Boy!" said the corporal, as he broke into
double time, "this looks like just another case of chuck-
ing 'em out". And so it turned out to be, but the
modus operandi was excellent.

The soldiers causing the bother had that day finished
a 'mounted infantry course' and were celebrating before
returning to their respective units. It was apparent that
some of them were a bit merry through drink, and had
decided to visit the brothels to spend a rupee on the only
'commodity' on sale there.

The firm and frictionless action taken by Corporal Smart
was a valuable lesson to me. He rose to the occasion
remarkably well, and in the manner expected of an experienced soldier in such circumstances. Here were several
men, excited, and potentially inclined to become riotous
unless carefully, tactfully and firmly handled. Calling
for the senior men of the party to step forward, the
corporal pointed out to them why and how their conduct in
refusing to leave the premises in the usual manner, they
had caused the womenfolk distinct alarm and fright. "We
aren't taking any names. We want you to fall-in, and
return to your quarters without more ado". They complied
with the corporal's request immediately. Of course it
was an order, an order, made to appear as a request.

I remembered this lesson from Corporal 'Titch' Smart,
and turned to it with success on more than one occasion.
Thank you, Titch, I'm sorry you can't hear me!

*   *   *

The battalion is shortly destined for Aden, Arabia,
where it is due to serve for about twelve months. In the
first decade of this century - and probably years before

54

it - four regiments of British Infantry, having served
in India for approximately twenty years, ostensibly
Homeward Bound, but one of them was chosen to serve in
Aden and its environs for about a year before actually
embarking for England, Home and Beauty. How this
particular choice was made - by lottery, or otherwise,
nobody seemed to know, but it was pretty certain that
none of the four units had been asked to volunteer.

India was a great country for learning the art of
soldiering, and, so far as I was personally concerned,
it would have suited me to continue to serve there for
several more years, but this was not to be. Just before
the date of embarkation for Aden became known, it was
announced that only five companies of the eight would be
going there, and that the other three companies would
remain in India and be stationed at Ahmednagar, until
they came to pick us up the next year, when some of us
would come home, while others would disembark at Malta
to reinforce the 2nd battalion of the regiment.

We heard some unwelcome rumours about what soldiering
was like in Aden, and of the climatic conditions there.
It was said that when compared with India, Arabia was
Hades and India was Paradise.

Like most other people in the world, we found that -
speaking generally rumour was a lying jade - but in this
particular case she hadn't perjured herself.

The effect of the Monsoons in India were, to me,
remarkable. Within two or three days of the first rains
falling, the transformation of the parched ground to
brilliant green was extraordinary. When I first saw the
change caused so rapidly by heavy rain, it reminded me of
the fairy tale 'Jack and the Beanstalk' in which Jack's
mother threw five beans out of a window, and found, next
morning, that a tremendous beanstalk - strong enough to
bear a giant's weight - had grown during the night. As
soon as a Monsoon makes its presence felt millions of
frogs come to life and advertise the fact by croaking all
night to show their pleasure and appreciation of what was
in store.

It was during a monsoon that I played golf with the
regimental schoolmaster and made many mistakes. This
fact caused me no surprise, but the silliest of them all
was when I allowed myself to beat him. He did not ask
me to give him another game.

Apparently, the Monsoons would have no effect in Aden;
frogs would not croak there because there would be
nothing to croak about, owing to the absence of ponds and
ditches containing the kind of water demanded or required

by such amphibious creatures.   Nor in those days would
there be any golf, nor would anyone have the inclination
to think of fairy tales, with the possible exception of
Ali Baba and the Forty Thieves.   But in the days of which
I write no British soldier of the rank and file, possessed
any property which could possibly appeal to an Arab.

*   *   *

My friend, the soldier who was unfortunate enough to
have had his ear punched - he preferred to say 'fettled'
instead of punched, - was one of those remaining in India.
But within a short time he was found medically unfit for
further military service, and discharged.   I was glad to
hear of this, and thought it just as well; for he seemed
to be developing into 'a persecution maniac', by imagining
that people whose conversation he couldn't hear quite
clearly, were speaking of himself.   I have kept him in
memory, and hoped that he enjoyed life with the assistance
of a Hearing Aid, as he deserved to.

IV

Arabia

It was in early February, 1910, that we disembarked at
Aden, a military station which at that time was regarded as
in the 'first three' of the worst in the Empire; but as it
had been in occupation of British troops since 1839, we
were not unduly discouraged.   What our predecessors had
succeeded in doing during the previous century, when
conditions must have been worse than now, we could do
equally well.

Viewed from the ship, it looked horrible and uninviting.
It appeared to be exactly what it was, the result of an
awful volcanic eruption, and likely to turn out an unhealthy
weight-reducing spot for British soldiers to learn that the
building of an Empire entailed taking possession of noxious
territories as well as good and productive countries.   But
as a common soldier, I felt that no such lesson was required,
and that it was pretty certain that the naval and military
authorities in Great Britain in 1839, considered Aden to
be necessary for their purposes, and that reason was good
enough for any British service man, I imagine.

There were mutterings and forecasts from a number of
'astrologers' who expressed opinions of things likely to
happen to us during our stay in Arabia.   One of the most
knowledgeable of these - a cockney - said; "Blimey, Charlie,
what a bleedin' 'ole, we'll all get the 'Deolali Tap'
before we've bin 'ere long".   My own sentiments were
somewhat similar, but being an optimist, I refrained from
expressing them.   The sun was shining brightly, and though
still on board, where there was some protection from it, all
the troops were sweating profusely.

Landing at a small pier situated nearer to the Crater
than to Steamer Point, we marched through a kind of Pass to
our Quarters at Crater.   The C.O. thought it necessary to
tell us what we were in for, and that we would find things
a little different than in India.   He needn't have bothered,
we could smell the difference, and were glad to get under

cover for a cleanup.

There was little delay before we were made to appreciate exactly what the C.O. meant when he said: "You will find things here a little different than in India". There was no fresh water; that for drinking was distilled from sea-water, and our daily allowance of it was two gallons. Water for washing was a mixture of sea-water and distilled water, in which ordinary soap wouldn't lather; so most of us used cold tea for shaving.

The heat was terrific, and drill parades could only be held in early morning and towards sunset. Two minutes in the sun was sufficient to make one's shirt and shorts wet through from perspiration, and whenever troops were in the open during daytime they had to wear Spine Pads to prevent the overpowering rays of the sun doing damage to the spinal column and causing other embarrassments. And when on the march, each time we were brought to a Halt we had to turnabout and face the sun whenever it was at our backs.

Aden had no virtues apart from the sea which, both at Crater and Steamer Point, was there by the merciful will of The Almighty. Personally, I blame Mephistopheles for that volcanic eruption, which, to my way of thinking - as the saying goes - ought to have been postponed until 1967.

In 1910-11, the period I can speak of, Sunstroke or Heat Apoplexy was usually fatal and meant burial of its victims on the evening of the day on which it occurred, for no refrigitant was available as a cooling medicine. Neither was there electricity nor any other scientific invention to bring aid to the populace.

Our daily rations consisted of tinned foods of all kinds; butter, dripping, cabbage, potatoes, etc., etc. Fresh meat came on the menu occasionally, but it was always from the same kind of animal - the goat - who had breathed his or her last a very short time before being cooked and made available for eating. It was hellishly tough - just right and appropriate for use in Hades - but there were no complaints; we had no desire to upset the Quarter-master. Bully Beef, of which there were tremendous stocks, was a luxury.

In Aden itself, nothing would grow. There was much evidence, however, of attempts having been made to remedy this, and clear proof of failure. Withered stumps of what had been saplings of various kinds of trees - probably from India - remained as memorials. And to these sad reminders, practical jokers of our predecessors had appended printed requests to their successors to kindly refrain from damaging the trees, plucking the flowers, and walking on the grass.

These details of some of the conditions in Aden may appear

to be the grumbles of a grouser, but please believe me
when I tell you that they are not.   I give them merely
to provide a true picture of them as they were at the
time when I was there.

At that time and for many years before, wives and
children of soldiers of all ranks, were not permitted to
live there.   And the only service men stationed there were
of the Artillery and Infantry, simply because the Royal
Air Force had not come into existence, so there was no
aircraft of any kind.   There were no buildings of much
account, no good roads and no mechanical transport.   And
the people with whom soldiers came in contact in any way
at all were Arabs and Somalis.

Conditions being what they were, the troops were
encouraged to take as much physical exercise as circumstances permitted, and this they did by swimming, playing
football, rowing and taking long walks along the seashore -
usually, when at Crater - in the evening to Marshag
Lighthouse.

Our first game of Soccer was played against a team of
Somalis.   It was the funniest match ever witnessed, and
I am certain that a talking cinematagraph record of it
would have been worth a fortune.

The Somalis, all six footers, were naked except for a
loin-cloth, and as there was no need for us to wear colours,
we played in vests and khaki shorts, boots and socks.   The
spectacle provided by the teams as they lined up was
extraordinarily ludicrous, and the few spectators - mostly
soldiers - gave vent to their feelings by loud and raucous
laughter, cheers, and rude remarks.

As we had expected, the methods adopted by our opponents
were crude, rough and unorthodox, but their kicking powers -
both at the ball and at us including the referee, whom they
thought was one of us - was marvellous and almost unbelievable.   Unencumbered by footwear, and having feet as hard
as iron, they could kick the ball the full length of the
field, and each of their shots at goal appeared to have a
heavy charge of cordite behind it.   They were powerful,
fast furious men, and their feet were so large and covered
such an area of ground, that it was impossible to charge
them off the ball.

In the early part of the game, the referee found it
necessary to use his whistle more often than he had ever
been required to do previously; and it was obvious that the
Somali team regarded him - if they had ever paid regard to
any referee - and his whistle, as general nuisances.   So,
in order to keep the peace and the game in progress, the
referee, with our team's concurrence, had to allow them much

latitude.

Our opponents indulged in much shouting at each other, especially when one of them failed to score, and whenever we deprived them of an opportunity to beat our goalkeeper. Their expressions of disappointment and disgust, were made, not, in Somali or Arabic language, but in Cockneyisma, such as 'Ply the gime', 'cor blimey', 'Lor lummy', 'stone me', 'stiffen the bleedin crows', and expressions of similar nature that put us out of step just as we were about to shoot at goal, and there was much laughter in our 'ranks' causing us to hesitate long enough to lose the ball and a golden opportunity to take the lead, as well as making us miskick when defending. In these circumstances we lost 2-3. Defeat was never taken so joyfully.

The Somali Players had picked up the cockney dialect from men of The Queen's West Surrey Regiment, our immediate predecessors in the station.

It was, I think, the amusement provided at this super comical football match that made me realise that life in Aden need not be intolerable, if one looked upon it philosophically and incapable of evasion. To me, laughter has always been good medicine, and I have learned to look for the bright side of things, and to retain a memory of them when confronted with disappointments for the purpose of striking a balance; and I have found that patience - following failure of expectation - has brought its reward.

*   *   *

DEAR OLD PALS

Private 'Dad' Sexton, the oldest soldier in the battalion by age, was Private Roddy's closest friend, and when not on duty one was seldom seen without the other. Dad, who was employed as a clerk in the quartermaster's office, was a dapper little man, about 5' 4" in height, and rather stout. Of very cheerful disposition, he was well respected by the quartermaster who trusted him implicitly.

I remember an occasion on which Roddy was waiting for Dad to leave his office to accompany him to the canteen, as was their wonted custom each noon, when the sun and their thirst reached the meridian. Roddy was broke, and his anxious inquiry revealed that Dad too was without visible means of subsistence. Roddy was not dismayed. "I have just seen something going on in your office which has given me an idea indicative of the manner in which we can avoid disappointment". Like Roddy, Dad was in need of his midday refreshment. "What's the shortest court-martial

NO SILVER SPOON

sentence the perpetrator of your scheme could get" Dad
asked.   Replying that no court-martial was likely to
ensue, Roddy gave Dad the details.
    Re-entering his office, Dad spent less than five
minutes there before rejoining his pal.   The two worthies
went to the canteen and Dad presented a chit, in exchange
for which they were given liquid refreshment.   Roddy
indicated to the manager, a German, that they would call
for the remainder that evening; and this they did.   But
somehow or other, Dad didn't seem to enjoy his beer like
Roddy did.
    Next morning, as he was about to enter his office, Dad
saw the canteen manager leaving it.   Can you imagine how
poor old Dad felt?
    Conscience-stricken and shaking at the knees, Dad
awaited the call that he knew would come at any instant.
It came before he had time to ease his chin-strap, and it
had a tone of great urgency about it.   Just one word,
SEXTON, uttered so loudly and sharply as if the owner of
the voice was annoyed at being unable to express it in
one syllable.
    Dad answered it with alacrity, came to an abrupt halt
in front of the quartermaster and sprang to attention.
    Waving a small piece of paper in the air, the officer -
in a voice intended to appear very angry - hissed, "what's
the meaning of this?"   Taking a deep breath, Dad explained
that he meant it as a joke and a cheap lesson, "Go on,
Sexton," the quartermaster said, "I'm interested".   And
Dad went on explaining.   "It was because I have seen you
signing papers without reading them, sir, so having worked
for you for a long time, I chanced my arm".
    The quartermaster stood up and looked towards the guard-
room.   "Taking a chance which could result in getting you
two years detention by court-martial seems too silly for
an old soldier like you Sexton", the officer commented.
And he expressed an opinion that Dad was not alone in the
matter.   "I think your chum Private Roddy had a hand in
this", he said.   Dad coughed, but remained silent.
    The quartermaster read the chit again and guffawed.
"Get out of here Sexton", he said, "before I change my
mind".   Dad was so relieved, that he saluted very smartly
when he oughtn't have done, he hadn't got his hat on.
    Why did the quartermaster suspect that Private Roddy
was partly responsible?   He knew, of course, of Dad's
friendship with Roddy, but his suspicion was made stronger
by what had happened a few days before when he saw Roddy
leaving the regimental library and had asked that worthy
whether there were any good books there, and Roddy had said:

61

"Yes, sir, there is one that will suit you particularly; it's title is 'Robbery under Arms'".

The chit by which Dad and Roddy obtained their beer on the previous day bore the words:

"Kindly supply bearer with one
gallon of Amber Ale and place
to my account".

The culprit Dad, at Roddy's suggestion, had put the quartermaster's rubber stamp mark on a blank indent form. The quartermaster following his usual habit of turning over the right-hand corner of the form and signed it above his stamp. Obtaining the signed form, Dad did the necessary writing.

*   *   *

EX-DRUMMER BOY SEXTON

Old Dad Sexton had seen active service with another regiment. As a boy of fourteen he had been a bugler and drummer in the Royal Fusiliers (City of London) Regiment, and during his twelve years' service in that corps he had served in The Egyptian War of 1881-2, for which he gained the medal and the Khedive's star. But having failed to report this previous service when he enlisted in the Northamptonshire Regiment, he had enlisted fraudulently, and for that reason he couldn't wear the decorations awarded for that campaign, and had rendered himself liable to court-martial.

When King Edward VII died in 1910, an amnesty was granted to all troops then serving, who admitted having been deserters or fraudulently enlisted men.

I was one of the few who knew of Dad's previous service, so I asked him if he intended to seek The Pardon. He answered in the negative. "I have a little more oil in my lamp for that", and he explained the conditions attached to the grant of the amnesty was one he dare not risk. "Like all men who admit previous service", he said, "I would forfeit all my service in this regiment and in order to get it restored to me I would have to keep out of trouble for three years. I couldn't take that risk boy". Knowing Dad Sexton, as I did, and that in four years time he would qualify for pension, I saw the wisdom in his decision.

*   *   *

RODDY IN LINE AHEAD

At Crater, Aden, a bather could go out hundreds of
yards from shore before the water came up to his waist,
and, owing to the presence of sharks in rough weather
there was A Brigade Standing Order which made bathing in
deep water a serious offence against discipline.

About a quarter of a mile from shore, there was a
breakwater, and it was between the shore and the breakwater that troops were permitted to bathe.   Usually it
was safe, but when the sea was rough, there was always
the possibility that sharks would swim over the breakwater and become dangerous to bathers, hence the need
for the Order.

It was owing to an alleged infringement of the aforementioned Order that Private Roddy got into a spot of
bother.   One evening, he and five other soldiers went
for a swim, and because Roddy was the senior soldier, he
was deemed to be in charge of the party.

Just before the party entered the sea, Roddy informed
his companions that as he was responsible for their
safety, he would lead them 'in line ahead' so that they
could keep him in sight the whole of the time, and come
to his assistance if and when necessary.

During bathing time, the regimental police kept watch
on shore for the purpose of warning and, if necessary, to
report offenders.   And it was because of the keenness of
the regimental police to do their duty, that Private
Roddy's party came under observation.

No sooner had they waded ashore than each man was told
to consider himself under open arrest on a charge of
'being beyond the limits whilst bathing, contrary to
Brigade Standing Orders'.

Next morning they were brought before the C.O., and
their crime was read   out by the adjutant.   The prevost-
sergeant and two of his staff gave evidence.

Private Roddy, who was standing at the right of the
line, was the first man of the party to be asked what he
had to say in answer to the charge.   "I wonder, sir",
Roddy asked, "if you would be kind enough to take the pleas
of my colleagues first, because I've rather a lot to say".

The colonel obliged.   All five of Roddy's colleagues
expressed their sorrow, and pleaded that they were unaware
of being in deep water.   The C.O. intimated that he would
postpone sentence until he had heard Private Roddy.   The
R.S.M. marched the five alleged offenders out to the
verandah.

"Now then Private Roddy", the C.O. exclaimed, "I'm ready

to hear you". Roddy cleared his throat and began.
"I regret, sir, having to say this, but the evidence of
the sergeant and his satellites is most unreliable, and,
with your permission, I'd like to cross-examine him."
The prevost-sergeant was re-called. I will detail the
interrogation of the sergeant by question and answer:-

Q.1. How did you know that we were out of bounds.
   A. I used my binoculars.

Q.2. Are there any buoys or floats marking the deep
      water.
   A. No.

Q.3. Did you see any of us standing up.
   A. No.

Q.4. Then how could you tell that we were ever over our
      waists in the water.
   A. I know where the water is deep.

Q.5. Is it the same depth at both tides.
   A. Not at the same spot.

Q.6. Did you think we were in danger.
   A. Yes, if there had been any sharks about.

Q.7. Did you see any sharks.
   A. No.

Q.8. Assuming that you did consider us to be in danger,
      why did you not launch the regimental boat and come
      to our rescue.
   A. I was about to do so, but at that moment you and
      your party turned towards the shore.

Diverting his eyes from the sergeant to the C.O.,
Private Roddy submitted most respectfully that he and his
fellow bathers had no case to answer; that no sufficient
evidence had been adduced to prove the charge, and that
like other alleged offenders, soldiers were entitled to
the benefit of any reasonable doubt.
The C.O. laid his pencil on the table, looked Roddy in
the face, and allowing a smile to appear on his features,
summed up, and announced that, having noted the answers
given by the sergeant put to him by Private Roddy, he was
satisfied that a reasonable doubt existed. "Bring in
those other men", he ordered.

The other soldiers were marched in and turned to face
the C.O., who addressed them and said: "Private Roddy
has convinced me that none of you were out of bounds.
Thank him; it was a near thing. March them out".

Happy at dodging a dose of cells, or confinement to
barracks from eight to fourteen days, each member of the
party expressed his appreciation of Roddy's advocature.
Roddy thanked them for their eulogies, and told them that he
refrained from charging a fee, but he would like them to know
that when off duty he spent an hour or so in the canteen.

* * *

I was finding life in Aden quite tolerable, and the
knowledge of the ways of men and of human nature broadened
my mind. Although having only just reached my majority,
I had gained much valuable experience, and, as time passed,
it became clear that lessons could be learned each day, not
only from one's own errors, but often from the known
mistakes of others, and the various kinds of trouble arising
from them. And I was appreciating the truth of the
saying: 'Experience is the great schoolmaster of life'.

As already mentioned, it was my intention to become a
police officer, and it being possible that I would be
returning to England within a matter of months, my thoughts
turned once more towards the police service as a career
when the time came for my transfer to the Army reserve.
But eighteen months were to pass before I became a policeman, and in the interval much more experience and fun were
to come my way, though not without tests, trials and
difficulties.

Early one evening I was one of a party of soldiers
taking walking exercise along the shore at Crater, in the
direction of Marshag lighthouse, when we came upon a
turtle making its way back to the sea. In all probability,
it was a female returning after laying its eggs and
covering them. We surrounded it, and one of the party,
a cockney, had a brainwave. "Blimey", he gasped, "if
we could get this to the officers' mess, we could flog it
to the mess-sergeant and make 'a few chips' (rupees). Then
he could make some turtle soup for the officers".

The project was considered for a moment or so, and though
the greatest optimist in the party could imagine that each
share of the money (if any) so obtained, to amount to more
than eight annas (pence), we decided to act as suggested,
and surrender to the lure of lucre.

Our task in getting the turtle to a spot as near as
possible to our destination without removing it from the

beach, was difficult, slow and tedious. Taking steps
to prevent it re-entering the sea, we left two men in
charge of it, and the remainder of us made our way to
the officers mess. Later, I was informed of an easier
way to deal with turtles.

The mess-sergeant was busy arranging the evening meal.
I didn't like the look of him. He was sweating profusely.
Acting as spokesman, I informed him of our capture, and
suggested that here was an opportunity to make a name for
himself by making and serving turtle soup to the officers
and their guests. "Where is it?" he asked. For a
moment I thought that he was interested, but for no more
than a moment. "It's on the beach quite near, sergeant",
I said, and at once noticed that his face registered 'no
sale'. Picking up an offensive weapon usually seen in
the kitchen where food is being prepared, the sergeant,
with an economy of well-meant, but impolite expressions,
told us what we could do with the turtle. "Get out of
this, and push it in the sea!" he commanded. "I don't know
the Turtle drill."

There being no point in staying where obviously we were
not wanted, and fearful of a reprisal in the form of fatigue
duties, we made a hasty retreat, realizing once more that
generous offers are not always acceptable. But there was
no anger in us.

Returning to the beach, I reported our failure to the
two 'sentries' bade farewell to the turtle, and, though
we had been prepared to take her life away, we wished her
good health and longevity and put her where the sergeant
told us to.

*   *   *

Life in Aden and its environs went on in accordance
with military routine. But rumour raised her head declaring
that an individual by the name of The Mad Mullah had been
raiding Trading Caravans in British Somaliland and stealing
camels and merchandise. And as the troops in Aden were
only a few hours sail away from the scene of his crimes,
they were certain to be under orders to proceed to the spot
and put him 'out of mess'. We didn't go after the Mullah.

Had someone blundered? We shall never know; and I've
not a clue.

At that period, 1910, a campaign of short duration or a
week-end war would have provided a welcome relief to the
monotonous and unchangeable turkish-bath-like climate,
which was beginning to tell on the health of the troops,
who were having more ultra-violet rays than was good for them,

and appeared to be losing weight and becoming sick.
It was not that warfare in that part of the world would
have brought much of a change in climate, but rather a
change of environment - a change of life - as it were -
calling for and giving opportunities for the display of
initiative, and real soldierly qualities which were seldom
if ever necessary, when on purely garrison duty.

Like every other regiment, our battalion had its quota
of 'characters' who - by their exploits, actions or omissions
- bring notoriety to themselves in a manner to be remembered
for all time.

In addition to Privates Roddy and Dad Sexton, there were
others whose conduct provided topics of conversation,
argument, general discussion and expression of opinions for
and against, with the best of intentions and always without
loss of temper on the part of anyone.

I have cause to remember a good and popular soldier who
paid his debts to comrades with photographs of Rupee notes.
He seldom borrowed more than five rupees at a time - usually
for the purpose of obtaining reasonable liquid refreshment -
and the lender of that amount received a picture of a five
rupee note when payment became due. Not a single creditor
grumbled or raised his voice in anger. So far as my
knowledge of these financial transactions goes no lender
expected interest nor paid more than five rupees for this
valuable lesson.

It has been said on innumerable occasions that a soldier
enjoys a solitary 'Right' - the right to grouse. Even so,
this so-called right is not absolute; in fact, it is a
dubious privilege depending on the nature of the grouse,
when, where and to whom the alleged grievance is presented.
In the vast majority of cases, whatever be its cause, I
have learned that it would have been wiser to 'forget' and
'forgive' the episode; for one's peace of mind is too
valuable an asset to gamble with.

In looking back to those days of long ago, when the
conditions of service in the army were not so good as those
obtaining today, one realizes how much more monotonous life
in Arabia would have been if certain officers and other
soldiers had not taken upon themselves the task of providing
entertainment for the troops.

Concerts and Boxing Tournaments - held in the cool of the
evening - did much in the maintenance of morale. The
former were particularly good, providing as they did popular
songs both sentimental and humourous; giving soldier
artistes unique opportunity for satirical reference to
various officers and non-commissioned officers, which in
other circumstances would have amounted to gross insubord-

ination.   The satire was well received and resulted in
much good-natured leg pulling, for a reasonable period.

A miniature soldier in the person of Private 'Joey'
Chamberlain, was the cause of much fun and merriment when
taking part in a Richard III sketch.   His effort, 'A
norse, a norse, my kingdom for a norse', was always
worthy of a request for a repeat performance.

The boxing bouts most enjoyed were those between Somalis
engaged on menial jobs in barracks.   They were given the
names of famous negro boxers, Jack Johnson, Sam Mc.Vea,
etc., though they neither knew nor cared anything of The
Queensberry Rules.   Whenever one contestant was knocked
down, his opponent invariably got down beside him, and the
fight went on until the referee saw danger of facial
disfigurement resulting.   The 'boxers' appreciated acclam-
mation, and some of them might just as well have been
satisfied with applause as a reward for their talent, for
though each of them - winner or loser - received a purse
of two rupees (2/8), their winnings were purloined - on
their leaving the ring - by their womenfolk, who, seeing
an opportunity to acquire wealth, took it while their
menfolk were dizzy, weak and bewildered.

*   *   *

THE ADEN TANKS

At Crater, hewn out of the solid lava, are some
reservoirs known as the Aden Tanks, which were probably
constructed centuries before the British Troops were in
occupation.

Ostensibly meant to catch and store rainwater, the
people behind the scheme must have been among the world's
greatest optimists otherwise they would never have
started on the work, for little, if any, rain ever came
there, a fact which must have soon become obvious to the
authorities, for they abandoned them to fill up with debris
and disappear from view.   Some years after Aden was
occupied by the British, Lieutenant - afterwards Sir Harry -
Playfair, of the Royal Engineers, discovered them, caused
the debris to be removed and restored them to view to
become of interests to tourists.   A number of stray pigeons
took up quarters of value and free from molestation in the
highest of the tanks.   The reservoirs had been well
constructed and in the aggregate were of the capacity of
many millions of gallons and were arranged so that when
the highest one filled, the overflow would enter the next
one below it, and so on until the lowest was filled, when

any overflow from it would enter the sea.

A rather remarkable thing about them was the nature of the plaster covering of the walls of the highest and biggest tank. It was polished and had been skilfully applied. At a spot - the most convenient for the purpose - soldiers of the various units previously quartered in the station had scratched and written details of dates, their units, ranks and regimental numbers. Some of the dates purporting to show when the particular unit served in Aden were fictitious, recording that it was there before it existed.

As already stated, we arrived in Aden in February, 1910, and it was then reported there had been no rain for seven years. During our sojourn of thirteen months, rain came on one day only, and it lasted for a quarter of an hour.

*   *   *

Conditions in Aden and its surroundings have changed tremendously during the past half-century. In many ways it has improved; it has been made a healthy place to live in, so much so that service personnel, their wives and children and members of W.R.A.C., W.R.N.S., and W.R.A.F., have been allowed to live there. In other ways it has deteriorated tremendously. Many millions of the British tax-payers money has been spent to improve living cond-itions for the Arabs, who, under British protection, have been enabled to improve themselves in status. They have been trained in the use of arms to defend themselves and have been fed on food they never expected to taste, or be able to buy. From being lethargic and drowsy people with small means of subsistence, they have - at the British tax-payers expense - become somewhat active under super-vision and under-cover; but when supervision is removed, they will slip back to lethargicalness. One thing is absolutely definite; they are incapable of fighting in the open, the whiz of a couple of bullets over their heads is sufficient to compel them to discard their boots, turn about and run like hell. What position they will be in when their guardians - the British troops - leave them to their own devices only Allah knows, and Time will tell, but thousands of British soldiers and other persons have an excellent idea. But one must be charitable to the Adenese Arabs when speaking of them and their ability to retreat at the slightest sign of danger, by saying: "Never having fought, they've never been defeated".

*   *   *

69

As an ex-soldier who has served in the East, I am, I think entitled to express an opinion regarding 'Suez, 1956'. To my mind, which I expressed before the six day war of 1967, all those who were responsible for preventing the continuance of the action against Nasser at that time, did Britain and the whole world, a colossal disservice.

In a week or less, Nasser would have been defeated and he would have become 'a dead duck', instead of a menace to the world at large as he is today. There would have been no closure of the Suez Canal, nor any further trouble of any kind from Nasser. And furthermore, there would have been no Terrorists causing death and sabotage in Aden which would still have been an important British base.

V

In the Railway Police

In December 1911, I obtained a premature transfer to
the Army Reserve for the purpose of realising my ambition
to become a policeman.

My first appointment was with The Great Eastern
Railway Company in London. At the age of twenty-three,
I was tall but rather slight in build, and felt full of
vim, vigour and vitality, and ready for any kind of action.

For the first fourteen days, during which time my
uniform was being made, my assignment was to patrol the
many platforms of Liverpool-street station to keep a
sharp lookout for thieves who were said to frequent railway
termini.

Here was a chance for me to show what I could do in the
'detective line'. Anyone standing around or walking
about without luggage was, to me, a person worthy of attention as a potential thief, and one to keep an eye on in
compliance with my instructions.

In the very first hour of my first day's duty, my
suspicions were aroused by the meanderings of an elderly
man. Like a Lynx I watched him and brought into play the
methods considered to be those of a keen dedicated and
efficient sleuth-hound, by taking advantage of all available
cover, and to see without being seen.

My suspect visited several platforms, and appeared to
be most active. I saw him lift and examine mailbags and
various packages, and my suspicions increased considerably,
so much so, that I began to think of the words to be used
by me to intimate to him that he was about to lose his
liberty.

In an endeavour to get closer to my intended prisoner I
stepped behind a stanchion, and by so doing lost sight of
him for an instant. Emerging from my hiding-place, I
looked up and down the platform. Suddenly, there came a
sharp and heavy thump on my right shoulder which made me
sink at the knees. Turning round, not without a feeling

of alarm, I found myself face to face with the man I'd
been stalking.

In a booming voice of authority, he demanded to know
what I thought I was up to, and told me that he had been
watching me for some time.   Recovering from the sudden
shock, and pulling myself together, I gave my answer by
telling him that I'd been shadowing him, also, for some
time.   A changed expression crossed his face, and because
of it, I took further courage.   I asked him if there was
any good reason why he shouldn't identify himself.   "No,
none at all" he said "I'm a detective, you see".   I was
not convinced so I asked him to prove his statement.
"There isn't any difficulty in that", he snapped, "but
what is all this?"   and without more ado, he produced
his warrant-card; and I produced mine.   He laughed aloud,
and shook hands with me.   "I've never kept 'tabs' on
anyone with such pleasant results", he told me on the way
to the refreshment room, in which we found a home for two
glasses of bitter beer to celebrate an occasion on which a
real detective appeared to have wasted his efforts in the
line of duty, and I, a mere apprentice as it were, had
been taught an invaluable lesson on his very first day as
a policeman.

My newly-discovered colleague and I became firm friends,
he too, had been a soldier, a trooper in the Life Guards.
Experienced in the ways of thieves who preyed on railways,
he taught me much about the tricks and devices they
employ.

I would have liked to continue the patrolling of passenger stations, but such was not to be.   Most of my duties
were performed at Bishopsgate goods station on night duty.
It was a dull and dismal place, and uninspiring.

Conditions of service in the railway police in 1911-12
were far more exacting than those existing today.   Tours
of duty each day or night were of twelve hours.   To be
cooped up for such a time in the precincts of a railway
station or goods yard, or patrolling sidings between rows
of dirty rolling-stock, was most monotonous and uninter-
esting.

There was no time for recreation, and not the slightest
thought was given to welfare.   Prospects of promotion were
extremely poor, and there was nothing to spur one to
greater effort.   I soon discovered that the railway
police offered little chance for me to achieve my ambition
to become a detective of note.

I longed for opportunity to display talents - which, I
felt I possessed - in the investigation of serious crimes.
The work of a railway police constable was too much like that

of a night watchman to suit me, I thought, and I made up my mind to become a real policeman if possible, at the first available opportunity.   But a change of circumstances was on its way for me, and I appreciated it.

After four months in London, I was transferred to Cambridge.   My fellow constables were three in number, and the four of us were under the supervision of an inspector who had jurisdiction over a wide area.

In clean and pleasant Cambridge, I found life much more interesting than in London.   The pranks and Rags of the undergraduates provided me with a variety of excitement, and I quickly found that members of the Borough police and ourselves of the railway police had to display the utmost tact, forbearance and fortitude, in order to prevent breaches of the peace.

CONSTABLE MAC GINTY

My first experience of the antics of undergraduates occurred one evening when I went to the railway passenger station entrance to relieve Constable Mac Ginty, an old and tried policeman, who always took the line of least resist- ence; being well in the ways of doing one's duty 'on roller bearings' with as little friction as possible.

Just as Mac and I were about to part company, we were approached by two young men.   "I say, Robert", said one of them to Mac, "can you tell us how you arrange traps for speeding motorists?"   Mac hadn't the slightest idea, but he concocted a story to fill the bill.   When Mac finished his narrative one of the undergrads dropped a florin.   The obliging Mac stooped to retrieve it, and as he did so, the dropper of the coin delivered a heavy push with the open palm of a hand on the top of Mac's helmet forcing it over his ears.   I stepped forward to grab the aggressor just as Mac extricated himself and gasped: "Do it again, sor, at the same proice".   The invitation was not accepted.   The young men proved their ability to sprint.

One night, MacGinty was on duty patrolling the platform when he saw a burly undergrad armed with a heavy walking- stick come on the platform and proceed to smash a number of gas lamps by using his stick.   Satisfying himself by taking a description of the offender, Mac took cover.

Next morning, the inspector-in-charge informed Mac that the superintendent in London would certainly require to know what steps were taken in the matter.   "Tell him the old one", said Mac, "------ long 'uns".

Another of my colleagues at Cambridge was known as Old George.   This ancient constable had spent many years in

the district, and had an excellent knowledge of the larks
and practical jokes of those attending the famous
University, for he had been a victim on numerous occasions.
Once, when doing his utmost to prevent a horde of students
gaining access to a part of the platform where their
presence was not desired, George found himself being
forcibly lifted to the top of a huge pile of baggage where
he was issued an ultimatum that in order to gain permission to descend to ground level, he must first make a
speech.

"Very well", said old George, "but it will be in
question form". There was no objection. "Why is it that
you educated young men take so long to grow into real and
sensible men?" George asked. "Very appropriate" somebody
told George; and old George came down to earth without
further molestation.

George told me some of his experiences with undergrads.
And it appeared that in his opinion, the young men intending to become parsons were more of a nuisance than others.
I asked him if he could give a reason for thinking so.
"No, not really", he replied, "unless it is a matter of
having a last fling before being compelled to act as a
parson is expected to conduct himself".

*   *   *

Years ago, on November 5th, it was not uncommon for
students to seize cabs and similar passenger-carrying
vehicles and burn them on the streets. But it must be
said that the 'fire bugs' were always considerate enough
to remove the horse and cabby, and passengers - if any -
before applying the match. And they always compensated
the owners of the vehicles.

After one or two experiences of this nature, the owners
of ancient and dilapidated hansoms and growlers arranged
to have them on the streets in the hope that they would
be captured, burned and paid for at a price in excess of
their market value. Like all rackets this one worked
for a period - too long, perhaps - before it was detected
and brought to an abrupt end.

*   *   *

At the beginning of each term, there were misdeliveries
of luggage necessitating inquiries by the railway police
in an endeavour to prevent claims for losses. On entering
various colleges one could not fail to notice the relics
of bygone days which were on display. There were hand-

74

cuffs, truncheons, helmets and other items of police equipment, all of which bore labels giving details of the occasion on which they had been taken from their lawful custodians.

The chief constable of the Cambridge Borough Police once took his men to task for losing their accountrements. His reprimands were made known to the undergraduates who made it their business to demonstrate how simple it was to purloin a policeman's helmet. On the first opportunity, they relieved him of his own as a reprisal.

* * *

In October 1912, my career as a railway constable was over, I obtained a post as a County constable.

VI

A Village Constable in a County Police Force

It was on October 12th, 1912, that I became a member of the Norfolk Constabulary. I was posted to Stalham a rather large village in the Broadland district, about five miles from the coast and sixteen miles from Great Yarmouth, my home town, where my parents still lived.

Arriving at Stalham on a Saturday afternoon with the whole of my police career before me, I wended my way to the police station in which I was destined to live during the chief constable's pleasure and wondered what fate held in store for me, and reported my arrival to the sergeant-in-charge.

He was a fine upstanding man, six foot four in height and of proportionate build, clean shaven and of fresh complexion.

His name was Roythorne. He told me that he had been waiting to meet me. I thought this was a nice gesture on his part and told him so. We were in conversation for some time, but my part in it was the answering of questions put by the sergeant. And it was obvious that I was under examination of a kind with which my superior officer was familiar; he was after getting as much information in as short a period as he could. I made up my mind to get some from him later.

Sergeant Roythorne knew that I had been a soldier and expressed the assumption that I had been under discipline. I admitted these facts. He told me that I should find some of it in the police service too. "We can't do without it", he said.

I felt that the sergeant and I would get along together all right. My ambition to become a policeman had been realised, and I was determined to perform my duties conscientiously and get 'to the top' by climbing the tree in legitimate manner. I didn't tell the sergeant of my intentions. I awoke from my reverie just as he invited me to meet his wife.

She was a pleasant little woman about five foot high,
and she soon put me at ease. Her questions were numerous, and within a short time she was in possession of
a good proportion of my antecedent history. She expressed
the wish that I would be very happy and comfortable and that
I would like being a policeman. "If you do as well as Ted,
my husband, you'll not do so badly".

Sergeant Edward Roythorne vacated his chair, and,
putting on his helmet, he indicated that there was duty
to be done. "Come on, young man", he said, "I'll show
you round the village". We went into the main street,
where it was very quiet. The few people standing about
seemed to be interested in me. "I reckon he's our new
Slop", I heard someone say. From the sergeant I learned
that Stalham wasn't the only village on my beat. There
were two others, but neither of them boasted a police
station. It was some time before I ventured to speak,
but bringing to mind the words of his wife: that if I did
as well as her husband I would not do so badly, I asked:
"How long have you been in the force, sergeant?" His
answer caused me some dismay. "Eighteen years", he said,
"and I've been a sergeant for twelve months".

If it takes seventeen years to reach the rank of
sergeant, I soliloquised, how long will it take me to
become a chief constable? For that was my intention.

The village of Stalham - a straggling one covering
thousands of acres - consisted of the usual stores, two
butchers' shops, two bakeries and three public houses;
The Maid's Head, The Black Swan and the Railway Inn, all
within a radius of a hundred yards or so.

My companion, the sergeant, steered me past the hostelries
without a word. I asked my guide whether there was much
drunkenness in the district. "No", he replied, "but there
are one or two cases when harvest wages are received, and
when the few fishermen living around here 'make up' after
the herring season at Yarmouth".

For a couple of hours we patrolled the village without
witnessing any occurrence requiring police intervention,
and it appeared that the sergeant had made up his mind
that I should not regard constabulary duty as simple or
easy of performance.

We returned to the main street near to the lane in which
the police station was situated. Thoughts of the possibility of a rest and a meal came to my mind, but they were
a bit premature, so far as I was concerned. The sergeant
informed me that he was going in for supper, and instructed
me to continue on patrol. "I think you should turn about

and patrol in reverse the ground we've been covering".

At first, I didn't think that the instructions given me were very good, for I too was in need of nourishment. But who was I, a mere rookey, to express disagreement? So I remained silent and got on with my job consoling myself with the thought that if any would-be offender thought himself able to commit an offence now that the police had passed-by I would be able to cause him disappointment.

On the first day of my service in the Norfolk Constabulary, I was made to realise that, like a soldier, a constable must fend for himself. For the past seven years I had been compelled to fight my own battles and was prepared to carry on doing so; some 'battles' give pleasure. Not yet in uniform, I took advantage of the fact and lost no time in satisfying my hunger.

An hour later Sergeant Roythorne joned me again. To his credit he asked me if I had eaten. "You can turn in now", he said, "I'll see you at ten o'clock tomorrow morning".

At ten o'clock precisely, the sergeant kept his promise. He told me that I was in charge of things until he returned from church. Fancy a recruit-constable being left in charge of a police district on the second day of his service. I felt my responsibility, but hoped in my heart that nothing beyond my capabilities would happen during the sergeant's absence.

My first thoughts were centred upon the possibility of a murder being committed and reported to me, and for a moment or so my mind was troubled. Consolation came when I remembered that the sergeant was close at hand in the parish church. But I wondered whether he would have been sensible enough to occupy a seat at the back where he could be reached without difficulty.

Crimes of a serious nature may have been committed while my superior officer was attending divine service that Sunday morning, but I heard of none.

On his return from church he did not trouble to ask whether anything unusual had happened. Perhaps he knew from long experience that nothing ever did happen in Stalham on the Sabbath. He did speak to me, however, "Have you a bicycle?" he asked. I told him that I had not. "You must get one", he exclaimed. It was a matter of Hobson's choice. There were many miles to be covered, and the County Police Authority didn't supply bikes, so to ease one's legs and feet, one had to acquire such a vehicle.

Next morning, a large hamper was delivered at the police

station.   It contained my uniform, some Acts of
Parliament and what appeared to be an Instruction Book.
I was soon donning the garments and making myself look
a limb of the law and admiring myself in the mirror.

Perusing the book, I found it told me little of my
duties to the public I had sworn to serve, but it did
inform me of many things a wise constable should refrain
from doing.

Within an hour I was patrolling the highways and
by-ways ready to do my duty without fear or favour,
affection or ill-will.

As I walked up the street, shopkeepers and their
assistants downed tools and implements and came out to
take a look at me.

Frankly, I admit my feelings of nervousness and
anxiety. But persuading myself that these feelings
were brought about by wondering whether or not I would
do the proper thing if required to act in a sudden
emergency, 'I took a point to march on, threw back my
shoulders in a soldierly manner and kept my eyes to
the front' except when I looked at my reflection in
shop windows.

Gazing into one particular window, I saw some new
bicycles, and in consequence a bell rang.   Entering the
shop I asked how one could acquire a bike if one had no
money, and to my delight received a favourable reply.
In thirteen months a bicycle could be mine provided that
a similar number of instalments were promptly paid.   Now
a mounted policeman with joy in my heart, I rode away.

Up to this time I hadn't met with a colleague of my
own rank from whom any advice could be gathered.

Constables in charge of beats covering long distances
from three to five miles with a similar number of parishes
were stationed within a radius of seven miles from my own
beat, while others were quartered upwards of twenty
miles, though within the same division.

It was on the fourth day of my service that another
constable came into Stalham cattle market for the purpose
of issuing movement licences under The Diseases of
Animals Acts, and from him I picked up some useful
information.

Among various matters upon which we conversed, I made
the welcome discovery that the County Police Authority -
the Standing Joint Committee of the County Council - made
an allowance to police officers for the upkeep of their
own bicycles used in the execution of their duty.   "They're
thorough spendthrifts", he said with a suspicion of
sarcasm.   "Five bob a quarter or a quid a year they allow

us, and one old buffer - I think he said buffer, but I'm not quite sure - suggested that the amount was excessive, and should be halved".

Knowing nothing about the cost of keeping a cycle in road-worthy condition on rough flinty roads, I expressed the opinion that the allowance was better than nothing. "I agree", he replied. "But you'll find it just enough to pay for patching your tyres".

This particular constable had seven years service to his credit, so he could be described as a man of experience. He asked me whether I had made the acquaintance of the superintendent of the division, and I told him that I hadn't had that pleasure. My colleague sniggered. "You'll see him soon enough" he said, "he's a dear old soul". Wondering whether my companion was still in a sarcastic vein, I returned to the station, met my sergeant, and, acting on his instructions, went on patrol.

Taking my bicycle for its first journey on constabulary duty, I covered the three villages within my jurisdiction. There was nothing doing. The roads were extremely rough - there being no tarmac at that time - and punctures were annoyingly frequent.

The lanes through which I rode were devoid of traffic except for an occasional tumbril laden with swede turnips and other roots for cattle being fattened for Christmas. That part of the county was entirely agricultural and I found the farmworkers very respectful and apparently care-free and contented with their lot.

On my daily travels through these villages I felt that crime was non-existent, and it seemed that as if there would be little opportunity for a police recruit to show his mettle.

The furthermost village was on the coast, but most of it had been swallowed up by the encroaching sea long ago, and no person then living there knew its original boundaries.

It was on the thirteenth day of my service that I met the divisional superintendent for the first time and the meeting will remain in my memory until time is no more. His headquarters were at North Walsham, eight miles from Stalham. On alternate Fridays all constables within the division were required to visit the superintendent's office to receive their pay, and noting details of orders from the chief constable at Norwich.

On my first visit to North Walsham the constable whom I had met on my fourth day in the force, introduced me to the other constables who were awaiting an invitation to enter the superintendent's office. "I wonder what the 'Old Man's' text will be today?" said one of the company. Judging from this rather urgent inquiry, I assumed that the superintendent preached a sermon occasionally.

Perhaps he really is 'a dear old soul' I thought. Nevertheless, I wondered what I was in for at his hands.

Suddenly, from within the office, there came the sound of heavy footsteps and a voice stentorian in volume bidding us enter. "Go in quietly, lads," someone whispered, "the old man's got a liver". We followed this advice, and, to show my respect - being junior to all of them - I took up a position in the rear and was the last to cross the threshold.

In our anxiety to be quiet we must have seemed somewhat slow in making entrance. "Hurry up, there", came the stern command, "and shut that door!" I obeyed with emphasis.

I looked over the counter and saw the superintendent for the first time. He was a tall, broad and heavily built man of dark complexion, and his eyebrows were black and very bushy.

My colleagues and I sorted ourselves out in order of seniority, a procedure necessary for the purpose of entering the inner office in the same order as our names appeared on the pay-sheet.

Each man was required to sign the sheet before getting his wages. The highest rate of pay for a constable was twenty-eight shillings per week and by virtue of this fact he wore a badge bearing the word 'Merit' on one of his sleeves. The average period of service before a constable was entitled to sport this badge was twelve years.

My pay as a recruit was twenty-two shillings and two pence per week. But I was happy and contented in mind.

The man whose turn it was to sign immediately before mine, sat down, took up the pen and with great care dipped it in the inkwell, gathered too much ink and made a blot where his signature should have been. Instantaneously, there came a terrifying roar from the superintendent.

"Stand back!" he thundered, and his big round face took on a crimson hue, as did his language. "Oh my heart", he gasped, "aren't you an awkward so-an-so". He was quivering with excitement, and it seemed that he was about to collapse.

To say that I was surprised is to put it mildly. Never before had I witnessed such a sudden storm over so trivial and accidental an incident.

The unfortunate constable sprang from his chair, just managed to avoid a collision with the superintendent, stepped back as ordered, came in violent contact with the office counter and slithered down to the floor in a sitting posture.

'Tragedy' became comedy, and I was involuntarily forced to laugh aloud though all the other men - who knew the superintendent better than I did - remained silent.

"So you think a blot on a paysheet is funny, do you?" bawled the super.

I wasn't sure whether or not the irate officer expected a reply or an apology, but feeling that courtesy demanded one or the other, I said: "I'm sorry, sir, it was not the blot that I thought funny, but what has happened since that catastrophe". And judging from the change that came over the superintendent's countenance, I realised at once that I had made a faux pas bordering upon insubordination.

Gradually, the atmosphere improved and there were sighs of relief. All of us in the office with one exception began to think of home. But before mounting our bicycles, we had some items of information and intelligence to enter in our pocket-books.

From my colleagues I learned that by laughing in the presence of the superintendent and my answer to his query about what I thought of the blot, an important precedent had been created.

The constables attending the pay parade came from various directions, but quite a number of them were travelling home in my direction. And it was from these men that I heard their opinions of our superior officer. Some of these were good humoured and others were most uncomplimentary.

While a soldier, I had heard many such remarks made about non-coms, but I was rather surprised to hear similar opinions expressed by policemen about their superintendent, even though the majority of them were ex-service men.

But judging from what I had observed that day, my first experience of the superintendent and his temperament, some of the opinions expressed by my colleagues were appropriate; as I was to find out as time passed.

One of my colleagues on that day asked me what I thought of the 'old buzzard', and others were obviously anxious to know my opinion of the gentleman under discussion, but the sergeant didn't want to know. However, I considered the time inopportune for me to give my opinion, and I said so.

Here is a synopsis of the sayings, opinions, etc., expressed by my colleagues, as, in turn, they rode up beside me from five to eight miles on my journey home:-

1. His mother was very fond of him!

2. He wasn't called 'black minorca' for nothing!

3.   You'll find he'll 'choke you off' before he asks
for an explanation. He must get in first, you
see, to show you he's the boss. Never expect him
to apologise!

4.   He was born a super; his father was one!

5.   His bark is worse than his bite!

What proof was there that his mother was very fond of
him? She had him christened "Welcome William!" I think,
perhaps, that people would accept this as a true statement.
His black, bushy and heavy eyebrows earned him the
nickname.
With regard to statements 3 and 5 I must wait and see
before expressing my opinion.
Statement 4 was true, and it probably gave him a good
start to his career.
It was from my earliest experience of Superintendent
"Welcome William" Basham, that I realised that my life in
the Norfolk Constabulary was not likely to be easy.
This pleased me, for I didn't want things to be easy.
Ease might suit lazy and irresponsible men, but I wouldn't
expect it.
It soon became apparent to me that circumstances would
compel me to meet Mr. Basham fairly often.
In those days, only divisional police stations were on
the telephone, so whenever my sergeant had need to get in
touch with the superintendent, he was forced to make use
of the permitted quickest and cheapest means available
by resorting to me and my bike.
The telegraph was available, but spending money on
telegrams being frowned upon, constables were used as
messengers on every possible occasion.
I was fond of cycling and found no difficulty in obeying
orders.
It was my misfortune to upset the superintendent's
equilibrium fairly frequently, but I was forced to the
conclusion that the super's bark was indeed, occasionally
worse than his bite.

*   *   *

After a few months service it became apparent that unless
a Crime Wave was in the offing, there was little chance for
any police officer to make his name as a detective of repute.
The reason is simple; there was little or no crime to
investigate.

In fact, so small was the amount of crime throughout the County that a Detective Department had never been considered necessary.

When, however, a crime such as Larceny or Breaking and Entering occurred, it was the duty of the constable on the beat to detect the offenders - for what crime there was was local - and he was expected to know the identity of thieves living in his district, and his efficiency was judged from the percentage of detections he made.

He was never able to 'pass the buck'.   But it must be admitted that there were cases in which no record was kept. These omissions were very few, however, for knowledge that a serious offence had been committed was 'news' worth spreading and talking about in a manner uncomplimentary to the local constable.

As time went on I learned a great deal from my colleagues when meeting them at 'conference point', at which we spoke of many things and our knowledge of local 'characters' and their pursuits and suspected activities in varying directions.

It was at such conference points that we used to talk about our powers as policemen, when we could make an arrest and when we couldn't.   And it was in this way that we learned our duty as Constabularymen, for there were no Training establishments in those days; yet 'unlawful arrests' were few and far between.

There were one or two instruction books on the market, but few policemen could afford them.   I was able to purchase them because, as an army reservist drawing sixpence per diem as a 'retainer', each quarter, I was more fortunate than many of my colleagues.

Men in county police forces were never anxious to make arrests.   And unless circumstances compelled them to take a person into custody, they preferred to proceed by Summons. For at the time when I was a recruit, there were no motor vehicles available to the police in county forces.   And conditions in cities and towns were little better.

Can you imagine the predicament in which a constable would find himself when circumstances compelled him to make an arrest at a place on his beat many miles from his home and further still from the nearest police station?

It was customary in such circumstances at that period for the constable to ask a farmer to provide a vehicle and driver to convey a prisoner to the lock-up, but it was a good thing that these occasions were rare.

*   *   *

One of the most important obstacles to the successful

85

making of inquiries in villages and hamlets, is the close
relationship between any family and another.   And unless
a newly appointed constables took care to ascertain, as
quickly as possible, the family relationships existing
within his jurisdiction, he would find some difficulty in
carrying out his work without friction; for I have discovered what a simple matter it is 'to put one's foot
in it'.

The first opportunity I had of displaying my ability
in detection of crime in Stalham came, as most opportunities
do, rather unexpectedly.

On a Saturday morning, when part of my duty was to make
the environs of the police station look nice and tidy,
a well-known and wealthy farmer called.

I was busy raking the shingled path when my attention
was drawn to the visitor.

His face was very red and he appeared to be angry.
"Where's the sergeant?" he shouted.   "I don't know",
I replied.   I could have told the farmer that the sergeant
liked to keep his movements secret, but in my wisdom, I
remained silent.   At that moment Sergeant Roythorne came
in by the front gate, in full view of the irate gentleman
whose temper was rising.

"It's about time", he said rather heatedly, "that you
chaps woke yourselves up".   The sergeant glanced at me and
winked.   "What's troubling you, sir?" he asked.   "I'm
losing a lot of eggs", the complainant said, "and if you
can't catch the thieves, I'll see about it".   How he
expected the police to know of the alleged thieving, he
didn't trouble to explain.

The sergeant promised immediate attention.   And I can
only think that he didn't regard the case as particularly
serious, because he instructed me - a mere recruit - to
deal with it.   In fact he told me exactly what to do and
showed me how and where to mark eggs - on the narrow end
with a pencil dot - so that I could identify them as stolen
ones should I find them in the possession of a thief.

Hopping on my bike, I went to the scene of the alleged
crime.   From the yardman there I learned that eggs had
been disappearing daily from nest-boxes inside a derelict
vehicle standing in the farmyard wherein hundreds of hens
of the barndoor variety roamed at will.

Marking a number of eggs, I placed them in the nests
and arranged with the yardman that directly after the
farmhands had left for home, he would examine the nests,
and, if any eggs were missing, he should fire two shots
from his gun as a signal for me to act.

The shots were duly fired, and I stopped the farm workers,

declared my identity, and with no difficulty detected the thief.

Throwing out my chest with pride, I took the culprit to the farmhouse, and found the farmer-complainant. "Here he is Mr. Ladbrooke", I said.

Mr. Ladbrooke took a deep breath, and said: "Damn my diddle, so my own nephew has to rob me".

There was no prosecution, even though the police could have proceeded against the offender had they wished.

When the complainant visited the police station a day or so after I had so 'sensationally' and annoyingly arrested his newphew for theft, it was noticed that he was sweeter in temper, and, as he received the stolen eggs from Sergeant Roythorne, he turned to me and said: "You're not so ...... silly as you look!" And as he tucked the eggs into his waistcoat pockets, he went on his way rejoicing at the fact that his property had been recovered.

The price of eggs in 1913 was one shilling a score, and a good chicken could be bought for a shilling.

*   *   *

Some weeks later, I was conferring with another and much more experienced constable at a village about three miles from Stalham, where the same farmer owned a second farm, when the complainant drove up to us in a pony car. "You're just the blokes I want", said he, "I'm losing a lot of ------ corn from one of my barns".

My colleague, who had known the complainant for several years, was very polite, as all policemen are expected to be, was in jocular mood, and promised attention to the matter. But he caused me - and the farmer too, apparently - some surprise, when he pointed out to the complainant that blood-stained corn would probably be regarded as being of no value and that 'things of no value' couldn't be stolen.

The complaining farmer didn't regard the constable's remarks as a joke, however, and lost his temper and dignity. "I keep such _____ as you", he snapped, as he gave his pony a flip with the whip and went on his way home.

My colleague told me that he felt that his statement to the farmer was necessary because of the complainant's habitual use of profane language.

*   *   *

Before I became a county policeman, I, like numerous other people, looked upon village constables as persons of little importance with precious little police work to do.

But it took a very short period of time to show me
what a serious and unfair misjudgment I had made.

How very true it is that much wisdom comes from
mistakes when appreciated and admitted before further
harm is done!

I soon found how necessary it was that a village
constable should perform his duties conscientiously and
thoroughly; that he must be a man of intelligence, and
one able to keep his own counsel at all times; and that
it is essential for him to know the characteristics of
the people over whom he 'keeps watch and ward' in order
to learn those facts which he will have to rely upon, if
he is to be successful in his work among them.

In every village and district he will find, if his
experience is similar to my own, that people have
differences of varying importance, while some seem to
be too talkative, others are wiser and appear to prefer
waiting to guesswork, before expressing themselves on any
subject which they consider worth talking about.   Such
differences in people are of course, inevitable.   But by
listening and keeping an open mind, the village constable
will learn many things, the majority of which - in his
wisdom - he will keep to himself.

From one particularly friendly colleague, I learned
how to question suspects without arousing their suspicions,
and how successful one could be in making inquiries if
one acted tactfully and discreetly.

My friend, Bill Cooper, never wasted words.   He told
me, inter alia, that his earlier mistakes were due to
talkativeness.   And he warned me of the dangers likely to
accrue from a 'wagging tongue'.

It was, I am sure, my regard for this advice that
prevented me from becoming insubordinate to the superintendent at times when his remarks were not conducive to
an appreciation of my efforts in the cause of duty.

*   *   *

Very late on night, a fire occurred at a farm in Stalham
and, on the instructions of Sergeant Roythorne, I cycled to
North Walsham to apprise the superintendent of the fact.

This action was absolutely necessary in order to comply
with a Standing Order made by the chief constable: "On an
alarm of fire, the superintendent will at once repair to
the scene of the outbreak to take charge of the constabulary there".

I rode as I had never ridden before; eight miles in what

must have been a policeman's record time.   Arriving
at the super's house, I found it in darkness, a fact
that caused me no surprise for it was well past midnight.
The time notwithstanding, I had my orders and was determined to carry them out.   I threw some pebbles up to
what I calculated was his bedroom window.   My calculation
was correct.   Whether I broke the glass or the officer's
sleep or had interrupted a call of nature, I knew not,
but the window was jerked up, and there came a violent
inquiry from a voice impossible to mistake.

"Who's there?" the superintendent barked.   I declared
my identity.   "I might have known it", he said with heat.
"Well, what is it?"   Remembering that I had been told
'That a soft answer turneth away wrath' I put the adage
to the test.

In my most gentle voice I reported that Sergeant Roythorne
had sent me to inform him that 'Blackacre Farm' at Stalham
was on fire.   "Does he want me to come and put the _____
out?" he snapped.

Before I could muster a reply - which in all probability
would have been considered insubordinate - the window was
brought down with a bang, and, without any better respect
for the superintendent as a leader of men by example, I
returned to the scene of the conflagration, assisted in
pumping the manual fire-engine and found the sergeant.

Sergeant Roythorne asked me whether the superintendent
was coming.   "No, sergeant," I answered, "he is content
to leave the matter in your hands and await your report".
Sergeant Ted Roythorne seemed to be pleased.   He sent me
home.

For a short time after this episode, I felt resentment,
but I've had many a good laugh about it with my colleagues
since.

In 1913, a few months after I became a constabularyman,
the Norfolk Constabulary, like most other police forces in
counties, cities and boroughs did not possess a single
motor vehicle.   In fact, the only kind of conveyance in
cities and boroughs was the horse-drawn 'black maria'.
And in county police forces, superintendents of divisions
were provided with a dog-cart and a horse to draw it.

And in this vehicle he got around on his visits to
outstations, which were not numerous.   But the horse was
kept in a state of physical fitness by its rider - usually
an ex-cavalryman - within a mile or so of its stable, and
the constables regarded it as a pet.

Motor cars in the possession of members of the public
and used on the roads were few.   The legal speed for the
motor car was 20 miles per hour under the provisions of

The Motor Car Act, 1903.   And it was common for motorists
who exceeded such a speed to be regarded as 'road hogs'.

Let me tell you of my first case against an offending
motorist.   It was in June, 1913, when a powerful American
motor car driven by a chauffer, came into Stalham on
several occasions.   Usually, there were two passengers,
a boy and a girl.

On one occasion when it had passed me, I noticed that
the driver had suddenly brought it to a stop as if something had gone wrong with its engine.   This was not so,
however.   The cause of the sudden stop had been brought
by a sudden request by one of the children to be allowed
to drive the car.

The driver complied with the request, and the vehicle
was driven away from my sight.

Next day I was on cycle patrol in the village of
Ingham, when I saw the same car - a Studebaker - coming
towards me.   It was being driven by the girl.   I caused
it to stop.   I asked the young lady her age.   She said:
"I am fourteen".   I asked her if she had a licence to
drive a motor car.   She produced one.   It was signed
by the then town-clerk of Birmingham.

For driving when disqualified - she being under age -
she had committed an offence, and the chauffeur had rendered
himself liable to prosecution for 'aiding and abetting'
in the offence, but it being considered that he - as a
servant - was merely obeying orders, no report was made
against him.

During the morning following this episode, when on foot
patrol in Stalham, I was approached by the girl-driver's
father who had made a special journey to see me.   He
appeared to be somewhat angry.   "Are you the constable",
he asked me, "who stopped my car when my daughter was
driving it?"   I answered in the affirmative.   "Don't
you think that you would have been better employed catching
some of those road hogs", he asked.   And he informed me
that by acting in the way I had yesterday, was not the way
to get visitors to come to the district.

At the hearing of the case at North Walsham Court a
week or so later, a solicitor from Birmingham appeared to
represent the girl and her father.

Pleading guilty, the solicitor mentioned that the father
of juvenile offender was a magistrate in the city of
Birmingham and that he had not appreciated that such an
offence could be committed, otherwise he wouldn't have
obtained a licence to enable his daughter to drive.

Lord Kimberley, the chairman of the bench, called me
into the witness-box and asked me how long I'd been a

policeman. "Eight months, my lord", I said.   Lord
Kimberley - long since dead - smiled and said: "This
constable knew that an offence was being committed".
I probably smiled too, realising that such knowledge
had come to me by having recently made sure by reading
The Motor Car Act, of 1903.

The case was dismissed 'on payment of costs, four
shillings'.   A case proved without conviction, and
quite satisfactorily.

I have mentioned this case with the object of showing
that in those early days of the motor car, steps were
taken to prevent children and other disqualified persons
driving such lethal vehicles on our roads which were not -
in those days - as fit to carry heavy traffic as they
are today.

And the law expected the police to do their duty to
the general public by taking the action necessary to
detect and prevent - where possible - infringements of
it.

As a village constable with three villages on my beat,
I was learning how necessary it is to be tactful and
discreet in performing one's duty, and how simple it is
to make mistakes which may occasionally be considered
detrimental to one or more members of the community.

*   *   *

On a Saturday evening during harvest time, when I was
on foot patrol in Stalham High-street, a barman from one
of the inns came and asked me to 'chuck out' a customer
who was making a nuisance of himself.

I went with him to the public house concerned, and saw
that several male customers were enjoying themselves.
There was no difficulty on my part to discover the 'Nuisance'.
And I began to wonder what right I had to 'chuck' him out.
His size compared with my own was the reason, I suppose.
To the licensee I said: "Ask him to leave so that I can hear
your request".   He acted as advised, and was met with a
refusal.   "Come along, sir", I said, "I don't want anyone
to see you being chucked out".   He raised himself for
comfort, and said: "I'll go".   He said the same words
again and again and as I moved closer to him, he said:
"but it's only because you called me sir".   And he stumbled
through the door.

Most of the other customers then left the premises.
Later the same evening, Sergeant Roythorne informed me that
the licensee had complained about having lost some of his
custom after I had dealt with the man who had been disorderly.

But a number of wives of the revellers thanked me for causing their husbands to return home at a reasonable time.

VII

Fellow Constabularymen

Perhaps, when passing through a village at various
times during day or night, you have occasionally noticed
two or more policemen congregated there, and have
wondered why it was necessary for them to be meeting
amid such tranquil surroundings, or you may have thought
that their presence had been caused by a road-accident
or a crime. And in such circumstances you have felt
inclined to ask the reason for the police being there,
only to find that they were complying with routine.

But I am writing of what used to happen in Norfolk, in
years gone by.

At these conferences information was passed on and
exchanged respecting crimes committed in various parts of
the country, with details and descriptions of suspects
and persons wanted, in connection with them.

These periodical meetings were considered important,
and there was always the possibility that a superior officer
would attend them to give adequate supervision. But the
constables never knew whether they would be visited by
such an officer. And, as most of these conference points
were compulsory, besides having to be recorded in each
constable's 'journal', a book which was often checked by
one's superintendent, there was a disciplinary risk whenever a constable 'chanced his arm' by dodging such a point,
he seldom took such a risk.

Only an emergency of consequence was regarded as
sufficient to excuse absence from these conference points,
and any such absence had to be reported to the divisional
superintendent, giving the reason for non-compliance.

One particular night which - owing to the circumstances -
I shall always remember, I set out to trek to one of these
conference points. It was due to take place outside a
church in a village about four miles from Stalham, at the
bewitching hour of midnight.

Although constables were allowed and expected to cover

their beats beyond the village in which they lived by
cycle during the day, the use of these machines was
prohibited at night. But sergeants - who were often
required to visit more than one of these gatherings miles
apart, were allowed to cycle at all times.

I had covered about three miles of my journey to the
church when Sergeant Roythorne overtook me, dismounted
from his bike, fell in step beside me and accompanied me
to the church where we expected to meet a constable from
a neighbouring beat.

We waited for an hour, but nobody came. It was a
glorious night and a pleasure to be out.

The church stood in its magnificence about half-a-mile
from the sea; and with aid from a light breeze one could
hear the waves as they splashed on shore. "I can't stay
any longer", the sergeant said, "so I'll say goodnight,
and get back home". And mounting his bicycle, he rode
away.

All was still, just ideal for spooks and other disturbers of the peace, but I saw none.

I kept my lonely vigil for a further short period, but
as the constable whom the sergeant and I had waited to
meet had not turned up, I decided to make for home.

On my way I examined some farm premises, disturbing a
dog or two in the process, but finding everything apparently
in order, I reached home and turned in feeling fully
entitled to reasonable repose.

As sleep was about to overtake me, I heard a tapping
noise on my bedroom window.

Sitting up with a jerk and listening, I saw something
being drawn across the window. What on earth was it?
Was a burglar about to commit a felony 'against the peace
of our Sovereign Lord the King, his Crown and Dignity'?
If so, I must get him.

Police stations were not usually the scene of burglaries,
but my station did not look its part. It was, in fact,
much like several of the larger houses in the village, and
quite likely to attract the attention of a travelling
criminal.

Up to that time I had not captured a burglar. As a
matter of fact, that part of the county had been free from
that kind of serious crime for a considerable space of time.

Now fully awake and alert, I decided to investigate,
and, if necessary, make an arrest.

Seizing my truncheon from the bedpost on my left, and
without donning my trousers, I crept downstairs, through
the kitchen, and out into the open air. Keeping close to
the wall, I went to the front of the police station where

I saw a dark object.

Gripping my offensive weapon tightly I closed with the object and was about to raise my truncheon with intent to make its presence felt, when a whispered voice asked: "Has Guy Fawkes been to the point?" The voice was that of the constable whom the sergeant and I had expected to meet at midnight outside the church.

This was the first time that I had heard Sergeant Roythorne's nickname, but I thought it inappropriate, for up to then I hadn't noticed anything 'explosive' about him.

The cause of my excitement and suspicions having abated, I felt quite chilly, and, more for my own benefit than his, I invited him indoors.

Lighting a candle - there being no gas or electric light available - I looked at my colleague. His appearance was most grotesque. And if he had been attending a 'fancy dress' parade, the First Prize would certainly have been his.

He explained his absence from the conference point was due to his oversleeping, but knowing that that fact wouldn't be accepted as a legitimate excuse, he thought he had better find out whether the sergeant had attended the point before deciding if the making of a non-compliance report was necessary.

I saw what he was getting at, and so can you. When I told him that Sergeant Roythorne was there, he said: "There's no alternative, Black Minorca must be told!"

Preparing some tea, I promised that his unorthodox visit wouldn't be recorded or divulged. Expressing his appreciation, he removed the woollen stockings in which his boots were encased, made himself presentable and left to start his six mile journey home; during which, no doubt, he gave much thought to what he would say in mitigation of possible 'punishment' in the form of a sermon from Super-intendent Welcome William Basham, for missing the conference point.

When we made our next fortnightly visit to divisional headquarters for pay and anything else the superintendent had to offer, a non-compliance report was mentioned. "What have you to say about the one that you made quite recently, Betts?" the superintendent asked.

In a quiet and seemingly sorrowful voice Constable Jonah Betts, answered: "Nothing, if you haven't, sir". And to the astonishment and surprise of other subordinates present, he got away with it.

An hour later, when all the constables picked up their bicycles outside the office, the defaulting constable received a 'standing but whispered, ovation' from his delighted colleagues.

The liver of the superintendent must have been in extra good order that day.

* * *

Gradually, I learned the characteristics of my fellow constables. Some of them had long since become resigned to the fact that their chance of promotion had passed them by, but they seemed content with their lot. Others - generally those with less than twelve years' service - were dedicated and hopeful of attaining higher rank.

The first step on the ladder was the appointment to Acting Sergeant. And from then on, it was a matter of seniority, and providing such an officer continued to do his duty correctly there was a reasonable chance that he would eventually reach the rank of superintendent.

But under the conditions then prevailing, it was by no means certain.

In those days there was no system of examinations in which a police officer could qualify for <u>consideration</u> when a vacancy in a higher rank occurred.

To obtain a chance of promotion a constable and a sergeant had to be recommended by the superintendent upon whose opinion the chief constable had to rely, for about subordinates, apart from those stationed at headquarters under his personal supervision, as it were, plus one or two alleged defaulters who appeared before him to be disciplined, he knew little.

Since the Police Act of 1919, came into force, and under which the Police Federation came into being, examinations to qualify for consideration when vacancies occur in the ranks of sergeant and inspector, have been compulsory.

During my long service, however, it has become obvious to me that the mere ability to pass such examinations or those set by universities, should not be regarded as proof conclusive of an examinee's fitness to hold higher rank in the police service.

I give reasons for this opinion, in another chapter.

* * *

Among my colleagues was one in particular who had given up hope of reaching a rank higher than that given him on enlistment. He was known as 'Speedy', and was the most unpunctual individual I had met, although as the years have rolled by I have had experience of many like him in this respect.

NO SILVER SPOON

Something always happened to delay him or to provide him with an excuse for being late, but he was never late for his pay.   A constable of experience and ability upon whom reliance could be placed in matters of duty, he dodged much criticism by his plausibility.

On one particular occasion, which I shall be unable to forget, three constables and I converged on a compulsory conference point at which we were to meet 'Speedy' at 1 a.m., some miles from the nearest police station.

At this conference Sergeant Roythorne put in a visit, but as usual, Speedy was adrift.

The sergeant didn't like unpunctuality, and he seemed to be a bit fidgetty when he said, more to himself than to the constables present, "I wonder what's keeping him now?"

None of us had any idea of the cause of Speedy's absence, but all of us knew that the excuse given by him would be unassailable.

Suddenly, there came the sound of footsteps and the smell of tobacco smoke.   Speedy reached the conference point twenty minutes late, and by then, the smell of burning tobacco had ceased.

"What's gone wrong tonight", the sergeant asked.   But there was a slight delay in Speedy's reply: "I can't think, sergeant", the late comer declared,   "why you should imagine that something had gone wrong tonight".

"I thought", Sergeant Roythorne said, with a firm voice, "that the cause of my anxiety would have been obvious to any police officer who was so late as you were in arriving at such an important point as this is".

Speedy expressed his sorrow, and said: "Just as I was passing down the lane running alongside 'thingammy wood', I heard a shot and went to investigate.   I scouted around a bit and then I remembered this point and thought that you ought not to be kept waiting, and that I'd better attend to the matter on my way back".

At the moment that Speedy had given his indisputable explanation I flashed my torch to check the time and noticed that the sergeant didn't appear to have been impressed to any appreciable degree.

When Sergeant Roythorne had given details of what had been discussed during Speedy's absence, he instructed us to accompany the late one back to his beat and deal with the poachers, if any, who had been responsible for the shot which had caused Speedy's late arrival.

When the sergeant was out of whisper range, one of my older colleagues had a few words to say to Speedy. "If you could manage to be in time for once in your life", he said, "it wouldn't be necessary for you to concoct so many of your fairy tales".

"I take umbrage at that remark", said Speedy. "And its a pity that I can't take him with me instead of you chaps", he continued, wittily. But he didn't expect to get away with his drollery, even though he hoped to raise a laugh.

In fact, Speedy had three 'umbrages' accompanying him, each of whom were getting further away from their homes and nearer to that of the one who was the cause of their unwelcome and probably unnecessary job of work.

To be fair to Speedy it must be admitted that he apologised for being responsible for the sergeant's instructions, though he certainly didn't improve our feelings, when he said: "It's good for one's experience, lads".

We trudged towards Thingammy Wood, and on reaching its fringe we opened out like Infantry on the warpath. At intervals of ten yards or so, we picked our way through trees and other growths like trained scouts.

A quarter moon gave us little help, and, except for the occasional breaking twig, all was silent.

Each of us carried a small torch which for obvious reasons, couldn't be used until we came up with those of whom we were in search.

None of us knew the geography of the wood, for none of us had ever had cause to be there before, and all of us - even including Speedy, I think, - thought that we need not have been there that particular night.

Suddenly, there broke upon the silent night the unmistakable sound of a heavy splash followed by a flow of words never expected to be used by a police officer. The possible unlawful presence of poachers was now of no consequence.

We thought of the possibility of a life being in danger. Our torches flashed and convered on a spot in the middle of a deep, muddy and smelly patch of water from which a slow-moving black object was rising unsteadily into view.

What a sight! Was the apparition a poacher or a policeman? Judging from the language used by it, however, perhaps it was natural for one to conclude that the object wading out of the evil-smelling and stagnant water, could not possibly be a member of the force.

I was hoping that the unfortunate one was Speedy himself, but I was disappointed, for at that moment I heard that individual ask the needless question: "What's up?"

There was a violent splutter from the 'diver' as he

cleared slime, weed and other foreign bodies from his
mouth and nostrils.   "What's up, you ask, you silly
_____, I was kicked in the shins by a pheasant".
   Any man in the state in which the speaker was, who
could give such an answer, when he must have felt like
the most miserable man on earth, proved beyond doubt that
he possessed a sense of humour.
   To our shame we - except of course, the luckless one -
laughed aloud; the circumstances being so compelling.
But it was our hope that our unfortunate colleague would
imagine our 'glee' arose solely from his surprising reply
to Speedy, and not, in fact, the whole episode at which
we were so uncharitably amused.
   With aid from our torches we retraced our steps and
hoped that Speedy wouldn't be 'disturbed' by shots coming
from Thingammy Wood or elsewhere, for a long time to come,
and wended our respective ways back to our beats, at a
pace set by our muddy, smelly and uncomfortable colleague,
who was compulsively expectorating at every few steps.

*   *   *

   Another colleague with whom I occasionally met at
conference points during my first year of service was
Billie Marler, stationed at Hickling, an important and
well-known village, three miles from Stalham.
   Bill had joined the Norfolk Constabulary twenty-six
years ago, a year or so before my birth.   He was one of
'the Old and Bold', who had served in several parts of
the county, and was looking forward to his retirement and
a pension of eighteen shillings and eightpence per week,
to which he would be entitled when he had completed twenty-
six years' service.
   Bill's 'manor' or beat covered five villages extending
over a distance of twelve miles, and it was probably the
largest 'one man' constabulary district in Norfolk.
   Three of the five villages - Sea Palling, Waxham, and
Horsey, were on the coast.   Extremely pleasant in fine
weather, but in winter and early spring they were visited
by fiercely violent storms which, in effect, were not too
good for a policeman's complexion.
   The prevailing winds came from the North, and Bill's
face was red and weather-beaten, through no fault of his
own.
   He was a jovial soul, and his greatest wish was that
nobody would commit an offence within his view,. during
the remainder of his service as a policeman.
   As a matter of fact, he had never been one to go in

<u>search</u> of law-breakers, and it was the reason explaining why few offenders had come within his grasp.

But though Bill's fervent wish was realised, there came a time when it was almost dashed to the ground. For in consequence of a complaint made to Sergeant Roythorne by a farmer, to the effect that some of his corn-ricks and haystacks had become smaller in size and mis-shapen, through the unwanted presence of Nomads and their live-stock in the neighbourhood, I was ordered to re-inforce Bill at night for the purpose of investigating the matter.

We met at midnight in the vilest weather. Bill didn't hide his displeasure or his thoughts. But he considered it necessary to inform me duty must be done no matter what the elements or circumstances. He told me that this kind of job was very good for training youngsters like myself; that he had done a lot of it in his time; but for blokes like himself it was 'no bottle'. I thought it prudent to remain silent.

This staid constabularyman had probably spent about a third of his service on Night duty, and was convinced that the 'clerk of the weather' paid no regard to the welfare of policemen, except, perhaps, to clear the streets for him in daytime. Yes "P.C. Rain" is a good Bobby; for he can disperse a crowd quicker than an entire police force can.

Bill and I patrolled conscientiously until we came to the conclusion that we were wasting our miserable time. I was very pleased when my colleague gave the verdict.

Tired out and soaked through, we came to a large house, which, to my colleague's surprise, displayed a light in a room on the ground floor. We thought of the possibility that a burglar was at work. Acting on Bill's whispered instructions, I went round to the back while he remained at the front.

It was our intention to be as quiet as possible, and we decided not to use our torches. On my way to the back door I kicked a bucket or some such utensil which rolled along and gave off a 'tinny' noise. Just as I was about to express my annoyance, Bill and another man came to me. For an instant I thought the burglar had been caught. But the man with my colleague was the householder.

There wasn't anyone else about; but the householder was good to us. He was a retired gentleman apparently well-known to Bill. "What appalling weather", he exclaimed, "pray come in, perhaps I shall be able to find you an antidote".

Within a minute or so, the three of us were partaking of a hot reviver in the form of rum and lemon-juice.

Thanking our benefactor, Bill and I made for home.

Somehow or other the journey home seemed much happier than otherwise would have been.

I asked my colleague whether he knew any resident on my manor who was as hospitable as the gentleman we had just left. "As you gain experience, lad", he replied, "you'll find 'em; but take care, especially in the case of those who offer you a drink to make it appear that they are friendly to you. Make sure that you know your man; for there are some, who, having given you a drink will presume upon the fact and consider that they have 'bought' you".

I am satisfied that there was justification for the warning.

When Bill retired I took his place. Although under the same sergeant, I was in charge of a beat of my own covering a long and wide important area, and experienced a feeling of great pride.

The five villages under my supervision were purely agricultural, but in Hickling itself there was, and still is, the largest Broad in the Norfolk Broads. And at Sea Palling, sometimes called Palling-on-sea, there were Coast-guard and life-boat stations.

I became friendly with the life-boat men who were always on the alert and prepared to answer calls from ships in distress under most trying circumstances, for in those days life-boats were sailing-vessels which were often difficult to launch.

Those who man the life-boats round our coast have surely earned the greatest admiration of all people who have had cause to call for help in storm and tempest, and those who have actually seen them answering such a call. I find difficulty in expressing my own appreciation of the services rendered by these intrepid men.

*   *   *

Bill's old beat - now mine - kept me busy. It was plainly my duty to do my utmost to prevent and detect crime, protect life and property as far as possible, and to keep the King's peace.

Being keen on my work, I did not fail to recognise the opportunity given me to show my powers of initiative, tact and discretion, and possibly, my ability as a detective.

I was still on a recruit's rate of pay, twenty-two shillings and twopence per week, but having had such tremendous duties thrust upon me, I thought that an increase in my remuneration was justly due. A month passed, however,

without any sign of an increase. Naturally, perhaps,
I began to wonder whether some act or omission of mine
had incurred the displeasure of the superintendent. My
mind was soon put to rest.

A week or so later, when my colleagues and I visited
the divisional headquarters at North Walsham, Superintendent
Basham intimated that he had an important announcement to
make - you may think that I am not telling the truth, -
but I am - "Listen, all of you", he said, "Police Constable
Number 137 Bunn is advanced in pay from twenty-two shillings
and twopence to twenty-three shillings and fourpence".
Looking in my direction, and adopting a fatherly and
confidential tone of voice, he said: "You see what I've
done for you, now don't abuse it".

Having received my first promotion in pay at the rate
of twopence per day, I had a feeling that my devotion to
duty had been rewarded and that it was up to me to show
appreciation. "Thank you, sir", I replied, "I'll not
let you down". And I meant it.

On my way home I felt distinctly happy with the knowledge
that I had achieved something. Increases in pay in those
times were not awarded automatically as they are in these
days, but only when one's superintendent was satisfied that
a subordinate had earned it. The ladder to promotion was
most difficult to scale, but having moved out of the
Recruit's class I was content. That is, for the time
being; one simply had to be.

*　　*　　*

The first case of importance with which I had to deal
after having been given charge of a district, was to inquire
into an alleged Criminal abortion. I had received an
anonymous letter informing me that a young widow had given
birth to a baby whose body had been buried in the garden of
the cottage in which the widow was living.

Making what I considered were discreet inquiries, I
discovered beyond doubt that no birth had taken place, but
that the young woman had aborted. With the friendly
assistance of a neighbour, she had obtained and made use
of an abortifacient which had done exactly what was expected
of it.

A serious offence had been committed by both women and it
was necessary for me to spend a considerable amount of time
in obtaining particulars for my report.

Among various things of which I took possession, was a
blue bottle from which the requisite doses had been taken,
and on my examination of it I found that some drops of the

concoction remained.   To protect themselves the firm
supplying it had marked the bottle: 'non-abortifacient'.
    In those days - most county police forces being without
C.I.D. - it fell to the constable on the beat to perform
the inquiry work now done by detectives, and, in so doing,
he learned the importance and necessity for evidence
sufficient to substantiate and prove criminal charges, or,
in fact, to give him the 'power of arrest'.
    The same day as that on which I was making inquiries
into the alleged case of criminal abortion I was due to
meet Superintendent Basham at Stalham police station.
By letter, he had previously intimated his desire to speak
with me on an undisclosed subject.
    Although I had come direct from the scene of the alleged
offence referred to, the time of my arrival at Stalham
that afternoon, did not coincide with the time scheduled
by the superintendent.   I had cycled ten miles.   "You're
late" he said, "this won't do, you know".   Being only two
minutes late, I felt like making use of a rude remark,
but I refrained, thinking, perhaps, he would apologise when
he heard my oral report.
    I expressed my sorrow for having kept him waiting, and
consulted my watch, hoping that his own timepiece recorded
was the same time as mine, and that if he checked the time
he would discover that I had arrived almost 'on the dot'.
    In a few words I told the superintendent what I had been
doing, and at the same time I handed the blue bottle
previously mentioned to Sergeant Roythorne.
    The sergeant removed the cork from the bottle and sniffed
at the bottle as if to smell and give a name to its contents.
The superintendent misinterpreted the sergeant's intention,
for, in a sharp and short manner suggesting urgency, he
exclaimed: "Blast it, sergeant, don't you drink any of it
or you'll have a miscarriage!"
    This was the first time that I had seen a sign of a
sense of humour in Superintendent Welcome William Basham,
of the North Walsham Division of the Norfolk Constabulary.
    Thinking that I would enjoy taking a 'rise' out of my
superior officer for his attitude to me when I arrived to
confer with him, two minutes late, after having cycled ten
miles in unusual circumstances in order to comply with his
command, I said: "Have you ever ridden a bike, sir?"   He
was ready with an appropriate and true answer.   "No", he
said, "in my day, policemen had to walk!"   He had deflated
me, and it served me right, and I had 'asked' for it.
    The women in the case were not proceeded against; so the
writer of the anonymous letter got no satisfaction.

*   *   *

Many people will remember a picture showing nine policemen in uniform sitting in an Inn. Each policeman had a pint of beer in his possession, and the Artist called his picture: "Nine P(o)ints of the Law".

The policemen must have been County constables, for it was not possible for a similar number of officers to be found together in any other police force.

As a Constabularyman I had - once a year - been in company with eight or more colleagues in circumstances almost like those depicted; except the fact that I wouldn't have had a pint, for I was a T.T., in those days, and though beer was strong and 2d. a pint, it didn't appeal to me.

Once a year our division consisting of Navy and Army Reservists were inspected because we were believed to know our drill.

When about halfway to North Walsham, a number of us would converge on a public house and enter for 'reasonable refreshment', we were allowed twenty minutes for the purpose. A colleague known as Jakey Scott, of Ludham, would partake of liquid refreshment that caused a smell at short distance. To destroy the odour Jakey would suck a peppermint so as not to cause the superintendent's nostrils to quiver.

On one such an occasion, Jakey's peppermint gave him away. As the superintendent 'walked the line' of constables to see whether there was anything for him to grumble about, he caught a whiff of Jakey's breath, stopped and said: "You've had a quart!" The super's assertion was correct. After the parade Jakey said a few suitable words about the superintendent.

Both of these worthies have passed on.

VIII

Villagers and Others

I found that when parents encountered trouble with
their male offspring, they preferred to seek the help
of the village policeman rather than that of the parson.

When youths appeared to be getting beyond parental
control, the constable was asked to have a talk with them
in the hope that his friendly advice would result in their
return to the path of virtue.

Each mother would declare that her son was being led
astray by some other mother's son.

"My boy used to be as 'good as gold' before he started
to go about with young So-an-so; but now I can't do anything with him", was a typical example of many a mother's
complaint.

Having a certain amount of regard for the timeworn
adage, 'prevention is better than cure', I always answered
a desire for help, but made it clear to the complainant
that to put fear into adolescents was no part of a policeman's duty.

Being aware that certain youths were ganging together
keeping late hours, I hit upon a scheme which I thought
would act as a deterrent.

One evening, at about eleven o'clock, I came upon the
gang as its members were shuffling rather noisily to their
homes. Telling them that, judging from the state of the
bottoms of their trousers, it seemed to me that they had
gone on land where they had been in unlawful search of
game, and that I intended to search them under The Poaching
Prevention Act.

In performing this rather unpleasant task, I discovered
that the suspicion I had pretended to have, was, in fact,
well established. They possessed a number of conies and
various 'engines' used in taking the rabbits.

I had not seen the boys trespassing, and refrained from
asking where the poaching had occurred, so there was no
prosecution; but I took advantage of the opportunity to

administer a stern warning, which was appreciated and of good effect.

*   *   *

People who have been fortunate enough to spend a vacation on the Norfolk Broads, and in the peaceful villages around them, must have been favourably impressed by the friendliness of the local inhabitants with whom they came in contact.

In summer, thousands of small parties of holidaymakers find healthful quietude and rest by cruising about the waterways in motor-boats and trim little sailing craft, and, should a little gaiety be desired, it can be had by mooring for the evening close to one of the delightful inns there situate.

Ornithologists derive much pleasure in watching and recording the habits of the numerous and various birds inhabiting the Broads and the surrounding marshland from February to September.

Whiteslea, on Hickling Broad, is a famous bird sanctuary. When I visited it the man in charge was the very respected Jim Vincent known and revered by thousands of bird-lovers to whom he was always willing to help in their researches. He was a good man.

Freswater fish of many kinds abound in Hickling Broad, but in order to enjoy a good catch it is advisable to secure the services of one of the local boatmen. These cheery fellows know where the fish are to be had and what requires doing to induce them to bite.

The most knowledgeable of the boatmen when Hickling was on my beat was Tubby Turner. He had always lived within sight of the broads, and for thirty years or more had worked on and around them.

In the season, he would pilot visitors to the best spots for fishing; and when asked his fee he invariably answered that he thought it could safely be left to the gentleman concerned.

At times he gathered substantial tips, at others, however, his clients appeared to have a poor idea of the value of his services, but on the whole he did fairly well in this respect.

In the course of my duties I made frequent visits to the staithe alongside of which stood the inn known by the sign of The Pleasure Boat, and there I conversed with numerous anglers to whom Tubby had given assistance.

Judging from what some of the Piscators told me, their day's catch - according to Tubby - was a record.

Each season was one of record-making or record-breaking;

but each 'holder' went home in a contented frame of mind
feeling confident, no doubt, that his particular 'record'
would stand for ever.

Tubby's other job was reed-cutting.   Reeds grow in
profusion on the edge of the broad.   After drying the
reeds are tied in bundles and sent to many parts of the
country to be used for thatching, and many other purposes.

As can be imagined, Tubby was a 'character' in the
Broadland district.   His clientele was large, and included
people of title and anglers of repute.

Whenever he could be persuaded to entertain the patrons
of the 'local' by telling some of his experiences, he was
most discreet.   He never mentioned names, but it was a
certainty that he had knowledge of many and various 'goings
on' during his life on the broads, though he recalled and
spoke only of episodes likely to create laughter.

*   *   *

Another well-known and highly respected villager of
Hickling was Bob Vincent - father of Jim Vincent.   He
told me that his christian name was Robert, but he had
always been called Bob.

"If anyone came to this village and asked where Robert
Vincent lived", he said, "he would be told that no such
person lived in Hickling".   And he told me of an occasion
on which a former acquaintance of his actually had experience of this fact.

After this man had been told that no such person as
Robert Vincent lived in Hickling, he remarked: "It seems
funny to me that you don't know old Bob."   "Cor!" replied
the man who didn't know Robert, "why didn't you ask me
for Bob in the first place, everybody knows old Bob, bless
him".

A religious man, Bob rendered inestimable service to the
community by the usefulness of the talks he gave to
youngsters in his Sunday School.   And I felt that indirectly
he probably helped me too.

Well over seventy, upright and sturdy in build, he had
been a game-keeper, but now earned his livelihood by
catching and selling eels.   Beside his work in Sunday
school he was a local preacher in one of the chapels, and
did his utmost to instill into his pupils that 'happiness'
should always be regarded as an important goal in life.

Bob's vocabulary - like my own - could not be considered
extensive, which was just as well, because those to whom he
spoke were able to understand plain and simple language.
Straight from the shoulder, was Bob.

I am tempted to explain how Bob set to work in the performance of his self-appointed task of directing young folk to the straight and narrow path and keeping them there to the best of his ability, but I must not digress. Suffice it to say that he made use of the word 'Right' in an admirable manner. He counselled them to do right; to think right; to play right and to work right. Do right to your parents and respect them. When you play games, play to win but play fair. Think only of the good, and when you go to work don't shirk. The Lord above wants you to have a fair share of the good things the world can give, but He expects you to earn it. Be happy in the knowledge that you are giving good and useful service by whatever kind of work you do. Make others happy, and you'll be happy. Don't just think of yourselves.

Bob knew when to stop, when he had said enough for one day, he avoided going on until his advice became monotonous, but he'd remember where he left off, before beginning his next instalment.

Bob was a philosopher as well as a psychologist, and it was obvious to an interested observer that he had made a profound and intellectual study of the Scriptures.

I liked Bob Vincent, and never missed an opportunity of having a chat with him, but to broach the subject 'eels' was unwise unless one had an hour or so to spare. He did his eel-catching on dark nights in late summer and autumn. And he knew exactly where those escaping his traps went to breed. What he didn't know of their habits wasn't worth knowing.

Knowing how difficult it was to convince 'unbelievers' of the size and weight of fish alleged to have been caught, Bob had caused the largest of them to be preserved as Exhibits to provide corroborative evidence of the truth of his statements.

*   *   *

At midnight on the 4th August, 1914, Army reservists were recalled to The Colours, so I became a soldier for the second time. It was pleasant to meet again, soldiers with whom one had served in peacetime. And there was much questioning respecting happenings since we parted. Most of us would be experiencing War for the first time, and though we realized the risks, we were all optimists. We would all come home. I did, and after two years I was a policeman again. But many of my chums did not.

It was on my return to police duties that I was fortunate enough to make the acquaintance and obtained the friendship

of the village schoolmaster, John Prickett.   This elderly
gentleman had lived in Hickling for many years, so long
in fact, that almost the entire adult population had been
his pupils.   He was a Special Constable, and as such often
accompanied me on my beat.

I confided in him that my ambition was to attain high
rank in the police service, and confessed that lack of
education - for which no one but myself could be blamed -
made it imperative that I should go to school again.

Without hesitation he volunteered his help.   "You have
the right spirit", he said, "and my house is open to you on
any evening you can manage to come over".

For about two years I took advantage of my friend's
tuition and derived much benefit from it.   I found him
most patient, and have always been grateful for his valuable
help.

The cause of many patrols performed in the pleasant
company of my tutor was the reported approach or presence
of enemy aircraft in the form of Zeppelin airships which
often crossed the Norfolk coast on their visits.

One of the chief duties on such occasions was to prevent
anything capable of assisting the enemy.   Thus the showing
of lights skywards or in the direction of the sea was
taboo.

My schoolmaster friend had the greatest respect for the
scientists of Germany, and credited them with the possession
and use of apparatus enabling them to pick up the slightest
sound emanating from the ground thousands of feet below.

"Whenever we hear of the presence of Zepps", he said,
"it behoves us to converse in whispers".   I found it most
difficult to comply with his exhortation on all occasions,
so there were times when an apology was necessary.

In Hickling there lived a score or more of young men,
who from September to December each year, were fishermen
sailing out of Great Yarmouth in search of herring.   These
men were hardy, tough and brave.   At the outbreak of war
they joined the Royal Naval Reserve, and were engaged in the
arduous and dangerous task of mine-sweeping.

Their periods of leave were short, and when a number of
these gallant fellows gathered together, they, very naturally,
made merry, but on many occasions their merriment was short-
lived and turned to grief when they learned of the loss of
a ship-mate.

In my conversation with them they appeared to be Fatalists,
for they were firmly of the opinion that all things happen
by inevitable necessity; perhaps it was because of this
belief that they were so strong in character and free from
fear.

One night, when the 'take air-raid action' signal had been disseminated, my schoolmaster friend and I were on patrol when there was much noise and striking of matches in the vicinity of one of the village inns. And it was on this occasion that my companion 'slipped up' by forgetting his own rule regarding the imperative need for silence. "Just listen to those foolish fellows", he exclaimed in a voice brought about by the seriousness of the event, "and look at the lights they are showing". Apologising for infringing the 'whispering rule', he immediately broke it again by saying - excitedly - "let us descend upon them". As we were already doing this as fast as a brisk walking pace would allow, there was no point in what he had said, unless he considered that we should break into a canter, but he made no such suggestion. He then resumed whispering and reminded me that this was a case in which extreme tact and discretion were necessary, because those offending were all old boys of his.

Before I could remonstrate with the offenders, my companion sailed in to exemplify his idea of tact. "Don't you know", he said, in a tone suggesting that his voice had gone, "that enemy aircraft are about". In a very deep voice, one of the sailors acted as spokesman and gave us a speech of welcome. "Well", he said, "if it int old John, and int he quiet", he continued. Special Constable John Prickett explained why he was quiet and informed the gathering that it was essential because the German aeronauts could pick up the slightest sound as well as detect lights from the matches so recently struck. And he asked them to be quiet and to refrain from striking matches.

The one with the deep voice spoke again. "We'll do that, sir", he said, "but don't you worry, there's nothing in Hickling to make the Jerries drop any of their 'confetti' on it".

Bidding us goodnight, the sailormen dispersed. The desired result had been achieved. A Special constable's tact, and the good sense of disciplined men who realized that duty must be done.

*　　*　　*

Although I had now completed five years service in the constabulary - my two years war service counting - few opportunities had occurred for me to demonstrate my ability as a detective, but I was busy looking after five villages covering a distance of twelve miles which was quite a job, but I consoled myself with the hope that my vigilance had prevented the commission of a number of crimes.

NO SILVER SPOON

It is very rarely that Crime gives a warning of its approach.

*   *   *

At Waxham, some fishing-lines had been taken from the beach. The complainant was a visitor. He told me about his loss, and said there was little hope of their recovery. The lines had been cast out to sea and left for him to pull-in when he returned.

On going to the spot from which they had disappeared, there was a clue telling me that schoolboys were responsible for the felony. On visiting a school about three miles away, and in another police division, I - with the assistance of the schoolmaster - recovered the lines but not the fish the lads had found on them.

The owner was surprised, and he rewarded me with a codling. My wife and I found it very nice.

Though 'a fair cop' there was no cleverness about it. The boys were not proceeded against!

*   *   *

I remember the characteristics of many villagers living on and around the Hicling beat, in the county of Norfolk. And, as may well be appreciated, there were many adult persons living there and in other similar agricultural districts, who had never been to school. One such person, lived in a cottage quite near my own, and I saw him almost every day or so.

Old Sam was a real and sound son of Norfolk and spoke its 'language' fluently, but though in conversation with him on numerous occasions, I had never heard him use a profane word. Although he 'didn't mind admitting' that he'd not been to school, he was well educated in the phases of farming, which he carried out with devotion, for less than a quid a week. In those days, however, a quid was a pound worth twenty shillings and, believe it or not, work was more productive, and there was more happiness in Britain then than exists now - more than fifty years later - when politicians talk so much about the importance of a university education for all, even for such as Sam.

Sometimes, Sam went shopping. He didn't buy much, for he grew most of the food he and his wife required. But having heard that some people had made mistakes when 'adding up' he checked the price of each purchase on the bill. How was he able to do this without having been to school? Sam did it all right. He used a special form of shorthand

111

known only to himself.   And he told me that nobody ever
'twisted' him.   And I believed him.
    Sam was proud of his country, his king who spent some
of his time each year in Norfolk, and he used to fly the
Union Jack on what he described as 'high days and holidays'.

*   *   *

    Another villager whom I feel is worthy of mention as a
'client' of mine in Hickling was a farmer in a small way
known as Chummy Bell.   It was said that he went to chapel
three times on a Sunday just because it wasn't open four
times.   He wasn't a bad old stick!   But he was careless
about his lights in War time.
    I had cautioned him three or four times about the danger
likely to arise from his display of light from a window
facing in the direction of the sea, but my warnings were of
no avail.   So I felt compelled to report him for Summons
for an infringement of the "Defence of the Realm Act".
I must confess that at least two of my cautions to Chummy
were made for my own personal benefit; for they prevented
the need for me to cycle to North Walsham to prove the two
cases against him, a distance of forty-four miles in the
aggregate.
    As I stepped into the witness-box to give testimony,
Chummy raised his arms roofwards and shook them.   "May the
Lord come to me, may the Lord help Mister Bunn to tell the
truth" he prayed in a voice shaking with emotion.   I gave
my evidence and it was corroborated by a special constable
who was also a farmer.
    The chairman of the bench consulted his colleagues and
said: "Case dismissed!"
    As Chummy was leaving the courthouse, the special
constable said to him: "The Lord did come to you, Chummy".
With a smile Chummy replied: "I knew He would if I asked
Him properly".   In reality however, it seemed that Chummy
had 'a friend in court'.   Chummy was told of this belief.
He smiled; in fact, we all smiled, and there was no ill-
feeling.   Since then, I have been fairly certain that
friends do sometimes appear in court, sometimes on the Bench.
Sometimes it was just as well.   We live and learn.   Most
of my lessons have been 'all to the good'!

A VILLAGE GROCER LOSES HIS PANTS

    One morning a grocer in the village of Hickling complained
that a pair of his Long John underpants had been stolen from
a line on which they had been hanging to dry.

112

As already mentioned, Larcenies were uncommon in my district, but when one was reported I was keen to discover the offender.

Visiting the scene of the crime, I found impressions of a man's boots, and noticed some peculiarities about them; this was fortunate for me, because unless there are peculiarities - such as to show that nails are missing on the sole of a hob-nailed boot or other special signs - they would have been of little use in identifying the wearer of a particular boot or boots, so many soles being alike.

Covering the impressions with upturned boxes - obtained from the victim of the theft - to prevent their obliteration before I could take plaster casts of them; was the first step in my investigation. But as it happened, there was no need to take casts, for just as I was about to leave in order to get the necessary materials, I saw a man digging on an allotment a short distance away. Going in his direction and hoping that he could be of help to me by answering my questions, I found it quite unnecessary to ask him a single one.

Glancing down at the marks his boots were making I was certain that he was the culprit. What a piece of luck! I accused him of stealing the grocer's pants and he, in turn, accused me of Slander, and he threatened to have the law on me.

I found the pants in his possession and seized them as Exhibit 1. He was fined.

*   *   *

About a year later, I arrested the stealer of the pants on charges of 'having carnal knowledge' of two girls under the age of sixteen years. The girls were sisters and of weak intellect. They lived next door to him. He had gained their consent by giving them florins which he kept in a vase on his mantelpiece. The Law said the girls were too young to give consent.

At the Norfolk Assizes, in January, 1919, when put on his plea, he pleaded 'guilty of some on it' which meant that a plea of Not Guilty was entered on his behalf. He was found guilty, the girls were not required to give evidence.

Mr. Justice Bailache, sentenced the offender to twenty-one months hard labour in each case, the sentences to run con-currently. The accused man had previously been convicted of Rape.

For some reason - probably known only to himself - the Judge found it necessary to point out that his name rhymed with 'eyelash'.

This was my last case in the Norfolk Constabulary, a police force in which I had been proud to serve.

On my way to the assizes I had deposited my civilian clothes at divisional headquarters, and later the same day handed in my uniform.

Superintendent Welcome William Basham told me that he was sorry I was leaving. "I'm sure you'll do well in the police service", he said, "and I'll watch your progress", he continued. Thanking him for his good wishes and the hard and useful training I had received during my service under his supervision I wished him well. But it wasn't until I was about to leave his presence that I realized how beneficial his methods of keeping me up to scratch had been.

I hope that my description of a conscientious Village Policeman's duties is sufficient to show how necessary he is to the community.

Next day I became a member of the King's Lynn Borough Police Force, with the temporary rank of Sergeant, which was not to become substantive unless and until I had qualified for The Board of Trade certificate authorising me to perform the duties of an Inspector of Weights and Measures. Such duties, however, were to be extraneous to those of a sergeant of police.

IX

King's Lynn

Two months after joining the King's Lynn Borough Police
Force it was necessary for me to attend the Board of Trade's
Office in London, to take the examination lasting two days -
the result of which would - make or mar my chances of making
headway in the service; for failure would mean that I would
revert to the rank of Constable.

After an anxious wait of six weeks, the Warden of the
Standards informed me that I had qualified.

The Watch Committee kept their part of the bargain, and
I became a fully-fledged Sergeant. And the chief constable
was good enough to recommend that I be paid a salary of ten
pounds per annum for the extra work I would have to perform
as an Inspector of Weights and Measures; although my
predecessor, a former chief constable, had enjoyed a salary
of thirty pounds for the same job.

My diminutive extra salary didn't worry me in the least,
for, what was of much greater importance, was the fact that
I had gained promotion much earlier than would have been the
case had I remained in the county constabulary; the conditions governing promotion throughout the whole police
service in those days being bad indeed.

*   *   *

My duties under the Weights and Measures Acts in the
borough provided little excitement, but I gained a great
deal of useful experience which was of help to me as a
policeman.   It was very interesting to learn the ways of
traders regarding practises - sometimes called 'tricks of
the trade' - followed by them in their efforts to avoid
bankruptcy.

To say that I was surprised, is to put it mildly.   Yes,
I was learning something fresh.   It was now necessary for
me to visit more shops and business establishments than
ever before, and it soon became evident - almost instantly -

that I, as a Weights and Measures man, would need to keep
alert whenever so engaged; and it was because of this
necessity that I could not help becoming a better policeman.

In a number of apparent trade dodges I found it sufficient for my purpose, to let the 'dodgers' know that I had
noticed the antic, and to intimate that its adoption did
not please me.

One evening, I met a colleague and, in a fit of hospitality, asked him to 'come and have a drink'.

In the hotel I !noticed' something that I had never seen
before, neither had my companion.

My first prosecution in King's Lynn, was against a
licensed victualler for using false measures in the sale of
beer. The measures had false bottoms.

The two 'half-pint' measures involved appeared to be
perfect. They were silver-plated on copper; were concave
in shape; and were stamped as required by law. The false
bottom to each measure had been made by inserting - from
the open top - a piece of metal which was pushed downwards
until it fitted tightly; it was then neatly soldered. We,
my assistant and I were deprived of 20% of the liquid for
which we had paid. A fine of £5 was imposed. Altogether,
the offender possessed eight such measures - all with false
bottoms - which I seized. They were confiscated. Having
been in use many years, the extra profit obtained must have
been substantial.

*   *   *

In a case against a tobacconist for possessing a false
weighing instrument, I found that he was using the wrong
kind of machine for that particular purpose, and that it
was two drams against any customer whose purchase of tobacco
was weighed upon it. When I had given evidence to this
effect, the Chairman of the Bench surprised me somewhat, by
saying: 'Two drams isn't much, is it?" Taking his words
as a question to myself, I answered: "Yes, sir, I think so,
because each time this machine was used to weigh one ounce
of tobacco, the customer would be deprived of $12\frac{1}{2}$% of the
quantity he would be expected to pay for; and when used to
weigh half an ounce, which would more often be the case,
there would be a deficiency of 25%".

The Chairman seemed to be in a hurry for without con-
sulting his fellow Justices, he said: "Have you anything to
say, or any questions to ask?" There was no response from
the defendant. "Well", said the Chairman: "The public must
be protected, you'll be fined five shillings". The
defendant smiled, no wonder.

Shortly afterwards, when the defendant had managed to pay the penalty so mercifully inflicted, he came back and asked for the return of his weighing machine for further use. Having asked for and been granted an Order for confiscation, I asked him to accompany me to my office. And there, in his presence, I destroyed the profitable and fraudulent instrument. Had he carried out his threat to sue me, his costs would have been much higher than the fine he had paid; but then, I think, justice would have been done.

These two cases were the most serious I was involved in at King's Lynn, a town in which I had little fault to find with its traders.

*   *   *

It was in 1919 that The Police Federation came into existence, and it was then that policemen were first required to pass Qualifying Examinations in order to be considered for promotion up to the rank of Inspector. From then on I was pleased to be able to assist those who required help.

I well remember P.C. Henry Kirby of the King's Lynn Police Force, taking the first examination. He did so after pointing out to the chief constable that he did so under protest. Kirby was a good and efficient policeman. He knew his powers, and when to 'bring them in' and when he hadn't the power enabling him to do so, and he was a 'character'. In his early days as a constable, he was under cross-examination by Mr. Ernest Wild, a barrister - afterwards Recorder of London as Sir Ernest.

Mr. Wild's first question to P.C. Kirby was: "Let's see constable, they call you 'chuckle head' do they not?" Kirby's answer caused a mild sensation. "What's that to do with this case - (one in which a licensed victualler was being prosecuted for permitting betting on his premises) - I refuse to answer any of your questions until you apologise".

The Chairman of the Bench remarked that he considered Mr. Wild's question offensive, so P.C. Kirby got his apology. Mr. Wild expressing his regret. The case went on.

*   *   *

During my thirty months service in King's Lynn, I gradually became a kind of factotum; a sergeant clerk, a detective, a patrol sergeant, and an instructor of sorts.

117

THERE'S SOMETHING ABOUT A HAT

As many people were aware, the late Queen Mary was very fond of visiting shops in which there was an opportunity of purchasing an Antique article that took her fancy. In King's Lynn High-street, there was an establishment - a combined pawnshop and jewellers - which occasionally provided such a chance. But the article had to be one of great rarity to cause Her Majesty to travel the seven miles from Sandringham in order to examine it.

On one such an occasion, I was detailed to be in the vicinity of the particular shop to see that the Queen was not embarrassed in any way. It was not a difficult task, for members of the Royal Family often visited the town or passed through it without causing any excitement. Her Majesty had just entered the shop, when two fishwives stopped at the shop's doorway, as if they intended to stay a while. I approached them, and in a quiet tone I said: "Now ladies", there was no need to say anything further. They were very co-operative and knew me well. One whispered: "All right, sergeant, its the same old Took (toque)", and the other said, almost inaudibly, "The same old violets".

They knew me well, because I had examined and tested their shellfish measures.

*　　*　　*

On one of my many visits to Sandringham, off-duty periods permitting, I was accompanied by a friend, an R.S.P.C.A. Inspector, who was in uniform, when we saw Queen Alexandra with a lady-in-waiting. Her Majesty was always pleased to see the Inspector and on all occasions he was asked about the welfare of animals in his district, which was a large one. On this occasion, when the lady-in-waiting intimated that Her Majesty wished to speak to the Inspector, I backed away: "Please do not go away, sir", Her Majesty said.

Miniature gravestones set into the outer wall on one side of Sandringham House, mark the resting places of many of Queen Alexandra's pets.

Her Majesty's kennelman told my wife and me that the Queen could never have made a surprise visit to Sandringham, for as soon as she stepped from the train, her dogs made such a fuss and didn't calm down until she paid them a visit.

*　　*　　*

NO SILVER SPOON

During my stay in King's Lynn, I had the honour of
'keeping an eye' on the movements of people when in the
presence of members of the Royal Family, including Princess
Mary, afterwards Princess Royal, at the time H.R.H.
unveiled the War Memorial, in 1920; and when Prince Henry,
afterwards Duke of Gloucester, on the day H.R.H. opened
The Royal Agricultural Show there.

*   *   *

A well-known and honoured 'character' at King's Lynn
was a fisherman who was the proud owner of his own ship.
Very few people knew him by surname, but everybody knew
who was being spoken of when 'Brookendish' was mentioned.

His wife and he were regarded as the happiest married
couple in the country.

However, there came a day on which they had a bit of a
barney.   Anyhow, that was what the neighbours called it,
though one or two of them said that it was only on Bonfire
Nights that an explosion was heard.

A few words were spoken by each spouse, and then the
gallant fisher found it impossible to take evasive action
against a missile aimed at him with great accuracy.

Then there was a cooling session and, after a brief
snooze, the fisherman put to sea.   Some hours later, he
called upon his cabin-boy to 'bring that there pie my
missus gave you to bring aboard'.   "Hi, hi, sir", said
the boy, and in a jiffy, the pie - piping hot - was laid
before the Skipper.

When the pie was opened, the gulls began to screech,
and the Skipper's countenance took on a crimson hue as
did his language.   "Cor blast, boy", he said, "the missus
has done it on me".   For within the pie crust were some
pieces of earthenware to remind him that he had caused
his wife to lose her temper.

Then the cabin-boy, acting on instruction, handed his
Skipper another hot meat pie.   Perhaps in his glee, the
boy mentioned the episode.   Hence 'Brookendish' for
evermore.

*   *   *

The burgesses of the ancient borough were law-abiding;
and the majority of the small number of crimes committed
each year were traced to strangers.   It was here that I
made my first contact with a Borstal Boy.   He was a
very smart young man whose education had been costly at
one of the country's famous schools.   But his mode of
life had caused his parents much anguish.

On his release from Borstal - where he had been sent
for a period not exceeding three years after having
committed a series of larcenies - he decided against
returning to his home.

Within a day or so of regaining his liberty, he had
committed a mean theft. When passing through Huntingdon,
he observed a priest leaving his presbytery. Having
ascertained the name of the priest, he gained access to
the clergyman's study on the pretence of a desire to leave
him an important message.

The maid servant was so impressed by the visitor's
good looks and his speech and demeanour, that she made
him a cup of tea. Before leaving the presbytery, the
plausible one had stolen the priest's fountain-pen and
his cheque book. He told the maid that he had so many
matters to attend to, that he regretted being unable to
wait for the priest's return.

Within minutes one of the cheques had been turned into
currency, and the young offender passed on to pastures
new to pass further spurious cheques whenever his exchequer required replenishment.

The signature he appended to the dud documents
purported to be those of persons of high degree. The
cheque in the case I investigated, bore the fictitious
signature Donald D. Lansdowne. The idea of the offender
being to impress the person cashing it to regard it as
an honour at being asked to do so by such a famous person.

His modus operandi in this case was to claim friendship
with a young officer in the R.A.F., who was courting the
daughter of the shopkeeper upon whom he imposed. He was
about to be demobbed, he said, and desired to entertain
one or two fellow officers before leaving for home. He
hoped that he was not being a nuisance to the shopkeeper,
but as the Bank closed rather early, he found himself in
a kind of a fix. He would make do with £8, enough to buy
a drink or two. So out came the cheque book, and the
deed was done.

Unfortunately for him his victim became suspicious and
reported the matter.

Instructed to detect the culprit, if possible, the
chief constable handed me the cheque. I wasn't very
hopeful of success, but my luck was in; he was still in
town.

Visiting hotels and comparing the writing on the cheque
with the hotel registers, I found a signature purporting
to be that of one Osborne, which caused me to inquire if
he was in.

In consequence of 'information received', I visited

the Theatre Royal.

On looking into a private box near the stage, I saw a well dressed young man. He seemed very pleased with himself and was waving to the chorus girls as they tripped into the wings.

"Good evening, Mister Osborne", I said, and to my surprise he didn't deny that that was his name. "You have the advantage of me, sir" said he, "but you look like a detective". Although admitting to being a policeman I had been trying my best not to look like a detective.

My prisoner was particularly cool, so crediting him with a desire to escape, I took steps to prevent this happening.

At the police station I found him most interesting and informative about life in Borstal. It was natural, of course, that much of what he told me was inadmissible as evidence. I saw no sign of contrition in him, but he gave me the impression that this was the first occasion on which he had adopted the 'dud cheque' racket as a means of livelihood; that he picked up its rudiments from fellow inmates of Borstal, and though he had found the Art simple to accomplish by one with 'the gift of the gab' he had no intention to take it up again on his release from prison.

In talks with him I gathered that shortly after his admission to Borstal he was selected to give instruction in English to boys undergoing training. The officers, he said, treated the boys very well, and did their utmost to turn the youngsters into good and law-abiding citizens, but their efforts in this direction were too often rendered abortive by the tuition, given on the sly, by some of the senior boys, as to the manner in which various serious crimes could be committed with the minimal risk of detection.

Since my contact with this particular ex-Borstal boy - and during a period of thirty-five years before my retirement from the police service - I have had scores of such young offenders to contend with, and have become convinced of the truthfulness of this statement. And it has been proved beyond doubt, that tuition given in this manner by older boys with criminal tendencies, has destroyed the desired reformative effect of Borstal training and has - so far as some boys of low intellect are concerned - provided, instead, a post-graduate course for potential criminals.

*   *   *

One of the most interesting cases to which I was

assigned was that in which a woman reported that she had
been attacked at her home by a burglar who had dragged
her upstairs by the hair, and had robbed her of a
substantial sum of money.   Much was made of her story.
An unofficial newspaper, pink in colour, and published in
London, depicted a woman being dragged upstairs in the
manner alleged by the complainant.   This seemed a bit
much and far-fetched.   With the lady's permission I
examined her scalp.   It seemed to be all right.   No
doctor had been called, and no cry of alarm had been
raised.   I recovered the money from a chimney.

It was an eternal - triangle - case.   The complainant
had taken the first step to run away with another man,
and had tripped.

Since then, I have wondered how many reports of thefts
are false.   Insurance Companies could tell of some,
methinks.

*   *   *

After two years and five months service in King's Lynn,
I was successful in obtaining an advertised vacancy in
St. Helens, a busy mining and industrial town in
Lancashire.   My experience in police matters in King's
Lynn had been of great help to me.

X

St. Helens

In July, 1921, I commenced duty with the St. Helens County Borough Police Force.   And it immediately became apparent that in this, an industrial district, conditions would be much different from those which I had experienced in the agricultural area of Norfolk and Kings Lynn.

My rank was that of Sergeant the same as it had been in the previous force, and I carried out similar duties, but my pay was higher.   It was pleasing to find that there were fresh things to learn.   The first of these being obvious from the beginning; the necessity to speak and understand the local dialect.   The first person coming to the Police Office at the Town Hall, and asking for help, was a lad in tears.   "Wilt thee send Bobby", he pleaded "t'owd mon is laying on Mither".   A Constable Clerk gave me an interpretation of the boy's request, and it was attended to.

The Chief Constable of St. Helens was a Yorkshireman, Mr. Arthur Robert Ellerington, who had previously been in charge of the Margate Borough Police.   He was a 'ranker' having originally joined the West Riding of Yorkshire Constabulary as a Constable.   And he had risen to the rank of Detective-Chief-Inspector at the age of twenty-eight.

Well over 6-feet in height and of proportionate build, he wore a stern facial expression and a well groomed walrus moustache.   A strict, but firm disciplinarian, he expected subordinates to carry out their duties in the manner which they had sworn to perform them; without fear or favour, affection or ill will.   I found that he was always ready to support them whenever they acted according to law; but he took a poor view of anyone who lacked courage or ability.

Human to a degree, he displayed a great love of children and dumb animals.   And to help the genuine poor and needy

he inaugurated - with the aid of voluntary contributions -
a charity known as "The Clog and Stocking Fund", the object
of which, was to fit out poverty stricken children with new
articles of clothing of all kinds.

In order that the Fund should not be imposed upon by
unscrupulous persons, all members of the force were instructed to inquire into and report upon the circumstances of the
family to which any poorly clad child belonged.   The
necessary inquiries were made with the utmost tact and
discretion.   As may well be imagined, investigation of such
cases sometimes revealed wanton neglect by parents of these
unfortunate kiddies, but in the vast majority of cases
parents were blameless and deserving of assistance from the
Fund, and got it without delay.

I was present on a number of occasions when boots and
other articles of clothing were issued to children.   Heart-
rending and tear-producing as the picture of such poverty
was, the expressions of surprise and joy on the faces of
the recipients, provided a sight to cheer the most morose
person to realise what a small amount of genuinely administered charity can do.

Appropos this benevolent work, I remember hearing of a
bookmaker, who, having suffered the effects of raids by the
police - including myself - on his several betting houses
in the town, called at the Chief Constable's office, and to
the Chief himself, made a proposition suggesting that if the
police would refrain from making a nuisance of themselves by
raiding his premises so often at inconvenient times, he would
be willing to contribute £100 per annum, to the Clog and
Stocking Fund.   "Outside, you", said the Chief Constable,
"that Fund will survive without corruption, and you may look
forward to more inconvenient visits from us".   And in a
matter of seconds the philanthropic bookie was in retreat.

                    *   *   *

THE CHIEF'S HOUSE IS BURGLED

Mr. Ellerington's house, which stood in its own grounds,
was known as "The Cottage".   It was regarded as on one of
the Beats, and was examined by the constable on patrol at
irregular intervals during the night.

On a particularly dark and somewhat stormy night the
constable - I think that his collar number was 22 - was
conscientiously examining the Chief's house when his
attention was attracted by a moving low-powered light in a
room on the ground floor.   Investigating - in a way expected of all sensible policemen - he discovered an intruder

was engaged in packing a suitcase with articles which were
not his property.

Knowing that no constable colleague of his was nearby,
the constable took steps to prevent the burglar's escape,
and to arouse the Chief, if he happened to be at home.
The Chief was within, and he came to a bedroom-window which
he opened with care.   He had responded to a secret alarm
signal.   "What's wrong constable", the Chief whispered.
"There's a burglar, sir", answered the P.C.   "Can't you
manage him?" asked the chief.   "I don't know yet, sir",
the constable said rather hurriedly, "he's in your house".
The Chief came down with alacrity.

After the burglar had been rendered hors-de-combat, the
Chief removed the burglar's trouser braces.   And he - the
burglar - was dealt with according to law.

*   *   *

During my service of three and a half years at St.Helens,
owing chiefly to the 'Leadership-by-example' of the Chief
Constable, I gained much useful knowledge and experience
which were to stand me in good stead.   He taught me a great
deal, and I have tried to emulate him.

In February, 1922, on promotion to Inspector, I took
charge of the Sutton Oak district of the force, and training
classes.   Sutton Oak was rather a wide area covering
mining and agricultural parts of the town.   There was always
plenty of interesting police work to be done, and I was
assisted by three sergeants, a detective-constable and a
small number of constables some of whom were in charge of
parishes and lived on their beats.   I mention these facts
because in 1967, this method of policing was described and
much publicised as being a new idea which was being introduced for the purpose of reducing Crime.

Only one murder was reported to have been committed in
Sutton Oak during my sojourn there; and the detection of the
murderer was a particularly simple matter, we found his
body and the evidence, in a bedroom quite near that in which
his victim met her death.

*   *   *

In a thickly populated industrial area like St. Helens, I
was not surprised to find that - when compared with the small
town in which I had previously served - there was much more
crime committed; that some differed from those which had
formerly claimed my attention, and that in carrying out my
responsibilities I had to rely upon my subordinates and show

125

my appreciation of their conscientious efforts.

One of the first cases with which I had to deal at Sutton Oak turned out to be more amusing than that which usually occurs when police are called upon to 'execute a Warrant'. It appeared that some one or more persons had been bragging that the people who were responsible for running an illegal Sweepstake - known as The Rolling Mill Sweep - were too clever to be caught by the 'Rusty Buttons', the Cops, in local parlance, for policemen in uniform. My Chief, Mr. Ellerington, told me of a challenge, which I was pleased to accept. But this was a job quite impossible of completion by one man, and yet, one in which too many operatives would probably lead to failure.

Choosing a constable - one whom I felt was a stickler for a job calling for initiative - to assist me in the preliminary steps, we set out on the task. We realised that those in charge of the gamble were prudent and cautious individuals, who, by means of a 'security service' of their own, could keep us at bay for a considerable period. We found that the weekly Draw was taking place at a different house each time it was conducted. So we thought, this fact was the source of the bragging. My assistant, the constable, discovered means by which he could ascertain the venue of the next Draw. He put it to the Test and was successful. Information was laid for a Warrant, and arrangements were made for a Raid, which was made the same evening. We saw the alleged offenders enter a terrace-house with their paraphernalia, and after a time-lag we paid our visit. It was on a Wednesday evening, and we found that the Draw was in progress and was being conducted in a business-like manner. We, myself, and five other policemen, took the action necessary to prevent any misunderstanding of the purpose of our presence, and I read over the Warrant. As this was happening, an elderly lady came into the room, and addressing her son - who was the conductor-in-chief, she said: "Ee Nobby, there's bobby sergeant at front dooer". Nobby, whose name was not Clarke, turned in my direction and replied in rather a pleasant voice: "That's nowt, there's six of the ..... here".

The effect of Nobby's statement was the temporary collapse of his Mother, an occurrence providing an opportunity for a couple of bobbies to show their ability as First-Aiders. I was pleased at her rapid recovery.

The offenders - most of whom were workers at the local Rolling Mill - took the matter philosophically, and Nobby himself was particularly kind. He told me that I had been remiss by failing to send him a Post-card telling him of our intended visit so that he could have had some refreshments ready for us.

Taken before a Justice of the Peace at police headquarters, they were remanded on bail. And when dealt
with by the Justices - though heavily fined - they were
not out of pocket; they had wisely taken the precaution
to collect one week's subscription before the start of
the season, for a contingency which 'the Braggats' thought
the police incapable of providing.

The moral emerging from this episode is obvious, but
worth mention. Over-estimation of one's own capabilities,
or under-estimation of qualities possessed by others, have
been the cause of many tragic mistakes.

*   *   *

In the first quarter of the 20th Century, the town of
St. Helens, (in which I was proud to serve) was the scene
of numerous breaches of the peace, which usually occurred
at week-ends. A breach of the peace may be defined as a
violation of the state of quiet, calm or tranquillity
guaranteed by law to the Queen's subjects. It is a misdemeanour at Common Law, which is that part of the law which
is not to be found in the Statute Book, but which has come
about by custom from time immemorial, i.e., beyond memory.
Persons arrested for this particular offence were usually
dealt with by the Justices on Mondays, and on most occasions
some of the alleged offenders faced a further charge of
'assaulting a constable in the execution of his duty'.
And it was not uncommon to see several constables wearing
bandages or surgical dressings when attending court as
witnesses. At the same time it was noticed that few of
the alleged offenders were similarly decorated. And it
was because of this state of affairs that the chief constable
deemed it necessary to lecture his men on 'the rights of all
citizens to defend themselves against aggression'. One
lecture was sufficient to bring about a spectacular transformation scene. On Mondays following the lecture, bandages
etc., weren't so evident.

Policemen, like other members of the community, have a
perfect right to defend themselves against attack. But
there are occasions on which it would be imprudent on their
part to assert this Right. In a crowd, such as at a football match or at any other events where large numbers of
people congregate, an attack upon a policeman would entertain
many people, but if the policeman retaliated, his action
could easily cause a riot, such is life today. To assert
one's rights is a necessity on most occasions, but there are
times when such an action could cause much inconvenience, to

say the least.   I have heard of a case in which a man
stepped on a pedestrian-crossing when it would have been
more sensible to have waited for a few seconds.   When he
regained consciousness, in hospital, two days later, the
first words he spoke were to the doctor: "I had my rights",
said he.   "Of course", said the Surgeon, "but the other
fellow had a lorry".

*   *   *

One of the most efficient and conscientious policeman
that it was my pleasure to work with at St. Helens, was an
acting-sergeant known by the nickname 'Teaser'.   Before
joining the Police Force he had worked at Pilkington's
glassworks, and I believe that the job he did there was
called 'Teasing', hence the nickname.   He served with me
at Sutton Oak, and though I was much his junior in age -
and in experience - I couldn't have wished for a better
subordinate.   Whenever I gave him a job of police-work to
do correctly, cheerfully and tactfully, no one could be
more precise or punctilious than Teaser.

On a particular occasion he had dealt with a man who had
unlawfully been catching birds.   After the court proceedings,
Teaser was told to see that the birds were reasonably dealt
with and released.   This was a very simple and pleasant act
for anyone, but Teaser rightly felt it necessary to show that
the task had been properly carried out; so he reported - in
the margin of the document recording the case:

> Sir,
>   I have to report that in accordance
> with your instructions I took the birds
> to open country and duly released them.
> You will be glad to know that on leaving
> the cage they chirruped their appreciation,
> soared aloft, and took wing to freedom
> across a field of waving corn.

The chief constable endorsed the report:

> "I'm glad they chirruped".

*   *   *

The length to which some people will go in order to retain
a seat on a municipal council have been revealed to me on
more than one occasion, in different parts of the country,
but a particular instance in St. Helens, is, I think, an

example in which decency of mind, and a moment's thought on
the part of the person concerned, would have suggested that
such an act would be distasteful and detestable.

It occurred towards the end of October, 1921, a few days
before the annual Municipal Election. A member of the Town
Council - who was also a Justice of the Peace - entered.
the central Police Station and after declaring his identity,
he asked the constable clerk on duty to hand him a batch of
Summonses which he, the Justice, had signed earlier in the
day. Unfortunately for the constable, the summonses
hadn't been served, so not knowing what the Justice had in
mind, he complied with the request. Taking the documents -
Rate Summonses - to another part of the office counter, the
Justice of the Peace erased his signature from every
summons.

When the summonses were returned to him, the constable -
having been taken aback - asked the Councillor Justice:
"Is there any particular reason for this action of yours,
sir". "Rather", replied the Justice, "those summonses
are for service on voters in my Ward, and I'm up for re-
election!"

Judging from this occurrence, I think that it wouldn't
be a bad idea to suggest that persons honoured by being
appointed to The Commission of the Peace, should be issued
a certificate in the form of a folder-card, which they
should carry in case they were asked to prove their identity,
if required. And in order that such certificate should
act as a Reminder to themselves of their having undertaken
a duty in the interest of justice, it should contain the
words of the Judicial Oath: "I do swear that I will well
and truly serve our Sovereign Lady Queen Elizabeth the
Second in the office of Justice of the Peace and do right
to all manner of people after the law and usages of the
Realm, without fear or favour, affection or ill-will.
So help me God".

The constable-clerk concerned in this incident, was the
late Arthur Cust, who served with me at Sutton Oak, and
eventually became Chief Constable of St. Helens.

It has been said on numerous occasions over the years
by Judges, politicians and others, that justice should not
only be done but should manifestly and undoubtedly be seen
to be done. Although this statement may appear gratuitous,
there have been occasions on which its importance has
seemed to have been forgotten. But when it is appreciated that more than ninety per-cent. of alleged offenders
are dealt with by the lay Magistracy throughout the country,
the importance of keeping in mind: 'Justice', is imperative. And when one realises these facts, it is remarkable

that so few mistakes are made in Courts of Summary
Jurisdiction.

Notwithstanding this fact, there are people who
think that the Lay Magistracy should be abolished and
that all Magistrates should be qualified lawyers, who
would be required to give all their working time to the
duties of the office and be debarred from Private
practice. It being considered by such people that such
magistrates - learned in the law - and acting alone
would be more likely to assess correctly the value of
Evidence adduced, and further, that the penalties
inflicted by them would be more uniform than could
possibly be in the case when the Court is composed of
different Justices from day to day or from week to week,
and whose decisions are arrived at by majority vote.
It follows, of course, that if such abolition came about,
many members of County Councils or Town Councils would
not be eligible. But whether the exclusion of such
ladies and gentlemen would be regarded as a calamity is
a matter of conjecture; but whatever one's opinion
happens to be, all law-abiding citizens, would - one
imagines - agree with those who would say, and mean:
"Let justice be done though the heavens fall", as per
the Latin maxim: <u>fiat justicia, ruat coelum.</u>

So far as the necessity to bring about Uniformity of
penalties for the same offence in which the circumstances
are 'equal' is concerned, I would respectfully suggest
that a fixed Minimum penalty be provided, as well as
the Maximum penalty.

*   *   *

Up to this time, there had been few cases of serious
Crime in St.Helens calling for special skill or knowledge
in the elucidation of them, or the consequential bringing
to justice of the offenders concerned in them. But one
afternoon a Sergeant brought in a man who had allegedly
been trying to dispose of some cutlery. The man was an
Irishman, and he was rather argumentative. He looked
at me, described me as a spurious child and told me
what sort of a bloke I was. He bore an honoured name -
if the one he had given me a year before at King's
Lynn when I had charged him with Burglary - was his
true name. I had thought that it was only in fiction
that such coincidences occurred.

*   *   *

NO SILVER SPOON

While in charge at Sutton Oak, I was fortunate enough to have two particularly interesting criminal cases to deal with in which luck once more came to my aid. The more urgent of these was that in which two women - mother and grown-up daughter - had been attacked by a man who, by striking them with an iron bar, had fractured their heads. Both women were critically ill in hospital.

Owing to the seriousness of their injuries, it was essential that evidence be obtained as speedily as possible. The luck in this case was the fact that the identity of the alleged offender was known, but he had disappeared. He had been associating with the younger woman at intervals to suit his convenience, but the irregularity of his attentions had caused her to lose interest him, which culminated in his being told she wished the association to end. Late one evening, the rejected man had called at the home of his victims, found his way indoors and belaboured them with intent to do them grievous bodily harm; for the weapon was one the use of which was likely to cause death. Apparently, there had been some resistance on the part of the women, as on making an examination of the kitchen, we found half of a watch-chain on the hearth-rug.

On making his escape from the house, the offender left by the back door and had taken flight across a small field in which there were some trees, and it was against one of these that the assault-weapon was found. It was a large bolt fifteen inches long, five-eighths of an inch in diameter, and had a wicked-looking nut on its end. It was bent, and its condition revealed evidence of the use to which it had recently been put. An examination of the ground near the back door revealed the mark of a rubber heel having a metal centre-piece of unusual shape. A plaster case of this impression was taken by me in lantern light, and when the accused man was arrested it was found that the heels of his shoes bore rubbers of similar size, shape and design.

It was apparent that when the accused man left his victims he had thought that they were dead; and that he hoped to escape detection, for he didn't leave the district, though he was in no hurry to return to his home.

Within a short time he discovered that his watch chain had broken, and realising that the missing part would, if found at the scene of his crime and compared with the other part remaining in his possession - would provide strong circumstantial evidence against him, he

lost no time in disposing of such an important link in
the chain of potential evidence that could lead to his
conviction and nothing else; he buried the piece which
he had been carrying, together with the watch to which
it was attached.   With his assistance, I recovered
both.

Brought to trial at Liverpool Assizes, he was found
Guilty but Insane.   Today, in such circumstances, he
would have been found 'Not guilty owing to insanity'.

Insane people are apt to be cunning in the extreme.

*   *   *

At about 3.0 a.m. on a New Year's Day, in consequence
of a communication made to me by a Sergeant in charge at
Sutton Manor, I cycled to the district in which he
lived, met him, and, working together, we began to
investigate a complaint respecting an alleged burglary
and theft of money.   The complainant had reported that
just before midnight he had left his house for the
purpose of taking part in 'Singing the Old Year out
and the New Year in', and that after being satisfied
that the New Year had in fact arrived, he had invited
his fellow songsters to his home to partake of refreshment as a grand finale to the proceedings; and it was
on going upstairs to get chairs for his guests, he
found that a safe in his bedroom had been tampered with,
and that the money it had contained was missing.

The complainant was asked if he could suggest how
the burglar had made his entry.   He seemed rather
hesitant for a moment, then he said: "I think he came
in over the roof of the lavatory in the backyard and
pushing the bedroom window up".   An examination of the
lavatory roof satisfied me that it hadn't given help
to anyone.   There had been a keen frost during the
previous evening, and it was still freezing hard.

I asked the complainant what occupation he followed,
and whether the stolen money was his own.   He told me
that he was Secretary of a local branch of a Trade
Union, and unfortunately for himself, the money which
was missing had been paid to him by members of the
branch.   Suspicion was beginning to show itself, but
the Sergeant and I were not quite ready to declare it;
the reason being, that the wife of the complainant was
using the house as a shop for the sale of drapery.
Our inquiries on the spot with regard to this business,
and an examination of certain documents, revealed that
pressure was being applied by wholesalers, for payment

of their accounts. I conveyed our suspicions to the
complainant, telling him that we were men of experience;
that we had come to the conclusion that no felonious entry
had taken place, and we believed that the money allegedly
stolen was still in the house. The complainant broke
down, admitted being in financial difficulties, and that
he had taken the money to free himself from debt. Opening
a bureau, he took therefrom what was left of the spoils,
and handed it to me.

At Liverpool Assizes he pleaded guilty, and was sentenced
to imprisonment for eighteen months.

A member of the Watch Committee had approached the
Chief Constable (Mr. Ellerington) suggesting that the
offender be charged with Fraudulent Conversion - a misdemeanour for which the punishment would be less than that
to which a person is liable for committing the felony of
Larceny (stealing) - but was unsuccessful.

The Agent of the Insurance Company with whom the Safe
and its Contents were insured, recommended to his employers
that the police officers responsible for the detection of
the offender and recovery of the money, might be rewarded
in some way. But nobody would co-operate to support him.
I heard that a member of the Committee to whom the
recommendation was made, turned it down in two words: "Like
hell", he said. It was good intent on the part of the
Agent, but we (the sergeant and I) hadn't given a thought
to the matter of a possible reward. At times I have
wondered whether or not the gentleman who had been so
emphatic was identical with the person who had approached
the chief.

A 'MEMORY MAN'

There was an occasion on which two "Hooks or Whizzers"
(pickpockets) were 'brought-in'; the C.I.D. men were all
out. Mr. Ellerington saw the men and their escort going
up the steps of the police station. "Bring them into my
office" said the chief. The chief sat down at his roll-
top desk and looked at the men. Addressing one of them,
the chief said: "Hallo Charlie". 'Charlie' gave a gasp
of surprise, "Blimey, Long Jack of Doncaster", he muttered.
Twenty years or more had passed since 'Long Jack of Doncaster' - in the person of Mr. Ellerington, had been so
close together; it was at Doncaster Races.

There was a case in which money had been taken from
several Offeratory boxes in churches, and the culprit or
culprits were making a nuisance of themselves. One
afternoon, a male suspect was brought to the police station

and questioned.   An Inspector released him just as the
Chief entered the room.   The Chief asked what had been
happening, and was told.   "Have you looked inside his
hat?" asked the Chief.   "No, sir", was the reply.   The
inside of the trilby hat was quickly examined, and a
length of wire bearing traces of bird-lime was found
within the lining, and similar traces were on some coins.

At. St. Helens, I was often in charge of the police
detachment at the Rugby League football matches, and I
remember a particularly amusing incident during a Lancashire Cup Match at City Road, between Wigan and St. Helens
Recreation.   Whenever these teams met the spectators
could always be sure of first-class entertainment.   On
this occasion, the 'Recreation' were in great form, and in
quick time had gathered 18 points to nil.   One particular
Wigan fan was saying rude things about the game as the
players were running off at half-time when an obvious
supporter of the home team, standing quite near the Wigan
grumbler, made use of a few profane words causing me to
mildly rebuke the speaker in order to prevent a possible
breach of the peace.   The rebuked young man saluted me
and said: "All right, Corporal, but all they Wiganers want
now is a Chinaman in their team, then they could play for
the League of Nations".   Having held the dizzy rank of
Lance-Corporal in the Army, I felt the 'promotion' was
well meant.

*   *   *

While serving in St. Helens, I gathered much experience
in general police work in most of its phases, which has
enabled me to carry out my duties in law enforcement with
minimal friction.
Law enforcement is not an easy matter by any means, but
from the very beginning of my police career I found that
while it required nerve and fortitude at times; there was
always the need for tact and discretion in performing one's
duties.
In making raids - chiefly on Betting Houses - my
colleagues and I have had cause to appreciate the good
conduct of the householders concerned.   None was troublesome, but the tricks some of them resorted to were
ingenious and amusing.   The places used for the conceal-
ment of betting-slips were those most unlikely to be
examined, and though they must have been ignored by searchers

on occasions, there were times when their discovery caused extra diligence on the part of those whose job it was to search for and seize evidence in accordance with instructions on the warrant. But in most raids, search was unnecessary.

On an occasion - not connected with betting - a detective reported having searched 'every likely place' without success. The chief constable endorsed the report: "Now try all UNLIKELY places".

*   *   *

In January, 1925, with permission of Mr. Ellerington, I went to Bacup with intent to become chief constable of the Borough Police there if and when the then chief constable retired or obtained a more lucrative appointment. Three years later, I returned to St. Helens, as a voluntary witness for Mr. Ellerington, in a Home Office Inquiry. When on the witness-stand, I testified that, <u>inter alia</u>, I had served under four chief constables (two in the Norfolk Constabulary, one at King's Lynn, and one at St. Helens) and I couldn't have wished to serve under a better chief constable. In cross-examination I was asked by a K.C., acting for the Watch Committee, "Why did you leave St. Helens?" "Exactly for the same reason that I would leave the force in which I am now serving" I answered; "for the purpose of possible promotion!" No further question was put to me.

Mr. Ellerington had been under suspension, it seemed to me that the allegation against him was that he had been too strict. He was re-instated.

XI

Bacup

My duties in Bacup commenced in January, 1925, and
within a day or so, it became very clear to me that it
was a queer place.

It can be said that there is no place in England like
it. There are springs of water on the tops of the hills,
and in order to enter the coal pits in the Parish of
Stacksteads and on the Burnley Road, one must go up.

The town of Bacup, seven miles from Rochdale in the
direction of Manchester, and a similar distance from
Burnley, stands at the head of the Rossendale Valley and
is shut in by some parts of the Pennine Range. It is
unique from its position, and water poured to one side
will flow to the North Sea and to the other side will
flow to the Irish Sea.

Gradually, I found the character of Bacupians is as
marked as are the natural features of the Rossendale
Valley, pronounced, individual and blunt. When once
known, they are not easily forgotten, and are recognised
wherever they go. Their dialect is peculiarly their own.
It has been said, so I've been told, that they possess a
two-edged wit and humour, and that they love like angels
and hate like devils, but during my sojourn there I saw
no particular sign of love or hatred.

Engaged in the making of cotton cloths, boots, shoes
and slippers, the people of Bacup were, when the Mills
were working full time, busy and hardworking folk, and
they were keenly interested in music in all its forms.

One of my duties was to visit all Cotton Mills to
examine their weighing machines, so I was able to learn
some of the characteristics of Millworkers and their
dialect, which by the way, was different from that of the
people of St. Helens, though in the same County.

The Streets of the town were not good for the feet of
policemen, paved with stone blocks, they made patrolling
a very weary job. And the hilliness of the terrain did

not improve matters in this respect.

I found Bacup much different from the other places in
which I had served.   And there were times when I
questioned my wisdom in moving from St. Helens, where I
had been kept busy and learned much.   It seemed to me
that though a feeling of disappointment came over me at
times, the fault was my own, and there was nothing I
could do about it.   But there was.   And I rectified
matters and obtained contentment of mind by passing
some of the knowledge which I had gained by my previous
experiences, to my subordinates.

At first sight, a stranger visiting the town would
regard it as of the 'one horse variety', not because of
its folks, but because there seemed to be nothing doing,
and he could be excused for so describing it, because, in
all probability, rain might be falling so heavily and
continuously during his stay, that his enthusiasm, if any,
would surely be dampened.

The weather experienced at Bacup would provide the
most radical test for the purpose of proving the efficacy
or otherwise of water-resisting materials, and such a
trial could be applied almost any day, for rain falls
there on between two hundred and three hundred days each
year.   And: Its the sort of rain that hits thee twice,
a Bacupian would explain.   I kept a record of Bacup's
rainfall and the hours of its duration in my pocket-book.

Whenever snow comes to England it comes to Bacup, and
there it remains for long periods on the rugged hillsides,
which, unfortunately, are too dangerous for ski-running.
There was, however, one place at which something akin to
that sport was practised, yet rarely was it performed in
public.   It was a matter of necessity rather than enjoyment.
The locus was between the police station at the top of the
slope, and the main street below.

After a night's snowfall, the descent became treacherous,
so much so, that in order to negotiate it in comparative
safety, a constable - especially if in the heavy-weight
class - would skid and bump-bump down it seated on a shovel.

One can imagine how funny it must have been to see a
shovel being hauled back for its next passenger.

*   *   *

As time went on I got better and better acquainted with
the people, especially those engaged in the retail trade.
They were friendly, witty, philosophical and patient.   And
it was good that there were some who were ready and anxious
to relieve the monotony by providing entertainment for

others; and their efforts were appreciated. Among these good people were several who had experienced want, worry and woe, but the majority of them had succeeded by will-power, energy and self-control, in overcoming the obstacles.

So far as my police work was concerned, I gained no further experience to help me on my way, but inspiration came to me by the desire to leave that district for more salubrious surroundings and greater responsibility.

Ironically enough, Bacup was the only place in which I suffered 'trespass against my person'. In 1927, during a Strike by footwear operatives, I was 'running the gauntlet' with a charabanc party of girls, who had the courage of their convictions, and kept at work, when it was necessary - for the safety of the girls - to run through a hostile crowd of about two thousand strikers in order to get our charges to their homes. A man in the Unlawful Assembly threw a piece of concrete through the windscreen of the vehicle and marred my complexion somewhat by pitting my face with minute splinters of glass of the type used for glazing windows.

I spent a considerable amount of time on and off duty in trying to trace the offender, but my ability as a detective wasn't good enough. If there was ever a time when I felt like taking the law in my own hands, this was it.

In Bacup, as in St. Helens and other towns in Lancashire, and over the whole country, the Fire Brigade was manned by the local police, and I became interested in the brigade, its personnel - all friends of mine - its equip-ment and the various kinds of appliances and their uses in varying circumstances. Most of the tuition I received came from the engineer, 'general' Jackson. He was a witty and well-respected man who - although he didn't know it at that time - helped me on my way! I'd like to meet him again, but that's impossible.

It was at Bacup, too, that the chief constable, Mr. E. W. Sturt gave me permission to write my first book of instruction to policemen. The Police Officer's Assistant. Mr. Sturt permitted me to take the examinations of the Institution of Fire Engineers'. I was thankful.

XII

Gravesend

A FORECAST INTENTION IS PROVED

In November, 1930, I applied for and was successful in obtaining my first chief constableship, and a month later left Bacup to take up my post at Gravesend, Kent, eighteen years after joining the Norfolk Constabulary as a constable, and I had already served in four police forces excluding the Railway Police.

At that time - and for years thereafter - Local Authorities were not compelled by law to maintain a Fire Brigade, though many - especially City and Town Councils - did.   And in the interests of Economy and Ratepayers alike, policemen became firemen too.   With, of course, an incentive in the form of extra pay for each turn-out. But no policeman was compelled to be a fireman.

In addition to my duties as chief constable, I was appointed chief officer of the Fire Brigade and Inspector of Weights and Measures.   Having these extra duties to perform, I was kept busy; but never was I overworked.   A happy and contented man, it gave me a feeling of satis-faction which came to me with the knowledge that my success was due to my qualifications and experience, and without influence from others in the slightest degree.

*   *   *

Gravesend!   What a name to give a town.   What conceivable reason could there have been for conferring such a title?   To me, it appeared so ridiculous a misnomer, that I went into research and discovered that in the Domesday Book, which was compiled by order of William the Conqueror, and contained a survey of all England for taxation purposes, it had the more appropriate name of Gravesham'.

There is nothing sepulchral about Gravesend; on the contrary it is a distinctly lively and interesting town.

Standing on the Thames, opposite Tilbury, Gravesend is,

in fact, the waterway gate to London, and one has but to
spend an hour or so in its waterfront to appreciate why
the Port of London is described as the busiest in the
world; for from the ant-like activity displayed by the
shipping of all maritime nations of the world, plying to
and from, presents such continuous panorama of industry
that appears unique. Yet no ship coming from abroad
gets past Gravesend without being subjected to rigorous
inspection as a precautionary measure against the admission of disease, and contraband of all kinds, so it
follows that Medical and Customs Officers who perform
these weighty and responsible duties must be highly
qualified and particularly vigilant and diligent.

I soon became acquainted with customs officers and the
methods adopted by them when searching ships in the course
of duty, and was struck by their thoroughness, which
brought back to my memory the words of my old chief at
St. Helens, 'Now try all unlikely places' when detectives
had reported having searched all likely places without
success.

Ships have numerous hiding-places for all kinds of
contraband, and, as may well be imagined, the smuggler -
knowing the risks - feels no sting of conscience when he
chooses a place likely to nauseate a searcher.

In Gravesend I had fresh experience in Criminal
Investigation and the ways of criminals, and regarded myself
fortunate in this respect.

The first case of importance came unexpectedly, and
arose from a burglary at Hawarden Castle, Flintshire,
North Wales, the home of Lord Gladstone - in which ivory
carvings of great value, beauty and antiquity were stolen.
Many of them were jewelled, and had been acquired by Lord
Gladstone's father, the late renowned William Ewart
Gladstone, former Liberal Prime Minister of England.

News of the crime had been diseminated in Great Britain
and abroad, and details with a description of the stolen
carvings were given to dealers in antiques.

I mention this case particularly because it illustrates
how simple routine work - if carried out conscientiously
by police in all districts - both inside and outside the
area in which a crime of this nature is committed, can
result in the recovery of stolen property when the chance
of success seems small and remote; and it clearly shows
how wrong detectives can be by not keeping an open mind
or by rushing to hasty conclusions.

A detective who convinces himself that 'that sort of
stuff wouldn't come here' or 'it can't happen here' or
'it can't happen to me or us', etc., may of course, be

right on most occasions, but he can never be certain.
Guesswork or wishful thinking is seldom of use to any
investigator. However, one thing that is certain is
the realisation that no person on earth possesses
supernatural powers.

Some weeks after the burglary referred to, news came
from a man living a few miles away, to the effect that
he had been offered the chance of buying some ivories by
a man living in Gravesend, who had told him that they
were unique and almost priceless. The offerer said that
the goods were being brought to his house next day by a
man coming from London. The man from Gravesend gave
his home address, and arrangements were made for a visit
to be paid at a time convenient to all, including the
police.

Having been in charge of the force for so short a
period and knowing little regarding the proficiency of my
new colleagues, I took charge of the operation. Accompanied by a detective-sergeant from Rochester and a
detective constable of my own force, and armed with the
necessary search-warrant, and an empty automatic pistol
to create an impression of determination should the
necessity arise, I visited the house in an orthodox
manner.

In the parlour on the ground floor we saw the householder, another man and a whiskery old gentleman - the man
from London - sitting near a sofa on which a number of
ivory carvings were displayed. The gentleman in whiskers
was endeavouring to dispose of the goods, and the man who
had been given the chance to buy them was acting as
instructed. The warrant was executed in the usual manner,
the ivories were seized and the three men arrested. But
only the householder and the whiskered one were charged.

'Whiskers' gave his name as Patrick Murphy, but though
it is almost as common as the one of Smith, it was his
true name. He was an old lag, then seventy years old,
he was one of the actual burglare, but there was no sufficient evidence to substantiate his being charged with that
crime. His criminal record included sentences of imprisonment and penal servitude covered a period of thirty-
five years; but he had committed many offences involving
dishonesty which had not been recorded against him, for
he, like numerous other criminals, had escaped detection
on many occasions. In this particular case he, like the
householder, was charged with 'receiving the ivories well
knowing them to have been stolen'. To the surprise of
all in court, including himself, Pat was acquitted, but the
the householder got eighteen months imprisonment. Mr.

Murphy's counsel had told the jury: "Gentlemen, I'm
really sorry for you, you look so tired that I'm sure
you'll be glad to get home".

When the jury had given their verdicts, the Recorder
of Maidstone asked me to give the antecedent history of
the prisoner Patrick Murphy. I declined. "Very well,
Mister chief constable", said the Recorder, "I will do it",
and he did. It seemed to me that the Recorder wished to
point out to the jury that they had acted unwisely in
Murphy's case. By virtue of the fact that Murphy had
been acquitted it would have been wrong on my part to have
given it.

Needless to say, Murphy was soon away, and his counsel
asked if I knew where he was. My answer was "No, did
you expect him to stay?" The barrister's language
astonished me. "I wanted some more money from him",
he said, and he asked me whether I had taken any money
from Murphy on his arrest. "Yes", I answered, "but for
all I know, it might be the proceeds of the sale of
stolen goods".

When I arrived back at my office in Gravesend, Murphy
was waiting on the doorstep. "I've called for my money",
he informed me. And when told that his counsel wanted
some of it, he smiled and said, "My mouthpiece has had all
he's going to get, the boys paid him well".

Being unable to prove that the money was not his, I
handed him the money; taking care to get his receipt in
the presence of a witness.

*　　*　　*

Another interesting case was that in which the offender
was detected because of a careless slip on his part after
he had taken the greatest care to avoid giving a clue to
his identity. Fingerprints have long been in common use
for the identification of criminals, and have provided
clues which have resulted in the bringing to justice of
many troublesome criminals. And, being aware of this fact,
the criminal fraternity do not intentionally "leave their
cards" at the scene of their nefarious deeds, but, like
other humans, they err on occasion to their detriment, as
did the felon in this particular instance.

When it is realized that the formation of the lines on
fingers differs for each person, and that the pattern of a
fingerprint never changes during life, the value of such
a clue as a means of identification is clear.

Fingerprints of criminals are taken in prison, and in
certain circumstances by the police. The impressions are

classified, recorded and filed; it will be appreciated, however, before his fingerprints are taken and registered as it were, the offender could commit numerous crimes before falling into the hands of the police. If, however, his fingerprints have been found they have been class- ified and filed for possible future reference; so if he continues in crime he will be fortunate indeed if he does not lose his liberty, possibly for a lengthy period, because it having been proved that he had been concerned in the commission of several crimes he would, of course, be liable to greater punishment.

The criminal in the case under review had broken into an outfitter's shop during a Saturday night and had remained on the premises until next morning, when he caught the first 'bus to London. He had stolen a number of suits and other articles of gents' clothing, together with two dressing-cases in which to carry them away. It was apparent that he had provided himself with gloves, and that he had made use of them during the whole time he had been engaged in taking and packing the stolen goods ready for removal. He then went into a room in which the female assistants usually took their tea, and made himself a pot of the beverage. The night was cold, and having removed his gloves, he placed both his hands around the teapot.

It was nice of him to co-operate with the police in such a manner, for he had left behind him the clearest set of 'dabs' it had been our luck and pleasure to see. The offender was an ex-Borstal inmate and he was arrested within twenty-four hours.

When he recovered from shock brought about by 'instant recognition' of his fingerprints, he said: "I've rumbled how you got me". We didn't ask him to explain his line of thought in this respect.

The credit for discovering the utility of fingerprints belong to several men, all of whom are long since dead. But one, who in my humble opinion, deserved special thanks was Doctor Faulds, who spent some years in the East as a medical missionary, before taking a Practice in Hanley, Stoke-on-Trent.

In classifying fingerprints, the <u>name</u> of the person from whom they were taken is not of paramount importance. This fact is just as well, for persistent offenders make use of many aliases. For example, if a person who has been previously convicted of a crime and has had his fingerprints taken in consequence, is arrested again and refuses to state his name, no difficulty in identifying him would be created, for his fingerprints now being taken

would be sufficient for the purpose; and with the
notification of verification would come his criminal
record and other details, up to the date of his last
conviction.

*   *   *

I have been in contact with many bullies, but 'Snipey'
of Gravesend was the worst of them all.   This huge,
hulking brute, of about seventeen stone in weight, had
convictions for cruelty to animals, and assaults, but on
each occasion it seemed that he had been too leniently
dealt with, always getting away by payment of a fine.
On the occasion under review Snipey had his first
experience of prison, and thoroughly deserved his fairly
long sentence of five years penal servitude, for he -
with two others, who were brothers - had been proved
guilty of 'Robbery with violence', a crime rendering him
and his confederates to penal servitude for life, and,
at that time, a whipping with the 'Cat o' nine tails'.
Snipey, the leader of the gang and the instigator of
the crime, was fortunate in escaping the flogging which
the presiding judge clearly had in mind to inflict as
part punishment, but which, in the circumstances, however,
could not lawfully be awarded.   The reason being because,
to the astonishment of the judge and others in court, it
was reported that Snipey was found medically unfit to
receive it.   The brothers were sentenced to three years
penal servitude and twenty-one months imprisonment,
respectively.
The victim of the crime was a merchant seaman of
foreign nationality, who had served in British vessels
for many years.   He had come ashore at Gravesend for a
little jollification after many weeks at sea, and with
this end in view, he lost no time in entering an inn to
obtain what he considered would be necessary to fulfil
his desires.   Possessed of much money and being in search
of merriment, he was in the mood for spending part of it.
A kindly and generous little man, he invited the other
customers to join him in a few drinks and met with no
refusal.   Unfortunately for him, Snipey and his fellow
criminals were the only others present, and they helped
him to dispose of a fair amount of his hard-earned cash,
but that he should dissipate the whole of it was not their
intention, for in a manner known by gangsters - they had
conspired to possess the residue for their own use and
benefit.
Had a keen observer been present, he would have noticed

that Snipey was paying particularly friendly attention to
the foreign sailorman by recommending to buy this and
that kinds of liquor, and that such drinks were duly
ordered, paid for by the sailor, delivered and consumed.
But if the observer had known of the effect of such
concoctions on one's bloodstream and nervous system, he
would have been very suspicious to say the least. However, no such person was present.

One would have thought that an experienced sailor who,
in all probability had visited most of the world's ports,
wouldn't have succumbed to such temptation, yet many like
him have yielded time and again.

Having succeeded in getting their intended victim into
the desired state of intoxication and helplessness, Snipey
and his servile satellites took him off the premises,
intimating as they left, their intention to see him safely
aboard his ship; but, of course, they had no such intention.
Taking, almost carrying him, to a dark and isolated spot,
they belaboured him unmercifully, took all his money and
left him - for all they knew - to die. But he was tough
and did not succumb. He was found battered, bleeding and
unconscious, and taken to hospital, where he remained as
an in-patient for several weeks before being certified as
being fit to attend Court.

The first clue to a line of inquiry in this case was a
cloth cap found by the police at the scene of the crime,
but it was only after exhaustive inquiries that its
ownership was traced to Snipey, who did not return to that
particular spot to retrieve it. Neighbours, acquaintances
and other persons who could have told us to whom the cap
belonged were many, but they refrained for fear of
reprisals from the offenders. They needn't have been
frightened; the police do not divulge the source of their
information. In fact - especially in the Metropolitan
district of London - detectives prefer that the public
should think that the police got the information by their
own endeavours, without help from anyone.

*   *   *

Snipey gave his occupation as that of a 'general dealer',
a designation of uncertain and questionable meaning, but
it seemed that he was not regarded as a person of integrity
by anybody who knew him. He was of a nomadic type,
travelling by horse and cart on the lookout for anything
worth buying cheaply, and easy to carry. His home appeared
a poor one, and there lived with a woman of the gypsy class
who, notwithstanding the fact that she hadn't had an easy

job looking after Snipey, was devoted to him.

On the day before Snipey was due to take his trial at the Old Bailey, his female devotee called upon me at my office. She was desirous of going to London to watch the court proceedings, and intimated her optimism by telling me that she would bring Snipey back to Gravesend when the trial was over. Informing me of her financial difficulties, she borrowed a pound, and departed. A few days later she came again, paid me the pound, and borrowed it once more. "I want to see Snipey again before they send him to the moor", she told me.

When she came to repay the loan, she informed me that Snipey wasn't looking too well, well not so well as he looked when she saw him in court. Her news didn't surprise me, but I was rather taken aback when she said: "He's doing some arithmetic", for Snipey was illiterate. Being curious, and aware of the fact that she had never been to school, I asked what it was that she called 'arithmetic'. She pointed to an almanac and said: "He's got one of them things, and each morning he chalks a figure aht, and he told me that he knows to the minute when he's coming home from the nick".

I saw no more of Snipey, but it may be taken for granted that long before leaving prison, he was able to write; the prison chaplain having been his tutor. Snipey passed on.

*　　*　　*

Gravesend, like any other town within a radius of twenty or thirty miles of London, was visited occasionally by a contemptible class of thief from the Metropolis, who came for a stay of an hour or so on a 'cheap-day-trip' to prey upon traders by means of a sharp and criminal practice performed in a manner so subtle, that the person imposed upon would find difficulty in discovering the fraud, and, in some cases, when shortage of cash did come to light, one or more of the shop assistants came under suspicion as an embezzler or petty thief.

This particular class of offence or swindle is known by the fancy name of 'Ringing the changes', but is nothing more nor less than stealing by trick. As may well be imagined, many offences of this nature are not reported to the police, the reason being that some persons are loath to confess that they have been outsmarted.

I call to mind such a case in which an old man from Camberwell Green was involved. He went into a bar of a good class hotel and placed a ten-shilling note on the counter at the same time as he ordered a glass of a well-known and rather expensive kind of ale. The idea of the old rascal was that the barmaid should see the note and bring the change at the same time she brought his beer. When she placed the change on the counter the old man put it on the ten-shilling note and said to her: "I don't like carrying a lot of silver about with me, I wonder if you would be so kind as to give me a pound-note instead". The barmaid, impressed by the dear old fellow's politeness, complied with his request. Two hours later, when she cashed-up, she found that she had been defrauded of nine-shillings and eightpence, plus a glass of bottled ale. Feeling herself responsible for her employer's loss, she made up the deficiency and said nothing of the episode, but it alerted her.

About three weeks later, the same old gentleman paid another visit to Gravesend, and on this occasion it seemed that he must have been suffering from amnesia, for he went into the same hotel, the same bar, as on the previous occasion, which was in charge of the same barmaid as before. He acted exactly as he had before, but this time - though getting his beer - he did not succeed. The barmaid acted wisely and he was arrested by the constable on point-duty outside the hotel.

At the police station the prisoner in his declaration of innocence, told me that he had never committed an offence of any kind in his life, and that he had never been in a police station, and that he had never been in the hands of the police for anything. So adamant was he that the police had made a serious mistake, that I disbelieved him. It was three days before Christmas. He asked for a glass of water, and this was given him in a perfectly clean glass. When he had put down his glass I dusted it, and his fingerprints were clearly defined. "Blimey", said he, catching his breath, "have I fell for that?" There was no beating about the bush. He gave me his real name and particulars of his previous convictions. After verifying these facts, I bailed him. We wished each other the compliments of the season and parted.

He came to Gravesend for judgment in January, was awarded four months imprisonment, and was so appreciative that he thanked the police for their kindness to him.

*   *   *

A terrible crime too seldom reported to the police is that of 'Demanding money, etc., with menaces', an offence

committed by unscrupulous and vicious criminals, who by
letter threaten to accuse their intended victim of
certain serious crimes unless money is paid by way of
ransom. This particular crime is wrongly called
'Blackmail', a term formerly used to describe a tribute
paid on the borders of England and Scotland to robbers
for immunity from attack; but for my purpose I will
adhere to this misnomer.

Blackmailers are persistent blackguards rarely
satisfied on a single payment of 'hush' money, for
they regard this as the first instalment of an indeterminate sum as 'Consideration' in a contract for silence
during an indeterminate period, and continue to make
further demands at irregular intervals until the victim's
means of paying are exhausted; but even then they have
been known to continue their demands in the hope that he
or she would succumb.

Judges who have heard evidence of the shocking manner
in which blackmail has been applied and have seen the
awful effect it has had on the human mind, have described
it as 'moral murder' and 'murder of the soul': certain it
is that many under its baneful influence have become
insane or have sought relief from their sufferings by
suicide.

There must be many unfortunates at their wits end
today, who are enduring pain, torture and distress of
mind, together with great pecuniary loss unnecessarily,
for they have merely to seek an appointment with the
local chief officer of police and report the facts to
obtain freedom from their soul-destroying bondage.
The fact that the victim of a blackmailer has committed
a crime or an indiscretion is no defence for the
extortioner, who, by the way, is never anxious to appear
in court to give evidence; besides, the police do not
require an informant (the complainant) in such a case to
incriminate himself.

In criminal proceedings against a blackmailer, the
Prosecution requests that the name of the victim be not
divulged; the letter X being used instead, after the
prefix Mr., Mrs. or Miss, as the case may be.

Blackmail takes many forms. Accusations involving
Homosexuality were frequently made against men of high-
standing, but since it has ceased to be an offence in
certain circumstances, a brake has been applied to the
activities of those unscrupulous rascals who specialized
in accusations of this kind.

*   *   *

Like other Ports of importance, Gravesend provides Pilots whose intimate knowledge of tides, currents and potential dangers to navigation is essential for the safety of incoming and outgoing ships.

I consider myself very fortunate in having known many Gravesend Pilots; for they were the most modest of men. Master-mariners all; they spoke little of what occurred when following their profession, though the older ones - many of whom had sailed before the mast on Britain's grand sailing vessels - could 'spin a bender' at times; some based upon a vivid imagination, and others upon yarns told them by shell-backs of long ago, and which lost nothing in the re-telling. But they were reticent to a degree if asked to relate their experiences at sea in storm and tempest, in peace or war.

The uniform worn by these Trinity House Pilots is very smart and compares very favourably with that of officers of the Royal Navy, except that there are no rings of gold braid to indicate rank. Pilots are a strictly disciplined body, and the slightest mistake or negligence in carrying out their responsible and exacting duties renders them liable to suspension or forfeit of licence for a period. The majority of Pilots are assigned to ships in accordance with a rota, which is prepared by or under the supervision of the 'Ruler of Pilots' who is usually an ex-pilot of long and varied experience. The Pilots who do not work to the rota are those retained by the various Shipping Companies, and are required to confine their services to the Line employing them.

Two of the senior pilots with whom I became acquainted were named Buck and Bishop respectively. They were such close friends that they always appeared to be off-duty at the same time, one seldom being seen without the other. So noticeable was this fact, that their colleagues and friends considered them entitled to comparison with two things well-known to go together, 'Bitter and Burton'. And this was the verdict of them all; a judgment thought to be fair, appropriate, and acceptable to the recipients. And it was so!

Messrs. Buck and Bishop, and other pilots were keen sportsmen, and by their conduct made it clear to all observers that they were proud of their profession and the great traditions of the British Mercantile Marine.

The companionship of B & B came to an abrupt and tragic end during the Second World War, when, unfortunately, Captain Buck went down with his ship, during enemy action. May he and other pilots who lost their lives in this way, without the means of retaliation, rest in peace.

*   *   *

151

In the days of 'Pussyfoot' Johnson, the American Prohibitionist, who attempted to deprive the populace of 'The Land of the Free' of freedom in the matter of the sale, supply and consumption of intoxicating liquor, a band of British adventurers of resource, seeing the opportunity to do good business, accepted an appointment to take a cargo of Spirit across the Atlantic and dispose of it surreptitiously at a price ensuring them a profit commensurate with the risks. The men prepared to undertake this hazardous task were ex-service officers, who had given distinguished service to this country. One at least had been decorated for .conspicuous gallantry at sea, and he was elected commander of the enterprise.

Realising the probability that others were preparing to take advantage of the opportunity to do a profitable bit of smuggling and that in order to be successful in making the first delivery of the contraband, speed and expedition were essential, they lost no time in putting their own particular scheme into operation.

They already possessed the means of transport in the form of a sturdy, powerful and seaworthy motor yacht, of which, for the purpose of security, they were themselves to be the crew.

Leaving the Thames in ballast ostensibly for a pleasure cruise, they made for Antwerp, where the cargo of ten thousand gallons of pure alcohol - in metal containers similar to petrol cans - was taken aboard, and the voyage of adventure began.

The Straits of Dover and the English Channel gave them no concern, but the mighty Atlantic was not at all kind to them. However, after what seemed to be more than the usual difficulties had been overcome by the maintenance of discipline, excellent seamanship and navigation, the coast-line of America between Boston and New York, came in sight.

It was now the time for the imperative use of a stratagem to deal with any possible contingency. And as the utmost credit for alertness must be given to the American authorities, the commander's first decision was to remain in international waters until the time arrived for the landing or rather the transhipment of the alcohol in accordance with the arrangments made respecting the <u>modus operandi</u> to be used in handing. it over to those who were to pay for it.

Keeping their engines running, and moving slowly parallel with the coast-line, they anxiously and hopefully awaited the sighting of the vessel they were expecting, but it didn't put in an appearance. Something had gone

wrong, someone had blundered; of this there could be no
doubt.

One can but imagine the depths of their disappointment
and mortification when they were forced to admit failure
of the hazardous and costly scheme and make an ignominious
retreat to avoid arrest, trial and punishment by the
American Authorities.

A single defeat, however, was not sufficient to deter
these men of courage, and as Finland was the other country
in which the manufacture and sale of intoxicating liquor
was prohibited at that period, they decided to go there;
but it was of no avail, for on arrival they discovered
that prohibition had come to an end.

What variety of luck would a sportsman call a single
fruitless and profitless voyage of three thousand miles
or so at the end of which he had expected a substantial
'tax-free' bonus?   And what kind of language would he
use to express his feelings after having experienced a
second reverse involving further serious losses, in
circumstances beyond his control?   Personally, I have
only a rough idea.

Now there was nothing for it but to return to England
with their valuable cargo and the optimistic hope of
dodging the Customs, which they intended to accomplish by
landing it at a creek on the Essex-side of the Thames,
where lorries would convey it to London; but alas and
alack, frustration was once more awaiting the venturesome
crew.

Having been informed of the probability that I would be
required to take the crew into my custody, I stood by in
my office for the purpose.   But neither I nor any of my
men took part in the arrest, which was carried out with
dignity by the Surveyor of Customs at Gravesend and his
officers.

My 'prisoners' were not placed in the cells.   They
spent an hour or so in my office, and after the necessary
steps had been taken they were bailed to appear before
the Justices a fortnight later.   They were dealt with
by fines which appeared to be inflicted according to
seniority; the Commander paying the heaviest and the
other men varying smaller amounts.   And the motor vessel
and its cargo was confiscated.

In Gravesend, I was a happy man, not only because it
was my first chief constableship - the target I had set
myself - but also on account of the good feeling existing
between my colleagues in the Force and Fire Brigade and
the good relations with the Town Clerk, the members of his
staff and the public generally.

GRAVESEND

The Town Clerk - the late Mr. H. H. Brown, a
Yorkshireman, and a graduate of Sheffield University,
was always helpful in matters of law.   He was a popular,
jolly and humourous gentleman, a stickler for correctness.
At Council Meetings he was often amusing but always
tactful.   He was very good at pointing out to newly
elected Councillors the obstacles in their way when
attempting - at the first opportunity - to fulfil a
promise made in their Election Addresses, but he was
genuinely trying to help.

*   *   *

As already mentioned, all Local Authorities were not
compelled to have a Fire Brigade of their own until
fairly recently.   So it was the rule for a Brigade to
cover a wide area of villages within a certain radius.
Gravesend Fire Brigade was no exception to that rule; so,
in consequence, it turned out on many occasions to fight
fires occurring several miles from the town.

On several occasions during the time that I was the
chief officer of the Brigade, we were called to Cobham
where the Earl of Darnley resided, sometimes to extinguish
fires on his estate.   He was a very tall man, and on
occasions would watch us at work and would ask to be
allowed to give a hand.

In the village of Cobham there is a famous inn under the
sign of The Leather Bottle.   It is regarded as famous
because Charles Dickens stayed there to write "The Pickwick
Papers".   The chair in which he sat is there, in a private
room.   And one may, with permission of the licensee, sit
in it and make a silent wish.

A former well-known Band Leader, the late Debroy Somers,
used to stay there to get inspiration.   On the shirt-front
of the Head Waiter he wrote:

> "What will you have, sir", the waiter said,
> Pensively picking his nose,
> "I'll have two hard-boiled eggs, you old ....
> You can't stick your fingers in those".

The owner of the shirt-front bearing this Ode,
framed it, and when he left Cobham to open a small
restaurant, took it with him.   I have since heard that
he displayed it with good results; it brought business
one supposes.

As a chief officer of the Gravesend Police Fire Brigade
I learned quite a lot, a good deal from my subordinates

who had had long experience of Fire duties and the difficulties met with in varying circumstances and conditions. They were a happy band of men in whom I had complete confidence.

During the Summer of 1934, an advertisement announced that a vacancy for a Chief Constable existed at Grimsby in Lincolnshire. I became a candidate for the post and was fortunate enough to find myself on the short list.

The night before the elected candidates were to be interviewed by the Watch Committee, I, with two or three other applicants, was in the smoke-room of the Yarborough Hotel.

A number of regular customers were also there. They were aware of the fact that a new Chief Constable would be appointed on the morrow. I heard one of the customers say: "I wonder who we will get as Chief Constable tomorrow?" I later discovered that the speaker's name was the famous one of Tickler. In answer, another said: "Some ...... fool, no doubt". A third customer thought it appropriate to say: "I wouldn't mind betting that Alderman Dick .... has him in his pocket!" It was rather nice to know that people were interested in the forthcoming appointment.

I got the job!

Mr. Tickler was a member of the well-known firm of that name. I had eaten some of their produce while in the Army.

Alderman Dick Kitching was Chairman of the Watch Committee.

I took up duty as Chief Constable and Director of the Fire Brigade, on September 1st.

XIII

Grimsby - "Girl Pat", etc.

I took over my duties as Chief and Director of the
Fire Brigade on September 1st, 1934.   My predecessor
had died a few months before.

A County Borough, Grimsby had a population of about
ninety-three thousand, and is situated on the South bank
of the Humber, in North Lincolnshire.   Regarded as the
premier fishing port in the United Kingdom, it is an
extremely busy town, though it has experienced periods of
depression.

One of the first duties falling to my lot in Grimsby
was the very necessary elimination of a number of
unscrupulous persons who were imposing upon the public
outside the town, and who, by their fraudulent behaviour,
were likely to bring honest fish merchants into disrepute.

These impostors advertised in National Newspapers, a
promise to send a basket of choice fresh fish to anywhere
in the Country for the sum of two shillings, which was
to be sent with the order.   The initial orders were
occasionally complied with, but in general those who sent
money got nothing in return.

To prove that these deceivers were committing the
crime of 'obtaining money by means of false pretences'
was extremely difficult - if not an impossible task -
for many excuses for non-compliance with the orders were
available to them, the principal one being that if any
'wrong' at all arose from the failure to supply the fish,
it would not amount to a crime but only 'a breach of
contract', which could only be remedied by a Civil action
in the County Court, and not by prosecution.   In any case,
none of those persons who had been victims was prepared
to come forward to give evidence.

Fortunately, however, inquiries revealed that the
impostors were trading in names other than their own and
that none of them complied with the provisions of 'The
Registration of Business Names Act, 1916', so action was

taken against them for infringements of this statute, and they were put out of business.

As you are most probably aware, it has been said on many occasions, that 'The Law is an Ass'. All I wish to say with regard to such an allegation, is: "Maybe it was before 1916, maybe still is, in certain circumstances, but I found it distinctly sensible in 1935".

*   *   *

That sailormen have always been superstitious is a fact well-known by all who have come in contact with them or have read of adventures at sea, and it may be taken for granted, I would suggest, that deep-sea fishermen, who are considered by some people to be the toughest, hardest-worked and the only real sailors of today, are no exception to the rule.

In Grimsby, however, I found that most people employed in the fishing industry, including some owners of fishing vessels, were addicted to superstition, believing in supernatural, spiritual or diabolic agency.

A white cat indicated misfortune to come, and that to walk under a ladder was asking for trouble; but they appeared to be unique in regarding pigs and rabbits or the sight or mention of these animals as an omen of some kind of tragic event bringing severe loss or disaster in its train, unless an antidote - said by some to have been effective - could be resorted to in order to counteract their irrational fear of the unknown or mysterious.

It was quite by accident that I discovered the nature of the antidote referred to. Accompanying the Grimsby Town Football Team to Manchester, I was sitting next to a Director of the Club.

As the train was passing through the countryside, I saw some pigs grazing. It was a very nice day, and the sun was brilliant. I called the Director's attention to the beauty of the surrounding country and mentioned the presence of the pigs. He seemed irritated by what I had said. "We shall lose now", he said, and immediately reached for and touched the metal frame of the window. I asked him why he had prophesied that Grimsby would lose the match. "You said something about pigs", he replied.

Grimsby Town lost all right, despite the use of the antidote - touching cold metal. Manchester City 1

Grimsby Town 0. It was a splendid game, but Grimsby lost because their opponents were in better form that day. However, I decided never to talk of pigs again.

I believe it true to say that no superstition has ever been demonstrated as trustworthy. Many 'lucky' individuals have studiously defied every ignorant superstition, and some of the 'luckiest' events of history have occurred on Fridays; yet there exist today thousands of people who hug their inane superstitions feverishly to their breasts, and still live as though the world were under the sway of Black Magic performed by the supreme spirit of evil and his satellites.

Grimsby is an ancient borough, for it received its charter in 1201, fourteen years before King John signed the Magna Carta.

The police force of Grimsby came into being in 1846, but perhaps its earliest guardians of the peace appointed were a small body of watchmen who commenced duty about the year 1514 following receipt of a letter from King Henry VIII, who called upon the Mayor and Burgesses of the town to appoint from amongst themselves "such as be of the honestest and best sort" to keep watch and ward from nine o'clock at night until five o'clock in the morning; and it appears that the period of night duty has been between those hours ever since.

At its inception, the force consisted of one Officer, and three men; in 1955, its authorised strength was 152.

The letter which contained King Henry's directive is in the municipal archives and, despite its tattered condition, it is possible to read that it was the duty of the night watch to deal with 'idle and sturdy vagabonds who do not labour and travail for their lyving' so that there may be 'quiet for our good subjettes' and punishment 'for the worste sorte'.

As was the case in some other towns, Grimsby's early policemen had a great deal to contend with, for not only had they to deal with felons of all kinds, but were often called upon to prevent breaches of the peace, especially at local and parliamentary elections, when riotous assemblies were more frequent than in recent years.

They were compelled to pay special attention to one particular individual who was given to inciting his fellow townsmen to acts of violence and destruction. So it seems that even in those days of long ago, troublemakers were about. But it is refreshing to note that no mention is made of Strikes. Perhaps men were more contented in those days.

*   *   *

159

In Grimsby I found matters - so far as my duties were concerned - very similar to those I had performed in Gravesend. There were the same kinds of crime to deal with, and there was little difference in the amount. My second-in-command was a Superintendent of long experience, and he carried out his duties conscientiously at all times. And having served in the town for many years, he knew the characteristics of the people and gave me all the help I required. The force was a good one, efficient and loyal.

But matters had not always been comfortable for Head Constables, as they were called a hundred years ago. In 1859, the second Head Constable of the force and his entire staff was dismissed. But there was no difficulty in recruiting more men, so the life of the constabulary went on.

From the few records remaining it would appear that several members of the force would have done well if they had signed the pledge containing an extra under-taking to refrain from abusing their superior officers.

The Watch Committee of those days was most tolerant so far as liquid refreshment was concerned, for it is on record that one constable was twice dismissed and twice reinstated after being found drunk on duty.

Getting 'tight', in fact, seemed to have been almost a pre-occupation in the early days of the force if one is to judge by the Standing Orders of 1892, because they devote considerable space to disciplinary offences involving the use of intoxicants, and go out of the way to stress that 'experience has proved that coffee is better for keeping the body warm and comfortable in cold and wet weather than spirits or beer'.

The same Orders give other valuable advice by counselling constables, when walking the beat, 'to keep on the outside of the footpath by day and next to the houses by night'. The object being to give the public the freedom of the footpath in daylight and to provide cover for the police at night, making it more difficult for offenders to see them.

The public houses of those days were open all day and far into the night, and as intoxicating liquor was extremely cheap, policemen not only had to deal with numerous drunks, but were called upon to resist the constant temptation of <u>taking</u> drink themselves. Besides, intoxicants were much stronger than now. But it is pretty certain that such a state of affairs was not peculiar to Grimsby. The conditions of service for policemen in those days were bad enough to drive the strongest minded man to drink.

*   *   *

The Grimsby Watch Committee - during the two years I
served under them - were very watchful indeed on all
matters touching efficiency, and were anxious to keep
the Force and Fire Brigade up-to-date.

Having been a signaller in the Army, I was interested
in wireless as a means of communication and, with the
aid of a young fireman I made experiments with a certain
degree of success; which was most encouraging. This
was in 1934-1935, before Wireless Telephony had taken
foothold in the police service.

The Grimsby Ice and Cold Storage Company, hearing of
my endeavours, loaned me a transmitter and receiver of
the kind used in trawlers. It was very good and of
long range. Placing it ready for action in the billiards
room at the police station, we listened-in with anti-
cipation. We hadn't long to wait. The first call
came from the Skipper of a trawler who was asking a
favour of the Skipper ·of the trawler 'Stoke City'.
"Calling Stoke City, Calling Stoke City" came through
loud and clear.   "I hear you're homeward bound with a
good catch Jack, will you give me the bearings, over".
Skipper Jack Evans, of the 'Stoke City' replied: "It's
not my bearings you want, there's not enough fish here
to feed a seagull". The kind of fish that weren't
there was mentioned, but there are so many different
sorts you know.

The Consolidated Fishing Company named some of their
ships after First Division Football Teams, but rele-
gations to other Divisions have not caused the Company
to change the names of their trawlers.

Grimsby fishermen are gallant fellows who behaved
themselves when home from sea.   And the majority of
them were good football fans.   One occasion on which
I was watching Grimsby Town play, the 'passing' was going
astray, so much so, that a fisherman shouted "Put the
Band on".

I was told of a case in which superstition was used by
a trawler crew for the purpose of giving their support to
Grimsby Town Football Club in an F.A. Cup replay, but it
was really for their own enjoyment that they desired to
watch the match.   They had tried legitimate means to
obtain permission from their Skipper, but he was not a
football enthusiast, so they didn't succeed.   Putting
their heads together, as it were, they decided to let the

Skipper 'see the rabbit', and made sure that he did.
The trip to sea was postponed, for a tide or two.
Need more be said?

Fishermen at sea on Saturdays frequently enquired
by radio telephony to outcoming trawlermen the result
of football matches and other sports.   The replies
were always definite one way or another.   The word
'good' was used when appropriate but it wasn't predominant.

The language commonly used by Grimsby fishermen is
certainly descriptive.

*   *   *

There was not a great deal of juvenile delinquency in
Grimsby, but I remember a spate of shopbreaking which
gave us trouble over a period of weeks.   The signs
seemed to indicate that adults had been responsible, but
a small gang of boys - agile climbers - came under
suspicion in unusual circumstances; the philanthropy of
a youngster nine years old.   He and a friend took a 'bus
to Cleethorpes, and when the conductor came to collect
fares from them, one boy tendered a one-pound note and
said that he would pay for the two of them.   It wasn't
often that a boy so young was entrusted with so much
money, so the conductor was a bit suspicious, but when
the boy said: "You keep the change, buddy", he was more
so.

When asked by the police how they got into the various
premises affected, their 'spokesman' seemed quite pleased
when he said: "We bunked each other up".   Juveniles are
often responsible for crimes in which adults come under
suspicion.

*   *   *

Many people will remember the trawler 'Girl Pat' and
the story of the exploits of her Skipper, Dod Osborne,
in 1936 who sailed away from Grimsby under his own
'Secret Orders' to an unknown destination, using a school
atlas as a navigation aid.   Her owners had to contend
with unmerciful leg-pulling and banter of all kinds from
the moment the ship was reported missing.   And many
fictitious stories were told and disseminated daily
respecting her whereabouts.

'Girl Pat' was a very small craft, and usually fished
in an area not too far from home, so when her master
ventured into the mighty Atlantic his action was considered
somewhat risky and daring.   Since then however, much

162

smaller vessels have braved the elements and turbulent oceans all around the globe when navigated by one man without a crew. Nevertheless, the Skipper of 'Girl Pat' was a true and brave sailor, just the sort of man to undertake the task of sailing round the world alone.

Rumourmongers concocted and spread all kinds of tales regarding the object or objects her Skipper had in mind when he took the little ship away from home, and there was much guessing as to the nature of the offence(s) he had committed or would possibly commit as time went on, but there was no evidence that would substantiate a charge of 'Barratry' - 'A fraudulent breach of duty on the part of a master of a ship' up to the time that I left Grimsby to become the chief constable of Stoke-on-Trent.

To give the lie to the chorus of an old sentimental song which was sung with gusto by some of the local jesters:

> "She never returned,
> She never returned,
> Though her fate is still unlearned,
> For from that day to this,
> We've been watching and waiting,
> For the ship that never returned"..

The 'Girl Pat' did return to Grimsby, and without a stain on her character. To 'show off' she went to other ports, and was well received.

XIV

Stoke-on-Trent - Trials, Tribulations, Some Crimes, etc.

On September 1st, 1936, I took charge of the Stoke-on-Trent City Police Force. This was my 8th police force and third Chief Constableship. I was happy at having attained such an important position within a period of six years of having held the subordinate rank of Inspector, in the Bacup Borough Police, in Lancashire.

In case it might be thought that my progress in the police service was unusually rapid, I must admit that there was nothing extraordinary about it, for at that time there were more separate police forces than those which have existed since April, 1947, when a large number of Borough police forces were abolished and absorbed into County Police Forces. The point I wish to make is: there were many more chances of 'rising from the ranks' in 1936, than there are today.

Having been Chief Constable of two Borough Police Forces before coming to The Potteries, I soon settled down and was ready to perform my duties in the prescribed manner; without fear or favour, affection, or ill will, like all police constables undertake to perform. It seemed to me, that the citizens would not be difficult 'to get on with'; law abiding people were all right!

I had been in the City but a short time when it was brought home to me, in no uncertain manner, that my task wouldn't be a pleasant one if I didn't 'stick to my guns'; for it became ·obvious that the legal adviser to the City Council - Mr. E. B. Sharpley, the Town Clerk, considered himself to be the head of all Corporation Departments, which, he mistakenly believed included the City Police Force.

County, City and Borough Police Forces are not 'Corporation Departments', nor are Police Officers Corporation employees; even though a Standing Joint Committee in the case of County Police Forces, or a

Watch Committee in the case of City and Borough Police
Forces, consisting of Aldermen and Councillors exist
as the Police Authority.   And it was clear to me
Mr. Sherpley regarded all officials - no matter how
highly qualified in their particular spheres and
professions - as his subordinates; so it fell to my
lot to disillusion him so far as the City Police Force
was concerned.

Upon entering my office one morning, I found my deputy,
Superintendent Clarke, receiving an instruction from a
member of the Town Clerk's staff.   I heard it distinctly:
"<u>The Town Clerk says that no police action is to be taken
against Mister so-an-so for receiving stolen property</u>".
I had never met with anything quite like this before.
"Who is that speaking?" I asked the superintendent.
"It's the town clerk's right-hand man", he answered.
The 'right-hand man' was a Mr. Coupland, and he was told
to tell the Town Clerk that I, as the Chief Constable
of Stoke-on-Trent City Police, would not tolerate any
interference with my duties.

A few minutes later, Mr. Coupland rang up to say:
"The Town says, all right".

The man on whose behalf the instruction of 'no action'
was made, came before the Justices some days later and
received three months' imprisonment.

It was this early attempt to undermine my authority
and to defeat the course of justice, that made me
appreciate what I was up against.   It was a good lesson,
I was glad that it came early.

*   *   *

I derive no pleasure in writing of Mr. Sharpley as I
do, but this being an autobiography, should, I think,
include unpleasant happenings in one's life, as well as
pleasurable episodes.   And I regret having to mention
his name so often, but this is necessary to avoid
confusion and/or misunderstanding.   My experiences
endured at Stoke-on-Trent were regarded as unique so far
as relations between Town Clerks and Chief Constables
were concerned.   And by having served in eight separate
police forces, I became the holder of a record which
will live for ever, simply because never again will it
be possible for members of the rank and file to have so
many chances of promotion offered for legitimate
competition.

As time passed, it became more and more evident, that
the Town Clerk had been looked upon as one possessing

166

great influence and one whom most people of intelligence
would not dare to antagonise.

I found that members of the corporation staff
considered themselves immune from prosecution and above
the law so far as Stoke-on-Trent (and its six towns)
was concerned.

If caused to stop by police for an alleged offence
against the Road Traffic Act, they would say: "You
can't do anything to me, I'm a corporation employee",
or "it will be all right, I'll see the Town Clerk about
you, I won't be summoned".

It was imperative, of course, that such persons be
taught that no matter what influence they had been able
to call upon to evade the consequences of their unlawful
acts, they were in a state of equality with other
members of the community, so possessed no special
privileges.

The requisite lesson was duly given in each and
every case in which employees of the corporation
expressed a reason why lawful action by the police would
be invalid or abortive by virtue of the fact that they
were employed by the municipal corporation or had a
'Cromwell' to protect them, soon realized their new status
and acted as ordinary well behaved citizens.

* * *

The Town Clerk, Mr. E. B. Sharpley, was also a
farmer, and possessed holdings in North Staffordshire
and Lincolnshire. And as an agriculturist, he had
numerous acquaintances and was well-known by cattle
drovers, fellow farmers, butchers, etc.

There was one occasion on which a farmer who lived
outside the city, and who had done business with
Mr. Sharpley, got into trouble with the police inside
the city, and asked Mr. Sharpley to assist him. Knowing,
by this time, that he had no influence over me, the Town
Clerk - through a subordinate in the customary manner -
got in touch with the divisional superintendent of the
area in which the alleged offence had been committed.
Referring to the particular case, he would declare his
personal interest in the case and ask if criminal
proceedings were necessary. And on being informed that
an arrest had been made, and the police could do nothing
except bring the alleged offender before the magistrates,
he would ask for the names of the Justices who would be
sitting on the day of the hearing; and, if any of them
happened to be members of the City Council, he would

endeavour to procure their help in the direction which
he would indicate.   But he met with little success in
this direction, I'm pleased to say.

There was however, a case in which two corporation
employees and a council motor vehicle were involved,
and the circumstances of the occurrence made it necessary
to issue summonses against the men, if only to avoid
allegations of favouritism.

For the city police to take action against servants
of the corporation for alleged offences committed by
them in the course of their employment was regarded by
most members of the City Council as unpardonable, if
not ultra vires.

The vehicle was an A.R.P. conveyance and I was the
A.R.P. officer.   Such was the consternation aroused
in the minds of those who considered I had exceeded my
duty that several attempts were made to get me to
withdraw the summonses.   The methods adopted did not
impress me.   The Air Raid-precautions Emergency Committee,
presided over by the Lord Mayor, 'had a go at me', and
the Lord Mayor himself tried his best to persuade me,
but to no avail.

The case - which could have been disposed of by
inflicting small fines or even dismissal on payments of
the costs amounting to four shillings in each case -
came before two Aldermen of the City Council, who,
without listening to the evidence, and against the
advice of the clerk to the Justices, dismissed the case.

I caused an appeal to be made by way of 'case stated'
on a point of law, but before this could be heard by the
Divisional Court which is usually presided over by the
Lord Chief Justice, though the Divisional Court can
consist of any three Judges of the King's (or the Queen's)
Bench Division, a special meeting of the Watch Committee
was convened for the purpose of passing a resolution
preventing me pursuing it, but instead of such a resolution
it was decided to send a deputation to the Home Office
and to call the attention of the Association of Municipal
Corporations to the matter, for the purpose of ascertaining
whether or not a chief officer of police had the power to
appeal in such a case without the permission of the Watch
Committee.   Both the Deputation and the Resolution failed.
But it seemed quite clear however, that the Watch Committee
would not have given me permission to appeal if their
authority had been required.

One can only imagine the nature of a state of affairs
likely to accrue if a chief officer of police had first to
have the permission of a police authority before he could

take lawful action. Could one possibly estimate the
amount of 'wangling' that would be practiced in such
circumstances?

The prosecutor in the case referred to was Superintendent
W. Hobson, of the Stoke-on-Trent City Police, and the
appeal to the Divisional Court was made in his name.

The appeal was successful, and the case was remitted
to the magistrates with an instruction to convict. They
did so by inflicting fines of forty shillings. Appeals
are usually costly, and this one was no exception. But
it was necessary in order to demonstrate that, notwithstanding views to the contrary, the law is the same for
all (justicia omnibus), and that not only should justice
be done, but should manifestly be seen to be done.

*   *   *

During the Second World War, in 1941, a junior
subordinate of the Town Clerk was arrested for being
under the influence of drink or drugs to such an extent
as to be incapable of having control of a mechanically -
propelled vehicle, and was so certified by the medical
practitioner who examined him.

On the evening of the following day I received a
telephone message from the steward of the local golf
club, of which I was a member, to the effect that the
Lord Mayor, also a member of the club, wondered if I
would come to the club and see him on a little matter.
I complied with the request, and on arrival found the
Most Worshipful engaged in a game of Bridge and I waited
for the rubber to finish. "I would like a word with
you chief", said the Lord Mayor, "we can talk during a
short walk over the course".

From some of my previous experience in Stoke-on-Trent,
there came to my mind a rough idea or prediction of the
subject about to be broached. "I hear", said my companion,
"that one of the town hall staff has been arrested for
being drunk in charge. Is it so?" "Not quite" I said,
"we do not allege drunkenness in such cases today, but that
the person concerned is under the influence of drink or
drugs to such an extent as to be incapable of having proper
control of a mechanically-propelled vehicle; but, my Lord
Mayor, why do you ask?"

By defining the actual words of the charge against the
person concerned, I did not wish to be awkward or to give
a lecture on law, but to put the Lord Mayor at ease. He
did not mention the name of the person charged, but he
asked me if that person would have to answer the charge,
and whether there would be a difference if he were sent
into the Army. My answers were to the effect that although

I had sympathy for the alleged offender, I had no authority
to withdraw the charge nor could favour be shown him, and
if he did enter the Army or any other service, he would
be compelled to answer the charge made against him.

The young man concerned pleaded guilty and was fined.
He has since died.

Who had informed the Lord Mayor of this matter, and
who had asked him to have a talk with me with regard to
it?

One can appreciate the desire of a charitable person to
help another who is in sore distress, and on whose behalf
he intervenes to obtain a concession; but when the request
- if granted - would render the grantor liable to prosecution and dismissal in disgrace, one is, I think,
entitled to ask why any person - whatever his status or
rank - should ever undertake the task of coming to the
aid of any person in such circumstances.

*   *   *

In the early months of 1943, I, having a case of an
alleged Attempted Murder to deal with, and being of the
opinion that in the circumstances as I knew them, it would
be imprudent to request the Town Clerk to detail a member
of his legal staff to present the facts at the preliminary
hearing before the Justices, I suggested to the Director
of Public Prosecutions that he should be represented by
a solicitor of repute who was in private practice, and
he agreed.

The Town Clerk took exception to this action of mine
and complained to the Watch Committee; and when the
complaint was being dealt with, it was obvious that the
majority of members were against me, for they had been
advised that a chief constable was bound to utilise the
services of the Town Clerk's department.   Some Aldermen
and Councillors alleged that there was a personal feud
between the Town Clerk and myself; so once again a
special meeting of the Watch Committee was convened, but
on this occasion for the purpose of investigating the
suggested existence of the feud; the proceedings to be
'in camera'.

The meeting lasted eighty minutes, and at its conclusion
the only official statement made to the Press was that a
resolution had been unanimously passed to the effect:-

"That in all proceedings other than those in which
the Corporation was interested, the Chief Constable
shall use the Town Clerk's Department".

In case it is thought that the time taken up to pass such a simple resolution was eighty minutes, I regard it as incumbent upon me to explain that there was some discussion, and that the Town Clerk made a statement in support of the proposition. He said that research had revealed the existence in the minute-book, thirty-three years old, of a resolution which laid down that the chief constable should have invited him to undertake the prosecution.

My answer to this statement was the submission that no council of a municipality had power to pass any resolution instructing the police in the administration of justice. I stated, too, that I had not encountered more obstruction anywhere than I had in Stoke-on-Trent.

With regard to the alleged feud I stated: "I desire to state at once that there is no personal feud between the town clerk and myself. I reiterate, however, that I have encountered obstruction and interference in my duties almost since I came here, and I have abundant evidence of this; but do not propose to say it here nor in camera. Moreover, with the greatest deference to you, gentlemen, your Committee is not competent to inquire into or adjudicate upon the alleged differences; and if you wish to pursue the matter, I would suggest that a public inquiry, presided over by a person nominated by the Home Office, should take place, when, I have no doubt, it will be revealed conclusively, that my actions have been rendered necessary in the interests of justice".

The Town Clerk told the Committee that he knew of no instance of obstruction by himself or his department, and that, if any allegation of obstruction was made, he was immediately prepared to meet it. But he did not!

The Chairman of the Watch Committee, Mr. Tom Flint, suggested that the Town Clerk, myself and he, should adjourn to another room and discuss the matter in a friendly manner; but this did not materialise. My own suggestion that there should be a public inquiry was of no effect. Nobody but myself seemed interested in it.

The Local Press had quite a lot to say about the Watch Committee's proposed inquiry in camera, which it described as a farce, and asserted that it was stultified by its own legal incompetence. "Stoke-on-Trent Aldermen and Councillors", he said, "have experienced too many shocks to be horror stricken by anything. In any event, it has been common knowledge for a long time that the Town Clerk and the Chief Constable have not exactly seen eye to eye. Reports of meetings - Council

and Watch Committee have adduced evidence of lack of
visual parallelism.   Or, to reduce the situation to
one of popular analogy, the two have not emulated the
boys of the old brigade marching shoulder to shoulder
and blade by blade.   On the contrary there have been
thrust and riposte on various and successive occasions.
Accordingly, the members of the Watch Committee will
not need a special meeting for inquiring and investigating,
with sealed doors and sentinels on guard, to discover
that the Town Clerk and the Chief Constable are not
exactly comrades in arms or bosom friends.   Most remarkably,
some members were perturbed by the fact that the Chief
Constable had 'wasted' a couple of guineas by engaging
a local solicitor to prosecute in an attempted murder
charge, instead of inviting the Town Clerk, or one of
his assistants, to undertake the task".

In a leading article, the Editor wrote: "I could write
columns about this business and about the successive
civil troubles of Stoke-on-Trent; but I am proposing to
be brief and to the point.   Unless the Watch Committee
supports their Chief Constable, the public will have no
confidence in the Watch Committee.   If the Watch Committee
do not support their Chief Constable, I think the Home
Office will".

I had but little further trouble to endure from
Mr. E. B. Sharpley, the Town Clerk, who, by this time,
appreciated that I, as Chief Constable, was not
subordinate to a Town Clerk.

An amusing - if not significant - incident occurred
one Monday evening at the Theatre Royal, Hanley, within
the city.· A well known comedian, the late Dave Morris,
taking the part of a Mayor in a comic sketch, mentioned
that he and his company had just come from Birmingham, a
city whose motto was "Forward".   And he suggested that
the motto for the city of Stoke-on-Trent should be
"Move Sharply".

There was a case against an alleged bogus doctor.   And,
though the man concerned had allegedly committed several
serious crimes, Mr. Sharpley wanted him to be charged with
an offence no more serious than one 'of obtaining money
by means of a false pretence'.   The motive behind the
suggestion being to prevent the public knowing that an
appointment to an important medical post at a Maternity
Hospital had been given to the man without having made
the necessary inquiries into his credentials.   (See the
second part of "Two Bad Men").

*   *   *

At times, when taking exercise by means of golf, I
would think of the 'spots of bother I was having with
and through Mr. Sharpley.   And remembering the words
of the adage: 'Keep your eyes on the ball' I complied
with it, and imagined it was Mr. Sharpley's chin.   The
'comforting' thoughts usually came to me immediately
after playing the first hole at Trentham.   I would
place my ball on a peg on the second tee, take my stance
in the usual manner - some would consider it unusual -
address it, and take a deliberately intentioned swing
and smite it - out of bounds - in most cases, at a loss
of two strokes, plus half-a-crown.   Later on, I used
the scruffiest ball for the purpose.   There was no malice.
I found that these harmless acts of mine were sufficient
to keep up my morale.

Mr. Sharpley retired while I was the Chief Constable
of Stoke-on-Trent.   His place was taken by his deputy,
Mr. Harry Taylor, a local man, and happiness came with
him.

Mr. Sharpley died several years ago.   May he rest
in peace.

*   *   *

SOME CRIMES IN THE POTTERIES

In writing of these, no claim is made to fame by the
police for cleverness in bringing evil doers to justice.
The conscientious performance of their duties and the
assistance of the public are chiefly responsible.

TWO BAD MEN

It was at Stoke-on-Trent that I came in contact with
two of the most persistent criminals with whom the police
in this country have had to contend.

Both used many aliases, and before inflicting their
unwelcome presence upon the people of the Potteries, had
completed many terms of imprisonment, during which, with
the aid of literature available to them and the ever-ready
help from chaplains, had acquired an education not sur-
passed by one obtainable at Oxford or Cambridge University,
so far as plausibility is concerned.

The first of these men had a most unfortunate start in
life in that he was illegitimate, and unwanted.   His
mother had co-habited with a coloured man, a fact, the
result of which, was not likely to be helpful to him as
he grew up.   He was brought up and cared for by his

grandmother who, however, could not properly control
him. His criminal career started when he was twelve
years of age when he stole something quite useless
to him - two thousand feet of celluloid film. His
grandmother was aware of this first offence, and as
soon as she knew that inquiries were being made with
regard to it, she threw the film into the fire with
the result that she and another woman lost their lives.
For this first case of larceny he was sent to an
industrial school until he reached the age of sixteen.
This was a school available in each town in those
days - provided by the Local Authority - to reform boys
who had 'kicked over the traces', and they served their
purpose, I think, better in all ways to the so-called
Approved Schools of today.

Before he reached the age of sixteen, however, he
was liberated for the purpose of joining the Army as a
band-boy. Here was a chance for him to retrieve his
character, one would have thought, but he was alone in
the world one should remember. The Criminal kink was
still in him, and five months later he committed an
offence of housebreaking, and though only sixteen years
old, he was sent to prison for two months. At that
time - so far as the criminal law was concerned - a
person was an adult on reaching the age of sixteen.

Upon his release he was found a job at a cinema, but
it didn't suit him. By this time he was approaching
seventeen, and having committed two cases of fraud of
which he was convicted, he was sent to Borstal for a
period not exceeding three years. That he had brains
there could be no doubt, but having found how gullible
people are, and how valuable 'the gift of the gab' can
be, he decided to continue in crime. Even if he had
desired to reform and lead the life of a good citizen,
a term in a Borstal Insitution was not likely to help
him; for there he would meet scores of young criminals
like himself from whom he would learn of criminal
exploits which he had not yet tried, but could have
a shot at when he came out; and he did just that.

His next move was to invest himself with a Title
as the son of a Peer of the Realm, with a view to
enhancing his chances of success in his crimes
involving fraud. However, he was again detected;
went to prison again, and his Borstal licence was
revoked. His periods of liberty were short, and the
fictitious titles and names he gave himself were
unusually long and high-sounding, so much so, that in
all probability, they led to his rapid detection on

more than one occasion.   The offences with which he
was most familiar were larceny and false pretences in
which he deceived many persons who considered themselves fraud-proof.

London, Glasgow and Aberdeen were the chief places
in which he practised his 'calling', and though he
met with much success, the methods he adopted were so
simple that they almost pointed to him, and he was
captured when he considered himself safe from
apprehension.   To his credit, however, it must be
admitted that when arrested he gave no trouble to the
police beyond trying his skill at the use of the gift
of the gab.

He always dressed well, and from the proceeds of
his criminal deceptions was able to obtain first-class
accommodation in hotels of repute, and it was within
such establishments that he found many upon whom he
could and did impose.

On an occasion within a few weeks of his release
from prison he obtained the use of a motor car by
pretending to be an officer of a foreign power who had
escaped from Russia, and in passing through Germany
had obtained information of such importance to King
George V., that it was imperative that it be passed to
His Majesty without delay, hence his need of a car.

When asked the nature of the information he was
somewhat reticent, but he eventually took the owner of
the car aside and whispered: "It's a plot to
assassinate him, and only I in England know the details".

He did not obtain an audience with the King, but he
did obtain accommodation in one of His Majesty's
establishments for a period of fifteen months for the
attempt, made a few miles from Balmoral.   A police
officer had - with the owner of the car - listened to
his story and recognised him.

Upon his release, this persistent, audacious, but
still young criminal descended upon the Guards' Depot
at Caterham and posed as an American millionaire who
had lost a near relative in the Guards during the War
of 1914-18.

He announced that he would like to subscribe to a
Guards' Memorial and invited the Colonel and other
officers to dinner at a local hotel.

Before the time for the meal arrived the pseudo-
millionaire asked to look at the hotel safe to see if
it were suitable and sufficiently burglar-proof to
hold his jewellery.   The proprietor had no cause for
suspicion; and when his back was turned his visitor

emptied the safe of its valuables, jumped into a
motor car - which he had hired in a fictitious name -
and drove furiously away. His freedom was short
lived, but he was fortunate on this occasion, getting
only six months imprisonment for so serious a crime.
Released after four months, he kept to his criminal
path.

Known as Piccadilly Algie and other nicknames, he
was strong in his criticism of the 'Ticket-of-leave'
system then in vogue and in which a person awarded
Penal Servitude for his crime could, by good behaviour
in prison, get a remission of one-third of his sentence,
but the period remitted was spent on licence and subject
to the condition that if convicted during the period of
licence, his licence would be revoked and the unexpired
portion was added to the sentence given.

It was at Stoke on Trent Quarter Sessions in 1938,
that he made his protest against the 'Ticket of Leave'
system after having been convicted of stealing a pad
containing rings of great value from a Hanley firm of
jewellers. In this case he posed as a colonial who
had just returned to England to find, with glee, that
a niece of his had just got engaged, and he wished to
buy an engagement ring, one of high quality, as a
special gift from her uncle. His bronzed face, which
had come to him in birth, corroborated his tale about
being a man from the Colonies. When the shop assistant
brought the pad of rings he was not quite satisfied;
he wanted to see some more expensive ones. The man
behind the counter went to get what the customer
required, the customer seized the pad of jewels from
the counter quite satisfied with his haul, dashed
through the door which he had left ajar and dived into
a car which was gently purring with anxiety outside,
and made his escape to London.

This happened on the afternoon of Wednesday; three
days later he was safely gathered in. I had sent a
plodding detective-sergeant to London with instructions
to visit certain garages at which such a vehicle could
be hired for the day. By a piece of luck, my sergeant
found that a car which had been hired on the day in
question hadn't yet been returned. When, however, it
was, it was plain to see that the registration plates
had been tampered with. The false number plates used
on the car were made by a firm in the Wolverhampton
district, and we had no difficulty in tracing it. I
sent my detective-inspector to London and he, with the
help of a detective-inspector of the Metropolitan

Police, arrested the then 'alleged' offender. None of
the jewellery was recovered, but a price-tab from one
of the rings was found on the person of the man arrested.

Brought to Police Headquarters at Hanley, Stoke-on-
Trent, the prisoner told us that we had made a grave
mistake; he wasn't the man we wanted; that we had made
ourselves liable to an action for false arrest; but,
notwithstanding our mistake, he could give us a gleam of
hope to get the right man if we would agree to take him
back to London. "If you will do as I suggest", he said,
"I am prepared to take my rest tonight handcuffed to one
of your men so I wouldn't be able to scamper, and in the
morning I will take you to the place where I will point
out the man responsible, and when you see him you'll see
how remarkably like me he is".

Judging from his facial expression, I formed the
opinion that he was hopeful. I told him that his offer
of help would be made known to the Court. It was.

His Counsel did his best, but to no avail. In the
gallery of the Court was a pretty and well-dressed young
woman and, the prisoner was pleased to see her there.
When the Jury had left the Court to consider their
verdict, I saw the prisoner signal to her by raising a
hand with fingers and thumb extended, signifying 'five'.
He was correct in his estimate. "Five years penal
servitude".

Ten years later, in 1948, penal servitude, and the
ticket-of-leave system were, with certain other forms
of punishment, abolished. It can be said, however,
that such abolition, though beneficial to the criminal
fraternity, had probably been partly responsible for
the great increase in crime.

The man of many aliases mentioned here is dead.

The second habitual criminal came to the City of
Stoke-on-Trent in the guise of an eminent Colonial
Medical Practitioner. When asked the reason for his
presence in England, he said it was necessary because
he had some very important business of a legal nature
to transact, and not knowing when the matter in which
he was interested would come before the Court, he
decided to keep in touch with his medical work and,
incidentally, earn some money to defray his expenses
which were bound to be heavy.

A plausible liar, he had no medical qualifications;
but he had such a way with him that he deceived medical
men of great experience, who believed him to be the
person he represented himself to be.

Obtaining posts in Stoke-on-Trent as <u>locum tenens</u>

to two doctors, he came in contact with a pharma-
ceutical chemist who happened to be an alderman and
a member of the Health Committee.

By his plausibility he impressed the alderman
referred to, to such an extent that the Alderman mentioned
his name as a fully qualified person to act as locum
tenens to the Residential Medical Officer of the Stoke-
on-Trent City Maternity Hospital during the absence of
that official on holiday, and he did in fact take over
the duties attaching to that position.

Apparently no person asked him to produce credentials.
But when he went to the City Treasurer's Office to 'sign
on' as an official of the Corporation and was asked for
his name and qualifications, he requested the production
of the Medical Register and, turning over its pages he
pointed to the name of the highly qualified person who
was actually practising in Australia, who he had decided
to impersonate.

He acted as locum tenens at the Maternity Hospital for
a calendar month, and during that period relied upon the
efficiency of the nursing staff for most of the treatment
given to the patients, for he knew nothing of midwifery
on gynaecology; but there came an event in which he was
compelled to give his attention or confess.

Late one evening, a real medical man who had been
called by a midwife to a woman suffering from ante-
partum haemorrhage realized that his patient was in a
serious condition, in consequence of which he telephoned
to the man professing to be the Medical Officer in charge
of the Maternity Hospital, requesting that she be
admitted there for immediate treatment.   The bogus
doctor informed the caller that the Hospital was full,
although, in fact, there were three empty beds available
at the time; and advised him to try to obtain admission
to another Hospital.   This advice was acted upon, but
that particular institute was not then dealing with
maternity cases, so the unfortunate sufferer became the
patient of this horrible pseudo-medico, and, through his
lack of medical knowledge and his gross negligence she
died within four hours of her admission.

This culprit left the Potteries two days after his
victim died; but we had little difficulty in tracing him,
for once again he was acting as locum tenens, this time
in Wales.

It was this criminal case in which the Town Clerk,
Mr. E. B. Sharpley, particularly wished to be confined
to proceedings for 'Obtaining money by false pretences'.
The false pretences being 'that he - the alleged offender -

was a qualified medical practitioner'.

The accused man himself, in an attempt to limit the proceedings to that same misdemeanour, went to great pains to point out to the two officers who were to act as his escort back to the City: "What a stink would hang over Stoke-on-Trent, and the deleterious effect his appointment to the Maternity Hospital would have upon those who were so 'negligent' by failing to ask for and check his credentials before employing him, if he were charged with manslaughter and other serious offences"; he failed miserably. Justice demanded that he must be made to take the 'medicine' which the Law prescribed for him.

At Stafford Assizes he pleaded 'Not guilty' and stated that he had qualified in Australia about the year 1889, and in his interest his trial was postponed until the next Assize.

In the meantime further enquiries were made which resulted in the calling of two young Australian medical men, then serving in the Royal Navy, who knew the eminent doctor who had been impersonated by the prisoner. They testified that the prisoner was not he. The evidence was overwhelming. But the prisoner remained adamant, and his Counsel put him in the witness-box. The answers he gave to questions put to him by the Judge and in cross-examination showed that he had little knowledge of Anatomy.

He was sentenced to ten years penal servitude for manslaughter, and three years penal servitude on each of eleven other charges comprising of false pretences; giving false death certificates; forgery of and uttering such certificates. The sentences to run concurrently, that is, within the longest sentence.

This callous, unscrupulous and persistent criminal had resided for varying periods in the United States of America, Canada, Australia and South Africa. And during his periods of freedom he mixed with high society, posing as a medical man and on one occasion as a Presbyterian Minister. But there was always the intent to defraud.

It was evident that he had great influence over women, inducing some to marry him and others for various pur-poses. In one instance, when serving a prison sentence in America he persuaded a lady prison visitor to marry him in his cell; the prison chaplain officiating. Whether he was permitted to enjoy a honeymoon on that occasion is not on record.

His numerous frauds were always performed in the most audacious manner. In America he once induced the conductor of a train to bring it to a halt and wait for him whilst he visited a bank to cash a draft which was afterwards found to be worthless.

In the earlier part of his criminal career he was regarded as one addicted to violence, for when under-going another sentence in America he conspired with other criminals to murder a night-guard in order to effect an escape.

It is known that his first sentence of imprisonment was awarded in 1893, in New South Wales. Since then he has been convicted of serious crimes in other parts of Australia; in California, San Francisco and other places in America; in Durban, Natal and Johannesburg in South Africa, and in various places in England. Between 1893 and 1940, the terms of penal servitude and imprisonment awarded him amounted in the aggregate to forty-two years. But having regard to the fact that about one-third of the sentences would have been remitted for enforced 'good conduct' the actual period of incarceration would be thirty years, nine months.

During his long life of crime he went through at least seven ceremonies of marriage, and though he deceived and deserted most of his 'wives', he had never been charged with bigamy.

It was a matter of good fortune that this particular criminal never served in the fighting services in Britain, though he often boasted of his connection with the Army when it suited his purpose. He awarded him-self the Victoria Cross and the Distinguished Service Order.

I had never had to deal with a man with a worse criminal record than this man possessed, and am pleased to admit the fact. But it gave me pleasure to realise that the action taken against him at Stoke-on-Trent brought his criminal career to a close.

He will sin no more!

FOX FURS

The funniest offender who passed through my hands in the Potteries was one who boasted of being a Cockney. I will call him Frankie the Furrier.

When the issue of petrol was restricted and obtained by the surrender of coupons, Frankie and his son drove a motor car from London to Blackpool for the purpose of breaking into a tobacconist's shop - which had been previously 'surveyed' - and stealing cigarettes, tobacco, pipes, petrol lighters and other smoker's requisites, which were then in short supply and in great demand on the black market.

Successful in their criminal act, and being not particularly anxious to see the sea, they lost no time in beginning their return journey.

On reaching the Potteries, however, they met with an accident owing to bad visibility. The vehicle needed repairs and while these were being carried out they took breakfast. The contents of their vehicle aroused suspicion, and as they were unable to give a satisfactory account of their possession of the goods, they were brought to the Police Station in Hanley.

During the time an escort was on its way, I had a little talk with Frankie. Refraining from mentioning the charge which he would be called upon to answer, I found him most interesting and informative. Amongst other things, he told me that he had experienced no difficulty in obtaining petrol on the way up from 'the Smoke', and wasn't anticipating any trouble on the way home.

I asked him his trade. He told me he was a furrier, and that his "farver" and "granfarver" had been furriers before him; "My missus is one too", he said, "but since the bombs have been dropping there's been nothing in that line, so I started this lark of a 'screwsman' (burglar). Then he asked me: "Has your old lady got one of them there fox furs?" I answered him in the affirmative. "I'll bet you it ain't genuine", he said, and seemed so cocksure about it that I asked him how he could possibly say so without having seen it. "Because", he replied, "I help to work the oracle, and I know that nearly all them white hairs, specially them in and around the tail, don't come from foxes at all. Me and my missus put 'em there". I expressed my disbelief - I wanted to know more. "Blokes like you", he went on, "don't know what goes on in rigging furs". As he was speaking, he drew a small envelope from a waistcoat pocket. Opening the envelope, he displayed a bundle of white hairs, each several inches long. "Now will you believe me", he asked. I told him that he hadn't quite proved his assertion, and asked him to show me how the hairs were inserted to deceive. "Cor blimey", he muttered, and nodded his head a time or two, as if surprised at my unbelievable scepticism.

He asked me if I had such a thing as an old fur in stock, and told me that if I had a tube of sticky stuff he'd soon show me. Both of these articles were produced within a few minutes.

Squeezing a little adhesive into a saucer, he
dipped the tip of a single white hair into it, blew
into the fur, and in the space so made in the skin,
inserted the hair and repeated the process many times
with great skill and a steady hand.   And the ancient
moth-eaten stole was much improved by this beauty
treatment.

Still a learner, I appreciated the lesson and told
my tutor so.

He told me that the hairs he had just used were horse
hairs, and that they cost a "Nicker an arnce", but, of
course, there's a lot in an "arnce".

At Blackpool Quarter Sessions, Frankie did his best
to relieve his son of blame for the part he took in the
felonious escapade, and so well did he 'tell the tale'
that a merciful Recorder bound both offenders over to
be of good behaviour.

*   *   *

A METH-ELATED MAN

A not so funny man as the Furrier was one who had
been presented at Court on almost three hundred occasions,
and though he invariably admitted the charges against
him, he seldom, if ever, failed to make use of the right to
address the magistrates in mitigation.

In this he displayed considerable ability but with
little success, for the Justices had heard his pleas and
of his good resolutions regarding his future conduct so
often, that they felt it detrimental to their prestige
to allow him to take them 'up the creek' by his
plausibility.

Most of his offences arose from his strong feeling of
affection for methylated spirit, which he would drink
until he became bellicose.   It was then that he became
most objectionable and disorderly, attracting attention
to himself, resulting in his inevitable arrest and a
prison sentence.

What had caused him to become addicted to methylated
spirit nobody knew, though many people had tried to
ascertain with the desire to help him.   He had been a
soldier and a gallant one, and his bravery had been
recognised and rewarded.

Now a broken man; he had lost his self-respect and
had sunk so low in the social scale as to be regarded as
just a piece of life's jetsam and a person to avoid.
Like all other such addicts, he was an unpleasant and

182

difficult man to take into custody, for not only was
he a stinkard, but a potential carrier of infectious
disease also.   And when comatose, he was a dead weight.
   But there were times when he was witty.   When he
had sobered sufficiently to understand the charge being
made against him, he would be asked his name - though
every constable in Hanley knew the one he went by - and
would give that of a popular person famous on stage and
screen.
   In the early stages of his intoxication he would rave
and roar to such an extent that women and children became
terrified and hysterical, especially so when he placed a
foot inside the door to prevent it being closed, when he
was begging.   On one occasion, however, he received a
shock which did the public a good turn.   It came when he
happened to call at the home of a police sergeant.   The
officer had just returned home from duty.   The knock at
the door was answered by the sergeant.   Recognising the
caller, the sergeant asked: "What do you want?"   The reply
- made rather shakily as the caller retreated keeping his
eyes on the sergeant the while - was "Ten yards start
down bank".   The shock was electrical and sufficient to
prevent any further bother on that particular afternoon.
   The name by which this man was known in the city -
although an alias - appeared so frequently in the local
daily newspaper as that of one sent to prison, that the
facetious and uncharitable local comedians referred to him
as being: 'in town tonight, in clink tomorrow'.
   When out of prison, this unfortunate individual had no
fixed abode, and during his brief periods of liberty would
spend his nights on the premises of various brickworks
to which he went for the comforting.warmth radiating from
the walls of the kilns.
   It was while sleeping under such conditions and the
noxious influence of methylated spirit that he met his
death from the terrible effects of burning.   A post-
mortem examination was ordered and carried out.   It being
known that the deceased had been drinking the dreadful
mixture of spirits of wine and methyl for upwards of
thirty years, local medical men were anxious to see and
record the state of his arteries and liver, which they
expected to be tough and leathery.   They were surprised.
   The remains of this luckless old warrior were laid to
rest, but there were few mourners at the graveside.
   On a wreath of beautiful roses, however, the inscription:
"To my darling Daddy" brought tears to the eyes of many
who read it or were told of it.

MURDER MOST FOUL

The victim was a soldier, nineteen years of age.   When he went away to join the Army, he left behind him a suit of clothes, a bicycle, and a cornet which he was learning to play.

He had been away about eight months when his mother took in as lodgers a young woman and the murderer who were cohabiting.   The man had procured the woman by a promise of marriage, but he already had a wife.

The murderer was a spendthrift, had a fondness for drink, and often illtreated his paramour when she failed to carry out his orders to obtain money for his personal use.

It was not long before he took command of domestic affairs in the household, borrowed money from his landlady, sold some of her furniture, pawned the soldier's suit and sold his bicycle and cornet.

The victim of the crime came home on leave, but before actually going home he went to visit his mother at a pottery factory where she was at work.   He was wearing battledress, a khaki beret and tawny brown shoes. This was the last his mother saw of him.

It transpired that he reached his home about 2.30 p.m. His mother came home from work in the evening but her son was not there.   She asked the two lodgers where her son was.   It was then that the female lodger replied that she had cooked him a meal consisting of eggs and bacon, after which he had put on his haversack and gone out.

It was true that she had cooked the meal for him, but the latter part of her story was false.   It was false because she was acting under duress applied by the murderer, but she had no knowledge of the crime at that time.

After cooking the soldier's meal she had left the house for the purpose of picking some coal from a colliery waste-tip which was about half-a-mile away.   At that time the murderer and his victim were in the house.   She was away from the house less than two hours, but in that period the young soldier had been brutally murdered and his body was being disposed of.

In a reconstruction of the crime we, the local police, came to the only possible conclusion that as soon as the woman left the house to go for the coal the victim had been attacked from behind as he was engaged in eating; the weapons used being a hatchet and a hammer; and the motive robbery; murder for a pound or two.

NO SILVER SPOON

As she was approaching the house with her burden of
coal the woman heard some knocking noise coming from the
house. And when she entered, the sound was coming from
the front room downstairs which was the room in which
she and the assassin slept.

The noise was being caused by the murderer himself,
who, on being asked why he had been knocking, replied
that 'he had been putting the lino straight'.

That night - a few hours after the young soldier had
been so violently done to death - when the two lodgers
went to bed together, the woman mentioned that she
couldn't understand why the soldier boy had gone away.
Her companion, the murderer pointed downwards, and said:
"He's under here". At first she didn't believe him,
but his threats of what he would do to her and how he
would accuse her of assisting him in the crime, convinced
her. And being of a nervous disposition she became
terrified and kept silent.

For three more nights the pair slept on the floor
under which the victim's body was decomposing, and were
then forced by the nauseous atmosphere to remove to an
upstair room, but whenever an opportunity presented
itself the murderer visited the burial place of his
victim to give extra cover to his crime. He intended
to put in a layer of cement, but found that material
difficult to obtain.

On the day following the murder, the victim's tawny
brown shoes and his fountain-pen were pawned for nine
shillings. The pawn ticket concerning this transaction
was found under a mattress of the bed used by the
murderer when a search of the house was made after his
arrest.

When the police were satisfied that there was a body
under the floor, they left the remains in situ, and got
in touch with the Home Office pathologist for the district
- Mr. James Webster - who came without delay.

In order to exhume the body it was necessary to
remove a grand piano, some linoleum and several floor-
boards. Under the remains, various articles of military
equipment were found and there was evidence that they
belonged to the deceased soldier.

The young woman with whom the murderer had been
living was at first most reluctant to make a statement
to the police. And it was abundantly clear that she
had an obsession brought about by fright, that she would
be charged as an accomplice or an accessory to the murder
under investigation. Persistence and persuasion
triumphed however and she told her dreadful story.

Our evidence to substantiate the charge of Wilful Murder was complete. When cautioned and charged, the murderer gave the reply expected: "I do not wish to say anything until I have had legal advice".

He had, of course, been asked if he wished to make a statement, and he had replied in the same words as those he used when charged.

It should be appreciated that statements made by accused persons - unless amounting to confessions or are made in mitigation - are of little value. It is much better for the reputation of the police if they are able to prove cases by adducing sufficient reliable evidence in support of prosecutions they bring.

He was convicted of Murder and sentenced to death. And his appeal was dismissed.

On the day before he met his death on the scaffold, the murderer telegraphed the mother of his victim asking for her forgiveness. His request was granted.

This was yet another case of Murder to add to the vast majority of those which did not call for any specially clever detective ability apart from conscientious police work of obtaining evidence sufficient to prove, beyond reasonable doubt, the guilt of the person accused.

A BRUTISH BOY CRIMINAL

In Stoke-on-Trent and district for a period of nine months, there was a spate of serious crimes which caused the police and the public great annoyance. Night after night dwelling houses and other buildings were broken into and large sums of money, together with valuable objects, mostly jewellery, stolen; and though special patrols were sent out to catch the criminal, he escaped detection.

During the time in which he operated so successfully he took care to avoid going to the same district on two successive nights, though on occasions, he would carry out two or three raids within a few minutes of each other.

The raids were carefully planned and it appeared that the offender was working alone. All the breaking-in offences with the exception of two, in which he committed assaults on women, were carefully timed to coincide with the temporary absence of the occupiers.

Once inside, though he varied his method of effecting an entry, he took little precaution to avoid leaving his finger prints which, when photographed and compared, satisfied the police that the same individual was responsible. But beyond filing these impressions for possible future reference and comparison with those of men who had been convicted of various crimes, they could do little more to identify the criminal who was causing them so much worry.

It soon became apparent that the culprit was a newcomer to crime and one for whom a special and constant watch must be kept, in order to apply a brake to his nightly escapades. Imprints of size nine shoes, with soles of common design were found in the houses attacked, but these were of little value except to indicate that in all probability the wanted man was tall.

It was not until he had committed 145 crimes that he was arrested in the act of breaking into a terrace-type house by using a hatchet, and it was the noise he made which attracted the notice of the tenant, who was returning home after visiting the house of a neighbour when he heard the sound of breaking glass.

The householder closed with the offender and though coming into contact with the hatchet he pluckily held on to his assailant, until the police arrived.

On being taken into custody, the offender gave his age as nineteen, but though he was over six foot in height he was only sixteen.

When at the Quarter Sessions he pleaded guilty to all the crimes he had committed, the Recorder said of him: "He had the age of a boy, the stature, mind and intelligence of a man, and the uninhibited cruelty of a brute".

The offences committed against the women were of a particularly revolting and brutal nature. The first happened at about nine o'clock in the evening when the victim, a young married woman, was sitting by the fire with her five year old daughter asleep in a chair by her side. The woman heard a noise and on looking round saw the offender standing inside the door. She was terrified when he rushed at her. He struck her on the head with a cosh, threw her to the floor and threatened to kill her if she made any noise. Her assailant was big and powerful and she became terribly frightened for her child. He dragged the terrified young woman into the hallway and ordered her to strip. And he tore off her clothing until she was naked.

Later, when in custody, he informed the police that he intended to have sexual intercourse with his victim, but changed his mind and indecently assaulted her.

As soon an opportunity presented itself the woman snatched a coat to cover herself and rushed to the house

of a neighbour where she was overcome by the terrible
nature of the assault upon her.

The nervous depression which followed was so serious
that she found it impossible to remain in the house
in which she had suffered so dreadfully, and it was
sold.   Her doctor stated that her recovery might take
twelve months.   Many people will wonder whether she
will ever forget her ordeal.

*   *   *

In the second case, a woman had fallen asleep in a
chair while watching a television programme.   The
offender entered by an unlocked door and went into the
living room where he stole two rings and some money
from a sideboard.   He told the police that he was on
his way out of the house when he noticed the sleeping
woman, got a billet of wood from the kitchen, went
back to the woman and struck her with the piece of wood
at least three times.   Her scalp was lacerated, and
one of her fingers was fractured, necessitating treatment
at hospital as an out-patient for three months.

This particular crime was committed quite near to the
offender's home, but the woman, having been attacked
from behind did not see her assailant.

The total value of the property and money in all the
cases was £2,592, of which less than half was recovered.
In the culprit's bedroom the police found £740 in notes
out of a total of money reported stolen.   And the
people from whom the paper-money had been taken received
back fourteen shillings and tenpence in the pound.

Why should a youth, who had led the normal life of a
school-boy up to the age of sixteen, turn into a cunning
burglar and a brutal attacker of women?   When I asked
him why he had begun to steal, he replied: "I wanted to
set up in business!"

His Counsel told the Recorder: "I cannot put this boy
as being other than completely normal in mental condition
and behaviour.   He began by seeking excitement and
adventure - that is his explanation.   His first crime
was getting into a house and stealing fifty cigarettes,
which, as he himself did not smoke, he gave away to
friends.   The pity is that he was not caught then.
Here one can see the depths to which an unchecked
criminal can descend after such a short period of nine
months.   It began as high spirits, tempered with a
touch of lawlessness, and became something infinitely
depraved and wicked".

The accused youth was sentenced to six years' imprisonment, the Recorder saying to him: "With your criminal instincts and lusts, I do not consider you are a case for Borstal. In paying lip-service to Borstal training you would be out in eighteen months and there is no likelihood in that time of removing the deep-seated instincts you have".

It should be noted that in sentencing a juvenile offender - he was under seventeen years of age - the Trial Judge must state a reason for doing so.

By good behaviour in prison this young criminal reduced his sentence by two years. A period of four years under discipline should have had a reformative effect upon him; that was the Recorder's hope.

It is difficult to believe that his parents had no knowledge of his criminal exploits, but they were very respectable people, and it is certain that they were devoted to him; but beyond knowing of his boyish pranks and fights with other boys when he was younger, there never was, so far as they knew, any suggestion of violence in his make-up.

Although they visited their son on several occasions between his arrest and trial - when he expressed his desire to get everything settled so that he could take his punishment and start a new life - it was in court that they heard more than he had told them, and, to their surprise, that Psychiatrists had found him to be aggressive and anti-social.

Let it be noted that most of the breaking-in offences could have been prevented if a light had been left on.

PART II

XV

In Retrospect, Questions, Answers, Since Retirement

I retired from the Chief Constableship of the City of Stoke-on-Trent Constabulary, on May 31st, 1955, after having completed more than forty two years approved police service in seven separate police forces in England, plus ten months as a constable in the Great Eastern Railway in London and Cambridge respectively.

In case it might be thought that by having remained in the police service for so long a period I had delayed the promotion of younger men, it should be explained that by virtue of the fact that my first appointment to a chief constableship took place in 1930, Legislation compelled me to serve until I reached the age of 65.

It also seems necessary for me to explain how it came about that I served in seven police forces.

In those days, various Police Authorities - in whose districts the police were required to perform extraneous duties such as those of an Inspector of Weights and Measures, and those pertaining to the maintenance of a Fire Brigade - often found it necessary to advertise for officers possessing the necessary and certificated qualifications to apply for vacancies occurring in those departments. And it was in consequence of these facts that I made a study of the subjects which covered these extraneous duties and became qualified to perform them. But neither qualification exempted me from any form of police work.

In thinking over my past, I have realised what a good thing for me it was that I came under discipline at such an early age; on the training ship when sixteen, and later from seventeen onwards as a soldier at home and abroad.

My life in the Army provided me with invaluable knowledge of the ways and manners of men of many different types which has stood me in good stead throughout my career as a police officer from P.C. to Chief Constable.

191

Lessons learned from my own numerous mistakes, disappointments and misjudgments, as well as those of my contemporaries, have pointed out to me, for urgent consideration, the fact that in order to make headway in one's career, one must turn such errors to good account, and use them as stepping-stones to better things, by taking the action necessary to bring about such a desirable state of affairs.

Experience gained in my travels as a soldier in India and Arabia, made me realise how fortunate I had been by having been born British. And it taught me to distinguish the important difference between the necessity for strict obedience to lawful orders and servility by which one is liable to be regarded as a 'Yes' man or as one displaying readiness to 'take the line of least resistance' to avoid any particular responsibility or issue, rather than take any form of risk; a kind of cowardice not good for one's prestige or reputation in the eyes of decent folk.

My life in the police service - when taken on the whole - has been a happy one, I must admit to having found the road to success somewhat rocky at times, causing me to wonder whether I had missed my way. But I was fortunate enough to realise that certain obstacles are placed in one's way as 'Tests' to be taken philosophically and as incentives to greater effort, and by accepting the challenge, I was able to surmount them.

*   *   *

On numerous occasions during my retirement from the police service I have been asked to make comparison between the work and conditions, etc., etc., within the police service in my day and those obtaining since.

Comparisons are believed to be odius, hateful and offensive; but those I make are certainly not made in hate or offensiveness. For to me the police service 'called' me to it, and I was proud of my membership, just as I was in the Army in the U.K. and abroad in peace and war.

But there have been many changes, some of which were said to be necessary for the sake of economy and increased efficiency, though neither of these objects has been achieved.

In my days as a recruit constable, police officers on duty in towns and cities were compelled to walk, there was no alternative. But as a county policeman, I was allowed to buy a bicycle and ride it during daytime - not

night time, though I and others did so in the hope of
doing so without the sergeant's knowledge - when travelling
from one village to another.

I think my sergeant had a rough idea that I had
developed the habit of riding my bike at night, for at
least on one occasion he had a desire to accompany me
for three miles on my journey towards home from a
conference point eight miles from my cottage, but, to
his credit, he didn't ask me where I had hidden my bike.
Perhaps he had had the common sense to use his bike when
he was a constable on his beat at night.

Motor vehicles had been in use long before the police
possessed any. Local Police Authorities throughout the
country did not see the need for the police to use motor
cars in their work in preventing and detecting crime.

But no blame could be placed upon the police authorities
for not appreciating that motor cars were a necessity.
For at that time there was not a great deal of very
serious crime, nor had the criminal fraternity made use
of motor vehicles in their felonious activities. Besides,
criminals were slower then and not so well 'educated'
and were usually caught by policemen on foot.

In 1918 there was a Police Strike. It broke out in
London and attempts were made to spread it, but the action
was so unexpected that it collapsed. Nobody had given
thought to the possibility of such a step to be taken by
any member of the police service, any more than the
public of those days would have imagined possible a strike
on behalf of the fighting services. The UNEXPECTED had
happened!

The pay of the police at that time was disgracefully
low, and when one thinks of it one realises that it was
only loyalty to the public that prevented the unexpected
happening years before.

It was because of this strike action that The Police
Federation came into being in 1919. As a sergeant in
the King's Lynn Borough Police Force I became one of the
original members of the Federation.

In those days the Police Federation looked after the
welfare of constables, sergeants and inspectors only.
And it is still supposed to represent those ranks. But
in reality, it is proving beneficial to all ranks,
superintendents; chief constables; and even those who
leave the police service to become Home Office Inspectors
of Constabulary, for whenever a rise in pay is granted
to the ranks represented by the Police Federation, Pro rata
increases in salary are awarded to those who are not
members of the Federation. So now, it's a case of

'All one body we'.

In the early days of the Police Federation certain chief constables and Police Authorities took umbrage at the power vested in members of the Federation. But things are better now.

Are the police of today better educated than they were in years gone by? Of course they are! But it does not follow that a person of good education is necessarily energetic and devoted to his duties.

There are 'artful dodgers' in the police service, just as there are in other services and other walks of life.

The most difficult comparison that I have been asked to make relates to efficiency. So I think that I must be particularly prudent and take an example from a former member of the Brains Trust by saying: 'It all depends on what is meant', by the question: 'Is the police service of today as efficient as it used to be?'

But feeling that it is up to me to stick my neck out, I do, so here goes! The police service today - so far as England and Wales is concerned - ought to be and should be, but isn't!

The police service today is better equipped and much stronger in number than ever it was. The public is being told that lack of success against criminals and prevention of crime is due to the shortage of manpower. This statement is just an excuse made with intent to mislead the public.

The success of any police service depends largely on the manner in which it is deployed. The rank and file of the police service are as efficient as in former times, but they are not seen in public as they used to be. The trying of shop doors and offices etc., by constables on night duty was as familiar as the postman's knock used to be, but the importance of beat duty in the prevention and detection of crime seems to be regarded as almost unnecessary owing to there being so many motor cars available and able to get to the scene of the crime on receipt of a report. But criminals work faster today and do not hang about to be caught. A man on the beat might have done something to prevent the crime. Less motor cars and more men on the beat would result in greater efficiency.

Britain's police service must not be a 'talkative' service.

Since April, 1967, when the merging of city and borough forces into county forces commenced, types of crime formerly more or less confined to the Metropolis have spread to the provinces, and a significant fact to be

considered as urgent is the realisation that the manner in
which beats have been worked and covered in London cannot
be regarded as satisfactory in the provinces.   So the
quicker this fact is realised, the better it will be so far
as relations between the police and public are concerned.

Many complaints have been made by people, traders,
etc., all over the country, arising from the apparent
absence of constables from the beat.   Complainants are
not convinced that police officers are standing by and
ready to pounce on offenders within a short time of a
crime having been committed.   They need to see that
the police are actually close at hand on the streets and
available.

Although I have been on the Retired List since 1955,
people who know me or remember having seen policemen in
the district in which they live and work, have, during
the last year or so, asked me to explain the reason why
constables, sergeants and even inspectors, are not seen
on the streets today as they used to be.

The explanation should be a simple one to give, but I
find it extremely difficult!   There is, in fact, no
legitimate reason for the absence of police officers from
the streets, for any length of time.   And one cannot
give satisfaction to people by suggesting a shortage of
manpower, for in most districts there are many more
policemen than there used to be; and people know it.

In my opinion and that of numerous ex-police officers,
too much reliance is placed on the motor car.   In these
days the majority of menfolk own such a vehicle and every
owner knows how annoying it can be when an engine refuses
to start.

Criminals don't let us know when they are coming.
TIME, to them, is of the greatest importance, and they
waste none.

Professional criminals - I leave out the petty thief -
are usually men of resourse who take advantage of any
weakness on the part of those whose endeavours should be
aimed to defeat them.   And they have been given a
distinct advantage over the police for many years.

All members of the police service, except, perhaps,
those employed on administrative duties, must be organised
as they were years ago, when every man was expected to
prevent crime as far as he was able.   Nowadays, police
officers of the Uniform Branch are not encouraged to
regard themselves as being necessarily in the fight against
crime.   Crime, they are told, is a matter for the C.I.D.
to deal with and investigate.   And it is only when men of
the Uniform Branch see a person or persons actually in the

act of committing a crime that they should take action.
    This fact is 'unbelievable'.   But then we all know
that many 'unbelievable' things happen today.
    For many years, uniformed police officers serving in
the Metropolitan Police who have arrested a criminal
'red handed' have been allowed to give 'evidence of
arrest' only, the C.I.D. having taken over the case from
the time that the culprit arrived at the police station.
This procedure would be normal of course if the person
arrested was a man 'wanted for questioning' for alleged
murder, and no uniformed officer would have grounds for
a complaint nor would any such officer imagine that he
had been treated unfairly.   But when he is prevented
from taking any further action in the case - such as
being allowed to accompany a detective in taking
statements of evidence from persons affected by the
crime - he is apt to feel resentment and to regard
himself as a Retriever, useful for bringing 'em in'
and nothing else.
    This is NOT a way to treat an energetic and
conscientious police officer.   Nor can it be conducive
to training, contentment or co-operation in the fight
against crime and criminals.
    Having served as a constable, sergeant and inspector
in the Uniform Branch, I think myself entitled to
express an opinion on its necessity and usefulness,
when properly deployed to carry out its service to
the public.
    To give confidence to the community I suggest that
more officers must be seen on the streets; that they
be properly supervised by those officers who were
promoted for that purpose, sergeants and inspectors,
and, occasionally, by a superintendent.
    In times of trouble with violent demonstrators in
which law-abiding citizens are annoyed and alarmed, I
think it would be nice to see a chief constable - not
necessarily in uniform - taking charge of the officers
under his command.   Every member of the police service,
whatever the rank he holds, is a CONSTABLE.   But today
it is beginning to appear that some officers, when
they become entitled to wear chevrons, stars, crowns, or
a combination of a crown and star, etc., forget this
very important fact and 'rest on their oars' as it were.
This is the kind of forgetfulness that causes comment.
    The Beat system as formerly adopted in counties,
cities and boroughs worked by officers on foot according
to changeable schedules is as necessary today as in
years gone by.   It kept men healthy, alert and energetic.

Cynics are entitled to call one's attention to the fact that there were many obese policemen to be seen in my day as a constable, but I venture to suggest that 'energy' was not the cause of their fatness or build.

XVI

Changes in the Police Service

Since my return to civil life, there have been changes
in Britain's Police Organisation. And, as one interested
in and anxious that it should not be devalued as a Public
Service on which so much depends, I feel that re-organisation now in the offing, would not be conducive to
greater efficiency or its reputation, notwithstanding
the fact that the status of certain officers has been
raised and the remuneration of the rank and file has
improved, all is not well with the Police Service! For
while some members of it have and will benefit, many
others have lost their status by being compelled to
accept lower rank and become subordinates of men with
less experience in the many phases of police work than
they have had. This state of affairs, already existing,
is frictional, most unfair, and detrimental to contentment
and discipline. And it has brought about the resignation
of many dedicated officers of great experience and
ability, who 'saw the Red light' of deterioration on the
horizon and considered it better to retire than remain
in a service in which influence was taking the place of
Qualifications.
City and Borough Police Forces are losing their
identity and traditions by being handed over to County
Police Forces. And with the handing over of such
compact and efficient Police Forces will go the important
knowledge of the characteristics of local people; the
knowledge of local members of the criminal fraternity,
their habits and associates.
I would suggest that Police Authorities of City and
Borough Police Forces who meet monthly as a Watch Committee
are to be preferred in Local Government to a Standing
Joint Committee who meet four times a year.
The regionalisation of Police Forces is a long step
towards the formation of a National Police Force. And

it is quite clear or soon would be, that such a police
force would not be conducive to freedom of the British
community.   For all of us have noticed the gradual
loss of liberties.   Dictatorship, whether we like it
or not, is already very evident.

Expressing my own opinion, I am satisfied that a
national police force in Britain would be more favourable
to the criminal fraternity than to law abiding people.
Why?   Because esprit-de-corps would disappear entirely,
and chief constables will be Figureheads.   These figureheads, some of whom are known to me, will be those who
obtained their police appointments by absorption from a
specially prepared 'short cut' under the auspices of a
'society' having no registered title, but which, for my
convenience, I will call 'The Inner Circle'.

The object of this circle, which hides its existence
and methods in a manner practised by professional
conjurers to prevent their tricks becoming known to all
and sundry, is to procure high rank for those within the
circle, in the shortest possible time without opposition
of any kind.   In other words, to enable them 'to gather
the plums of the police service without having to climb
the tree'.   For the Inner Circle regards the performance
of actual police work such as involves necessity to
work the beat, make inquiries, attend court to give
evidence and the likelihood of being cross-examined, as
<u>infra dig</u>, and unbecoming.

Owing to the fact that members of the Inner Circle -
having a minimal experience of actual police work - obtain
chief constableships in counties, it is obvious that, by
force of circumstances, they must require much help;
which they obtain from experienced subordinates and by
brain picking.   In actual fact, chief constables of
most counties have been very fortunate in receiving
invaluable assistance from the chief constable of the
city or borough force which they - the county chiefs -
took over.

There can be no doubt that the police service of
Britain today requires leaders; leaders who are so
qualified in practical police work in all its phases
as. to be able to 'lead by example'.   But how can a man
become a 'leader by example' if he has never experienced
the rough and tumble of life?

Real leaders of men must be of courage, men of
initiative, and men who show that they can and do carry
responsibility, by refraining from 'passing the buck',
a practice more rife than it used to be.

Recently, a well known national newspaper displayed

the headline: "Brains on the Beat", and the public were told that a small number of university graduates had applied to join the Metropolitan Police and the Birmingham City Police, and had been accepted, as constables.

Having attended a university, these candidates will naturally and rightly have a fair start over men who have not had the good fortune to attend a university, but the graduates should, in the interests of fair play and efficiency, be required to perform the work of a constable by attending the same classes of instruction respecting police law and practice and what is required of them as police officers. It should not be taken for granted that a university graduate is bound to make a good and efficient, conscientious, constable.

Even if a new entrant to the police service has been a law student and obtained his degree in law, it must be appreciated that his studies did not touch upon the duties and powers of the police. Such being the case in fact, he should, I think, be required to pass the same examinations on the duties of the police and their powers, etc., just like all constables who are expected to qualify 'for consideration' when vacancies in a higher rank occur. Promotion on merit is fair; it brings respect too.

Ability to pass examinations does not necessarily prove fitness or suitability.

The words: "Brains on the Beat" were facetious, but could have been regarded as having a different meaning; for today, a certain class of comedian still tries to amuse his audience by making it appear that the constable on the beat is capable of taking the risk of contracting 'lead poisoning' by licking his pencil. I know the individual responsible for the newspaper heading previously referred to. And he knows me. He is a member of the Inner Circle, has a degree, but never worked the beat in the whole of his police career. Perhaps his possession of 'brains' kept him off.

Of course, a good education is an essential asset to a member of the police service who is dedicated to it and expects promotion.

But all people must know that almost the whole of the real and practical work of the police is done on the highways and by-ways in close contact with the public, rather than from behind the Blue Lamp.

There can be little doubt that the chief part of a police officer's education - when he is performing duties in close touch of the public, businessmen, motorists and

pedestrians alike, - is knowledge of the manner in which
they should be treated with a view to gaining their
co-operation in varying circumstances.

At school I learned that 'friction causes heat', and
as a policeman I have discovered its futility.

Loss of temper has been the cause of much bother; but
a policeman - to satisfy everybody - shouldn't have a
temper to lose.   I have known 'temper' to make all the
difference between a Caution and an invitation to Court.
Politeness pays.

When a person is 'sworn in' as a constable, he
undertakes to do his duty 'without fear or favour,
affection or ill will'.   But it is later that he finds
it necessary to know that all members of the community
have a right to his protection.

> "True liberty can only exist when justice
> is equally administered to all - to the
> King and to the beggar".
>
> Chief Justice Mansfield.

The primary duties of the police are: The prevention
and detection of crime; the protection of life and
property as far as it is possible, and the keeping of
the public peace.

The efficiency of any police force, whatever its
numerical strength and/or area it covers, depends to
a large extent upon the manner in which it is deployed
to carry out its functions; and its reputation as a
Public Service is calculated, not on the number of serious
crimes committed within its jurisdiction, but on the
number of crimes detected in which the criminals concerned
are brought to justice.

*   *   *

The Royal Commission on the Police Service convened in
1961, suggested, inter alia, that England and Wales should
be divided into a number of Police Regions.   There was
one dissentient however, and he favoured the formation of
a national police force.

Certain of the Commissions' recommendations have been
implemented, and it seems significant that the dissentient's
view is being preferred to those agreed upon by the
Commission.   For at least two well-known persons - one of
whom is an ex-Military officer - have written and spoken
in favour of a national police force as a 'necessity', and

a newspaper has reported that the ex-Military gentleman
has given the impression that a national police service
would be an established fact within five years from
1967.

It seems rather significant too, to discover that the
dissentient to the Commission's recommendations, the
ex-Military officer who predicted the coming of the
national police force within five years, and a 'witness'
who gave evidence before the Commission are closely
connected - one way or another - with Cambridge University.

Members of the 'Inner Circle' are known as 'Wanglers'.
Wangling is practised everywhere in the world and by all
classes of people. To some people it is regarded as a
natural thing to be just one of those things to be
endured. But it can amount to a dirty trick at times,
especially when it is adopted to defeat a man or men
possessed of proved and certificated qualifications
higher than those, if any, possessed by the wangler.

In ordinary and usual circumstances, an applicant for
an important post submits testimonials, and hopes for
the best. But when a vacancy in the 'Inner Circle' is
caused by retirement or death of a member no candidate
from the 'Inner Circle' is required to submit testimonials.
Firstly because the vacancy has not been advertised to
attract competition from members of the police service,
and secondly, because there is no need; for he, having
been ear-marked, is automatically absorbed, and his
appointment is announced in a manner intended to make
it appear outside the Circle as a promotion earned by
meritorious police service; whereas, in fact, it is
nothing of the sort.

I am prepared to substantiate this statement before
any Tribunal or Court of Inquiry, in which I would seek
the Right to ask questions of a small number of persons
whom I would name in good time and, if necessary, subpoena.
For it is within my knowledge that they have a controlling
interest so far as appointments to Chief Constableships
and higher ranks within the police service are concerned.

This 'controlling interest' is spreading, so much so,
that there is evidence to show that promotion to the
higher subordinate ranks - those of Superintendent and
Chief Superintendent - are becoming much more difficult
to attain than formerly. Such state of affairs is
causing much discontentment among the lower ranks of the
police service, constables, sergeants and inspectors -
the backbone of the service - who are bound to feel
resentment, when they see their chances of promotion
slipping away, because of the absorption of officers from

police forces outside their own force.

It is right and proper of course that a Chief Officer of police upon whom rests the responsibility in making promotions should have discretion in the matter, for he should know those officers who are deserving of promotion in his own force; but on occasions difficulties arise, and there is need for the introduction of 'new blood'. Such an excuse, however, is not always a good or reasonable one. The source from whence 'new blood' comes has been known to create suspicion and ill feeling.

Over the years, chances of promotion to the very high ranks in the Police Service for men who genuinely joined as Constables and dedicated themselves to it, have been becoming less and less, and, so far as high subordinate ranks were concerned in provincial Police Forces, the first block to promotion came in April, 1947, when many small Borough Police Forces were abolished by being merged with the Police Force of the County in which they were situate. The necessity for these merges was said to have been in the interests of Economy - the usual bait used to catch public support - and increased efficiency. Economy did not result; as any Borough Treasurer soon realised. But the officers who had served in the Boroughs were able to teach their new County colleagues that there were occurrences in the towns that were unknown in the villages. It was in this way, that County policemen became more efficient.

I am not alone in the realisation that the abolition of those was a retrogressive step; for those forces were compact and efficient; their personnel knew the characteristics of the inhabitants; and had a knowledge of local criminals, their methods and associates. All the small forces were stepping stones to promotion; for in most City and Borough forces had certain extraneous duties to perform, and this fact made it necessary that the police officers' performing those particular duties had to possess certificated qualifications. And as these extra duties brought extra pay, they were incentives, to men who wished to qualify. These incentives were fair and reasonable because they were voluntary, but they did not exempt a qualifier from the performance of police duties.

By qualifying for and doing such extraneous duties, I was able to obtain three important posts in three separate police forces in six years; but as expected, there was extra responsibility. Incentives in the police service in the 'Seventies' are not of a nature requiring extra work or responsibleness.

Frequently, almost nightly, television asks us not to invite Crime. This is an urgent and necessary request which all of us should keep in mind and comply with. Yet, when we read our newspapers, we find that invaluable information is being given to criminals, by advertising and giving details of the steps that are being taken by the police in order to keep a curb on criminals.

We read of what certain chief constables are planning to do to catch the crook. The officers are named and their plans described in detail. He is called a Crime Buster or is given a title indicating to local members of the criminal fraternity that they are in for a rough time at his hands, and he is good and helpful enough to tell them that he is organising a special squad of picked men in a fleet of cars always ready to dash out as soon as a crime is reported as having been committed.

Criminals who organise serious crimes such as robbery with violence, hi-jacking, hold-ups, raids on banks, etc., are grateful for any 'tip' indicating that it is only After a crime is committed that the bogies will be after them. And, knowing that time is very important, they act in a manner and at a time and place from which a getaway can be made before the Crime Buster can get his Busters into action.

Today, people who organise crimes for their under-strappers to commit must be given credit for the possession of active brains. They know all about the possibility of Road Blocks set up to capture runaway criminals, so this possibility is taken into consideration when their plans are being made.

Talkativeness by police officers of any rank is a pernicious habit. I have learned that a talkative person falls into many mistakes and misunderstandings, which a little judicial silence would obviate. And it has been noticed that the gift of the gab is often used to disguise a lack of knowledge of a subject under discussion.

In my day - not so very long ago - the police service was regarded as a silent service, and this was all to the good. But changes have come about, and the Press is given items of 'news' which, in days gone by, were considered 'strictly Secret and Private', and if any member of the force communicated them to any person outside the police service he was guilty - and would still be - of a disciplinary offence against Police Regulations;

the offence being known as Breach of Confidence.

To my knowledge the police did much better against crime and criminals when it was a silent service.

Surely, before one has earned the title of 'Crime Buster' one must prove that he has done some crime busting!

Since 1967, the public have been told that a special kind of police vehicle has been brought into general use in the fight against crime and criminals.

It has been given the name of Panda, and is said to be the invention of a Pedant.   And numerous claims have been made respecting its potentials.   To give an example of its usefulness, a national newspaper of repute described one of its powers as the 'rounding up' of sheep.

It is hinted, too, that it carried wonderful innovations in the form of equipment so marvellous that the detection of crime and criminals has become an extremely simple matter, so simple in fact, as it is to catch and bring criminals to justice by Script as depicted on the television screen.

Useful as motor vehicles are, both to the police and criminals, the most unfortunate failing of the Panda, is the fact that it is incapable of 'jumping a wall'.

Like the animal bearing its name, the police's Panda has not proved to be productive.

*   *   *

Boastfulness cannot be regarded as a worthy trait in any police force or branch of one.   In fact, it ought, I think, be considered reprehensible.   But in recent years bragging seems to have become necessary in order to make amends for failure.

An ex-provincial policeman I am able to say - with pleasure - that there is no 'shouting from the housetops' so far as the rank and file of provincial police forces are concerned.

What seems rather significant to me, however, is the fact that a number of London newspaper reporters have been responsible for bragging about the power that certain London detectives held over London members of the criminal fraternity.

Over the years, crime reports have called public attention to the commendable activities of various Scotland Yard detectives of high rank, with whom they have the privilege of calling by their christian names.

We read that Detective-Superintendent Tom, Dick or

Harry Blank has been so successful in bringing dangerous
and daring criminals to justice, that many crooks of
the Underworld have given him a special nickname, and
have become so panic stricken, that they have been
forced to 'seek pastures new' in order to maintain
freedom.

Such reports suggesting the fear felt by criminals,
is pure bunkum.   And so far as nicknames are concerned,
these are given to detectives by their colleagues and/or
reporters.   And the words used by criminals to describe
their opinion of detectives whose evidence has convicted
them, are unprintable and often accusative.

Over the years, many misunderstandings have arisen
as to the status of Scotland Yard in relation to the
whole of the police service of Britain.

For instance, many people - including Members of
Parliament apparently - imagine that Scotland Yard is
the headquarters of all the police forces of Britain;
that all chief constables throughout the country are
under the control of the Commissioner of Police of the
Metropolis and work under his directions; that the only
Criminal Investigation Department in Britain works from
there, and that Scotland Yard Detectives enjoy greater
facilities enabling them to perform much more efficient
detective work than those available to detectives in
the provinces.

Such beliefs are of course, erroneous, and could
sometimes be unfair to Scotland Yard detectives by
causing members of the public to expect too much success
from them in the detection of criminals.

Apparently, such beliefs have arisen from the constant
publicity given by newspapers to inform the community of
what the Yard is doing in probing this and probing that,
and the steps it is taking in shadowing persons 'wanted
for questioning', with regard to certain matters.

And it is possible, of course, that such ideas have
come about by the twice-weekly television programmes
showing the various ways used by criminals in their
nefarious escapades, and how 'detectives' set to work
to bring them to justice.

But whatever the means by which these impressions have
been created, it is imperative that they be dispelled,
because of their falsity and unfairness.

The facts are: Scotland Yard is the headquarters of
the Metropolitan Police only, and deals with all manner
of police work within the Metropolitan Police District
only; no chief constable of any other police force works

under its direction; every police force has its own C.I.D.;
and no detective working from the Yard has greater
facilities than any detective in any provincial police
force to help him in the investigation of crime.

There are, in fact, Forensic Laboratories in various
parts of the country in which the services of scientists,
chemists, etc., with the same qualifications are available
to provincial police forces to give the same aid as is
given to Scotland Yard. And it is for this reason that
it is unfair to Scotland Yard Detectives - who are of
the same 'material' as detectives in provincial police
forces - to expect them to work wonders in bringing
criminals to justice.

And it was because of my appreciation of the fact
that the detectives of Scotland Yard had more than enough
to do in investigating crime in London, that during the
whole of my twenty-five years as a chief constable of
three separate police forces, though there were several
killings, I did not ask for assistance from the Yard.
My own detectives were trustworthy and successful. So
I was not compelled to 'pass the buck'.

Calls for the assistance of Scotland Yard Detectives
are not numerous though each such request is well
publicised.

Why it should be considered necessary to inform the
public of police action being taken from the moment a
crime is reported, I have never been able to understand;
perhaps I'm a bit dull. But in my periods of wakefulness
I have found it necessary to put a seal on my lips as
well as those of my staff of detectives most of whom
found cause to be grateful.

What does a murderer do within a reasonable time after
committing his crime? He buys a newspaper to find out
how his crime is described and whether he has left a
clue behind him.

If he is a local man and is known to have been an
acquaintance of his victim, he will not help the police
by running away. And if he is a stranger to the district
and the newspaper has given a <u>true</u> description of him,
he would be grateful for the 'tip' and would take full
advantage of it.

A somewhat recent change which has certainly not
assisted detectives in their inquiries into serious
crimes, came in 1964, by the latest Judges' Rules made
in January of that year, which lay down conditions under
which the police should act in the interrogation of
suspects.

These Rules, though said to be not Rules of Law, are believed by many people - including a number of eminent jurists - to be obstructive and unhelpful to the police in their difficult task of bringing criminals to justice.

Perhaps it would not be imprudent if I described a hypothetical case as an example of a difficulty met with by the police when interrogating a suspect.

WANTED FOR QUESTIONING

Every minute of every day - and every night for that matter - in any police district, at least one person is 'wanted for questioning' in an endeavour to solve a crime of one sort or another.

In the vast majority of cases of a criminal nature reported to them, the police find themselves on the horns of a dilemma: whom are they to look for? The scene of the crime has been visited and the routine search for clues has been carried out, but without success. The detectives are at a loss. How they wish that someone would come and tell them where to look or for whom to look.

Occasionally, however, especially in Murder cases, it appears to them that a known person or one of whom a good description has been given, could be interviewed with a possible chance of success in their investigations.

In any event, nothing would be lost by arranging to have him interrogated.

It is in such cases that the Press, the public, and in fact, the murderer too, are asked to help the police in their inquiries. And judging from the details given and published, it would appear that the person 'wanted for questioning' is suspect Number 1.

Over the years, however, detectives of experience have found how dangerous and bewildering over-optimism can be; for time after time the principal suspect has had to be eliminated because he was able to satisfy them that he could not have had any connection with the crime they were investigating, so the hope of an early solution is shattered completely - necessitating a search for other lines of inquiry, which, if found and followed, have often ended in a cul-de-sac of disheartening frustration.

Who is next on the list for questioning?

And what of the questioning?

As inquiry after inquiry fails to bring the investigation any nearer to success, and all chances of making a detection seem to have been lost beyond recall; a little bit of luck in one form or another - which every detective must have to bring him success in most of his inquiries and investigations - appears on the horizon and all seems to be well! But is it?

In most cases, there is much more to be done. It is not sufficient to 'know' the identity of an alleged offender, for though such is enough to provide a very good reason for interviewing him, it is inadequate for his arrest; there must be Evidence - satisfactory legal evidence - to substantiate the charge. Suspicion alone, no matter how strong, is never accepted as evidence of guilt.

The detective officer placed in charge of the investigation in a case of murder or other serious crime, must be particularly skilful as an interrogator; but it does not follow that he should always be one holding the rank of Detective-Superintendent. He requires to give much thought to the nature of the questions he put or causes to be put to suspects, for his task in this respect may be one of some difficulty. There are Rules - The Judges' Rules - with which he is expected to comply if the answers to these questions are to be admissible as evidence. Although the Judges' Rules are made for the guidance of the police when questioning suspects and obtaining statements from them, the same rules - if known to criminals - serve as a reminder of the proverb: 'Silence is golden'.

It is axiomatic that men differ in many ways: be they detectives or persons of any trade or calling, or profession. And when two of similar type and temperament are confronting each other - one an investigator, the other a suspect to be interrogated, that is, if he submits to interrogation, - progress, if any, may not be appreciable.

These two individuals are on the alert, and each of them appreciates the necessity for diplomacy, tact and discretion. The detective of experience will endeavour, perhaps by means of putting two or three preliminary questions, to ascertain the nature of his task; but he will not be impatient. He has come across many awkward customers before this, and knows the importance of stepping warily until he feels it safe to start his Quiz in earnest.

If the suspect is a person of intelligence, he holds a distinct advantage over the detective; for it is probable that he has learned, from various sources, that while the police are entitled to ask him questions, he,

as the law stands at the moment, is not obliged to
answer them.   Although at first sight, this state of
affairs appears unfair to the Police, it is imperative
that suspects who may be innocent of the offence under
investigation should be treated with scrupulous fairness,
in order that 'justice is seen to be done'.
    It should be appreciated, too, that the road to
Crime Detection is seldom clearly defined.   More often
than not there is nothing to point the way.   What is
perfectly clear, however, is that the bringing of
criminals to justice never is as simple a task as is
suggested in thrillers or as depicted on cinematograph
and television screens.   While it is true that professional
detectives often attain success by way of 'information
received', never do they have the good fortune to work
by Script informing them of the identity of the 'crooks'
and where they can pick them up.
    Actor-detectives display skill in following instructions
given by script writers and producers, though they seem
to possess greater powers than real detectives; but it is
very noticeable that they are spared the necessity to
give evidence or to undergo cross-examination in the
witness-box.   That these concession are necessary in
such circumstances, no real police officer would doubt;
for the Rules of Evidence cannot be learned in a hurry;
and in any case, all that requires to be done is to show
how quickly criminals can be brought to book - no evidence
required.   It's as simple as that, so far as the
intention of the film is concerned.
    In reality, however, professional detectives, no matter
how well trained or the name of the Police Force to which
they belong, find by experience, that in order to meet
with success in their work, they must have the co-operation
of the public; for not being super-men endowed with special
powers enabling them to do things which no other person is
capable of doing.
    Today, most unfortunately, Crime is so much on the
increase and of such a serious nature, that law-abiding
citizens are not keen to help the Police.   This attitude
of the public is becoming more and more understandable as
time passes.   Most people are scared of having to attend
Court to give testimony and take the risk of cross-examination; other people fear reprisals against themselves
or against members of their family.   But it should be
understood by all people that the giving of information
does not necessarily carry such fears; the Police know
how to keep secrets.
    Imagine that a girl has been found murdered.   The

Press has intimated that the Police desire help from
the public in tracing a man of whom a detailed
description is given.   It is stated that he is wanted
for interview because it is thought that he could help
the Police with their inquiries.

Imagine, too, that a Constable on his beat has seen
the 'wanted' man and has taken him to the Police
Station to be interviewed by the Detective in charge
of the case.

On arrival there the man is taken to a small room,
where, in a kindly manner, he is asked to take a seat
and offered a cigarette.   Being a non-smoker, however,
he declines the offer, but thanks the officer.   After
some delay, he is asked 'to come this way' and is
conducted by the Constable along a passage to another
room where someone says: "This is Detective Superintendent
Johns of Stockton Brook".

Mr. Johns puts on a smile, and bids his visitor to
make himself at home.   Then, by way of making a start
and 'weighing-up' the suspect, the Detective-Superintendent
says: "I have asked that you be brought before me so that
you can answer a number of questions I desire to put to
you - just routine - you understand?"   The suspect was
all attention.   "Yes", he said, "I understand, I presume
you mean 'just routine on your part' is it so?"
Detective Superintendent Johns doesn't answer; but he
realises that tact is called for.

Sitting at the table, within a yard or so from the
Superintendent, is Detective-Sergeant George Gumption
with an open pocket-book before him.   He is here to
take notes of what is about to take place.

Judging from the nature of the preliminary questions
put by Mr. Johns, it appears that he suspects the man;
but beyond admitting that he was acquainted with the
dead girl, the man being interviewed is reticent.

Mr. Johns is a patient man, but he is beginning to
show signs of annoyance.   "I wonder if you know that to
withhold information from the Police is an offence?" he
says quietly.

Turning his head in the direction of Sergeant Gumption,
the man addressed, asked: "Has he written down what you
have just said about withholding information?"   Mr. Johns
did not answer.   "All right", said the man, "I'll make
a note of it myself, and of anything else you say to me!"
And, taking a diary from an inner pocket he began to
make an entry.   Mr. Johns now realised that in the man
he was interviewing he had caught a 'Tartar'.

Placing his diary on the table before him and looking

at the Superintendent, the man asked: "I wonder if you would be kind enough to allow me to ask <u>you</u> a question". This was an unusual request, but Mr. Johns saw no harm in granting it. "You may", he said.

Fingering his diary once more, the man wrote a few words and said: "I'm very interested in what you've told me about withholding information, am I right that the offence is known as 'misprision of felony, and means concealing a felony'?"

A long time had passed since the Detective-Superintendent had been asked to define such a misdemeanour, but he said: "May be". Making a note in his diary, the man stood up, and asked: "Have you finished with me now?" Mr. Johns also came to his feet. "Yes, for the moment", he answered, "but I would like you to make a statement". The man smiled. "What is your object, sir", he said, "is it because you think - as the papers say - that I can assist you in your inquiries?"

Anticipating the Detective's answer to be affirmative, the suspect asked: "Am I to regard myself as being in police custody?"

Detective-Superintendent Johns sniffed his annoyance and said: "You were invited to come here to answer my questions! The suspect was very cool. "Invited, you say!" What would have happened to me if I hadn't accepted the invitation?" he asked. Mr. Johns knew the answer, but he didn't think it necessary to express it; for he thought that the suspect knew the answer before he asked the question.

The suspect made another note in his diary.

It will be appreciated, I think, that interrogation of suspects in accordance with the Judges' Rules, 1964, has its difficulties.

What can be done to render the Judges' Rules less burdensome to the Police? A simple amendment, it seems.

Could there possibly be any unfairness in requiring a suspect to acknowledge having been given the opportunity to state his whereabouts at the time the alleged crime was believed to have been committed; that such opportunity was given him when he was being interviewed with regard to the offence at the actual time that interrogation was in progress. Or if refusal - in certain circumstances - was regarded by law as supporting evidence on behalf of the prosecution or as rebutting any evidence on behalf of the defence?

Such an amendment, however, would be efficacious where an alibi had not been rigged beforehand. But, owing to the fact that criminals make mistakes occasionally, amendment would be worthwhile.

*   *   *

FOOTNOTE

<u>Early production of a Policeman's notebook.</u>

During my long experience as a Policeman
I have had cause to question the wisdom of
a Detective who, when talking to a suspect,
produced his pocket-book too early.   Somehow
or other it has seemed to turn a human being
into an oyster.   Circumstances alter cases,
of course, but it is wiser, I think, to wait
a bit before creating a feeling of nervousness
in a person.

XVII

Changes in Types of Crime

Since I left the police service, there have been
changes in the types of crime committed, and it appears
that Highway Robbery has become vogue once more, to
test its efficacy as a means of defeating the police
in the War against Crime.

And when one reads of the many crimes of this nature
and of the apparent ease in which they have been committed
without hindrance, one wonders whether those whose job
it is to investigate them, are doing their utmost to
catch the culprits.   But people are permitted to criticise
any public service which seems to be failing in its task;
so when many crimes of the same kind are successfully
committed without detection, criticism of detectives is
fully justified.

On the other hand, people must appreciate that the
detection of criminals is by no means so easy as it is
made to appear on cinematograph and television screens.
Most adults realise this fact, but they know, too, that
many detections result from 'information received'; and
such people can be excused if they wonder what's gone
wrong with the Nark system.

But today criminals are getting wiser.   They are
getting more violent too, and would-be 'grasses' or
informants know what it means to them and theirs if they
pass on information to a detective or any other person.

Hi-jacking, and most other serious crimes, are
seldom committed on the spur of the moment, but only
after much thought and deliberation; except of course,
when there is collusion between individuals in charge
of the vehicle which is to be 'held up' and those who
are to do the 'holding up'.

Ironically and disturbing is the fact that professional
criminals have been alerted by the efficiency of the
police wireless communications system.   They are quick
to learn, and they know how dangerous it is for them if

they stick to the road for any length of time after committing a crime. So they naturally act in a manner calculated to render the police communications system abortive. And, judging from what has been happening in London, its environs and other parts of the country, in the form of hi-jacking, raids on banks, etc., there is distinct and unchallengeable evidence, that the criminal fraternity have been very successful in making a 'Getaway'.

In recent years, it has become increasingly apparent that much futile and unrewarding work is being performed by the police.

The much advertised 'putting up of road-blocks' is being treated as a joke by criminals who always take that hazard into consideration when organising their crimes.

THE GREAT TRAIN ROBBERY, OF AUGUST, 1963

This was the first occasion on which a crime of this nature had been committed in Britain. It took place in the county of Buckinghamshire. And all people who have read about it, must have realised how definite and precise the plan of action must have been prepared and adhered to, right up to the time at which the train was brought to a halt. But immediately after that moment, mistakes began to be made by the thugs actually at the scene. First of all, the driver of the train was set upon and seriously assaulted, and threats were made indicating things likely to happen to the driver and his mate in certain circumstances. But one of the criminals 'requested' that no alarm should be raised within half-an-hour of their leaving the spot. This request might have provided a Clue to the belief - by the police - that within that short period of time, the stolen money would be dumped or transhipped at a place within a few miles from the scene of the crime. Apparently, however, the police didn't regard the thugs' request as a clue of significance.

'Time' is very important to the criminals, and the place at which the train had been stopped was an isolated one, carefully selected by the Organisers of the coup, to ensure that the police would take some Time to get to the spot. Yet, experienced as the organisers undoubtedly were, there were 'slips' of various kinds, which they had not foreseen, and which brought about the early arrest of some of the criminals concerned in it; and this fact gave the impression that

the police were ahead of those responsible for organising
what has been described as the most diabolical robbery
of all time. But, unfortunately for the police, that
impression was false; for those particular arrests came
about because of the gross carelessness of the criminals
themselves, in attempting to obtain accommodation at
Bournemouth, by offering terms which seemed so excessive
for men of their type, and which created suspicion
against themselves, during the Hue and Cry. Further, the
arrest of at least one of the other culprits, came about
from the negligence of those whose job it was to scour
the dishes used in the meals served to the gangsters, at
the farmhouse which they had taken for their headquarters,
a short distance from the scene of the crime, where the
share-out of the spoils was to take place. But this
evidence did not become available until the gang's
hiding-place had been discovered by a farm worker, some
days after the crime had been committed. And it came
to light, probably during an examination and identity of
finger impressions on the aforesaid dishes or utensils,
seized by the police at the farmhouse, a considerable
time after the gangsters had taken flight. The farmhand
who discovered the gangsters hiding-place, rightly
deserved a substantial reward.

The actual organisers of this outrageous crime, in
which £2,500,000 was stolen, contributed to its partial
failure, by under-estimating the intelligence and
wakefulness of country folk.

Five years later, in August, 1968, a former Head of
the Metropolitan Police C.I.D. - though he had never
been a detective or a member of the police service -
Sir Ronald Howe, wrote to The Times expressing his
opinion, that owing to the urgent need to deal effectively
with criminals (there had been several cases of hi-jacking
in London, in which no arrests had been made) a National
C.I.D. should be formed by joining all detectives of all
police forces in the country together under One Head
with authority to employ his own methods without question.
His article: "MY WAY TO FIGHT THE GANGSTERS" was amusing
to me, as it probably was to many others with police
experience. He declared with emphasis, "That had there
been a National C.I.D., in August, 1963, at the time of
The Great Train Robbery, hundreds of detectives would
have been sent to the scene without delay, and the result
would have meant the instant arrest of the gangsters and
the recovery of £2½ millions". How splendid for the
reputation of the police this success would have meant;
and what a pity it is that Sir Ronald was a retired civil

servant, at the time of The Great Train Robbery?   But
one must not be satirical about such a great idea.   For
IF the robbers had been 'given away' or 'grassed' by an
informer, the Buckinghamshire Constabulary could have
arranged for a Special Reception Committee to welcome
them with open arms.   And, what is a matter of great
importance - if the police had done their duty in 'the
prevention of crime' - this terrible 'first time in Britain
crime' would not have been greater than an 'attempt to
steal' or one of 'loitering with intent to commit a
felony'.   There wouldn't have been an assault on the
driver of the train, nor would there have been any cause
for Sir Ronald to worry about the necessity to form a
National C.I.D. or where such an organisation should
have its headquarters; nor would the taxpayer have been
forced to find expensive accommodation for the robbers,
for any great length of time.   Though there may be
other IFS, I will refrain from suggesting them.   But it
is certain that hundreds of detectives at the scene of
one crime would have required a field ambulance and
staff to deal with casualties caused by detectives
falling over one another.

A National C.I.D. could not possibly have done any
better than was done at the time of The Great Train
Robbery in the circumstances existing at the time.
A mere Change of Name would not have brought with it,
the slightest chance of greater success in dealing with
any crime of a type which had never before been attempted
in this country; nor would the fact that such an
organisation would be under One Head with special power
to act as he pleased, have made any difference, for
IF tradition were followed, he would be a civil servant,
a Home Office Official, and just a Figurehead, who
would appoint Deputy and Assistant C.O.'s to carry the
burden (if any); a procedure, which is known in the
police service as 'Passing the Buck'.

Where would Sir Ronald Howe and his fellow believers
in the need for a national C.I.D. have its headquarters?
Would they be satisfied with one in London, or would
they prescribe eight (one for each region, too)?   But
wherever located, it would require time to get into
action.   In my experience, criminals of all classes never
wait to be picked up by the police, and it is very seldom
that 'they leave their card', for they are getting cleverer
and cleverer day by day.   Besides, in order to be ready
for any contingency, a number of active detectives would
be required to stand-by, at all times of the day and night.
Crimes like the Great Train Robbery will not happen very

often, and any police officer who has done any 'stand-by duty', knows its snags. There would be long periods of forced idleness amounting to boredom, which would inevitably cause sluggishness and lethargy, two of the worst ailments detectives can suffer.

The Buckinghamshire Constabulary acted well in The Great Train Robbery and did all they were allowed to do.

When one gives sober thought to the question of detection of criminals and bringing them to justice, it must be appreciated that outside Fiction, there is not a single detective in this planet, or any other for that matter, who possesses a sixth sense enabling him to say, as Sherlock Holmes and Sexton Blake were allegedly able to say, who had committed a particular type of crime, by discovering a clue of a kind so rare, that made it impossible for a professional detective to recognise or follow. But it is a fact that any trained detective, in any part of the Globe, can have a 'hunch' that certain individuals could have been concerned in a crime of a particular nature. I have known such a hunch to materialise, and give pleasure to the detective who had it and followed it.

XVIII

The War against Crime

The War against Crime and Criminals is interminable,
and although all sorts of suggestions have been acted
upon with a view to reducing it and to bring the Criminal
Fraternity to the path of virtue, no success can be
anticipated.

Theorists and Criminologists have been consulted
with respect to these very serious matters, but to no
avail.   Let's face these problems and ask ourselves
to explain the causes of Crime and give a reason.

As one who has had the opportunity of studying the
ways of criminals, the answer is really a simple matter!
Greed accompanied by work-shyness, plus the receipt of
leniency from the Courts when dealing with them.

There is no cause for serious crime today.   And it
is serious crime of which I am writing.   Leniency to
first offenders in cases of petty larceny is essential,
but young offenders should not be treated by being
patted on the back and told - in too kindly a voice -
that they are forgiven.   It is much better, I think,
to tell them that by having acted as they did they had
let down their parents, themselves and their school.
Too much kind talk does more harm than good.   If male
delinquents are nearing school-leaving age, it has been
found quite a worthwhile deterrent to point out that
other boys who have behaved themselves would stand a
better chance of getting a good job than boys who steal
or do damage to property.

But leniency shown time after time to persistent and
hardened criminals is futile.   In actual fact it
encourages crime.

Some well-meaning psychiatrists have suggested that
the treatment of criminals should be of a nature likely
to cure, instead of punish.   How simple it is to
express such an opinion, and how splendid it would be
for society if 'kindness' could be relied upon as a

remedy.   But when administered to criminals upon whom
it has been absolutely ineffective, great expectations
of Reform are most disappointing.   In prison circles,
the psychiatrist who gives advice to 'old lags', is
regarded by them to be wasting his time.   Prisoners
listen, but they have received good advice so often that
they have become immune to it.   In fact, such men have
escaped detection so often that they consider it worthwhile to continue in crime.   In fact, they are satisfied
that Crime pays.   All people must realise that no-one
is free of risk from crime or accident.   Such thoughts
as: 'It can't happen to me or mine' are absolutely
ridiculous.

I have become aware of detectives saying: "Such a
crime couldn't happen around here" or "the wanted men
won't come here or hereabouts".   Such remarks are 'hopes'
and only hopes; but detectives must have open minds, and
should keep their own counsel.   A good detective keeps
himself ready to cope with any sudden and unexpected
occurrence.

In reading of crimes published in the Press, it seems
that they are committed with such ease, and with so much
success, that readers must wonder whether or not those,
whose job it is to investigate them, give criminals
credit for the possession of brains.

ESPIONAGE, CASING THE JOINT

Professional criminals are progressive.   And there
can be little doubt that they make a study of police
methods, from the manner in which Beats are worked and
covered, to the ways of detectives for the purpose of
gaining information, which they consider likely to help
them in their investigations.   I have known 'scouts'
for criminals to sympathise with a constable during
inclement weather, for the sole purpose of finding out
the extent of his beat, and other details useful to
would-be thieves.   And criminals have been known to
give detectives a 'tip off' about a crime to be committed
in a certain district, when their intention was to do a
'job' in a different place.   Hi-jacking and similar
serious crimes in which criminals have been successful

in committing and getting away without hindrance,
suggests that the successful ones must possess and
act in accordance with an efficient Espionage System,
which enables them to carry out their felonious
activities with a minimal risk of detection.

And it is now obvious that Espionage is widespread
and so efficient that the utmost secrecy is absolutely
necessary whenever valuable goods and large sums of
money are in transit, for, as time passes, violation
of allegiance, or of faith and confidence has become
common if not usual.

Today criminals are given more chances to reform
than ever they were, but in the majority of cases they
treat such advice with contempt; they have listened
to good advice so often that they have become immune
to it.   In fact, criminals have escaped detection on
so many occasions, that they consider it worthwhile to
continue in crime, and have come to the conclusion
that they are entitled to regard themselves as members
of a legitimate profession, which offers them good
remuneration free from the attention of the Inland
Revenue Authority; and, if they have any conscience at
all, they find consolation in the knowledge that the
Exchequer would have no hesitation in taking its share
of their ill-gotten gains if it could be evaluated.
So, patting himself with pride, burglar Bill, like an
ordinary honest member of the community, thinks that a
Receiver is a worse criminal than the thief, and is not
beyond saying to himself: "If it weren't for the likes
of me, there'd be millions of unemployed!"   Like many
a decent bloke, Bill is very fond of himself.   Criminals
who think like Bill does, are satisfied that Crime 'does
pay'; and while they can keep free from the crippling
effects of Arthritis or other afflictions affecting
their mobility or alertness, they will carry on 'working',
and making a nuisance of themselves.   Many criminals -
of low degree - carry tattoo marks: "Death before
dishonour".

*　　*　　*

Most of the serious crimes against the State and
people of this country are committed in London and its
environs by criminals living within its boundaries; and
there is little doubt that much of the crime committed
in the provinces is the work of Londoners, who work and
act on 'information received' via the Espionage System

previously mentioned. I have had some experience of these criminals from 'The Smoke'. There is nothing special about them. I found the majority of them somewhat bumptious. On being questioned, the answers they gave were just as I expected, and gave me the impression that they regarded themselves as being too clever to be caught by country policemen. They were not really clever; their pretended knowledge of the law; their threats to sue and get damages, and other bluffs were too hot to deceive. I found that 'bringing them down to size' was quite a pleasure. Let me give you an example: Two Londoners came to Hanley, Stoke-on-Trent, and bought a load of china and earthenware from a pottery factor. They took the load from the factor's house and paid for it there. Their purchase was on behalf of two or three customers of theirs. They noticed that the money which they had paid was taken upstairs; and learned that the factor and his wife would be out for the evening. The Londoners drove away with their load ostensibly for London; but they had gone no further than Newcastle-under-Lyme, a nearby town where they had lodgings. They came back to the factor's house and stole the money which they had paid as well as other money, from a wardrobe. Coming under suspicion, they were interviewed at the Police Station. They took umbrage at being suspected of such a dirty trick. "Fantastic", they said, and were so emphatic in their remarks, that it became clear to me that their intention was to make us nervous. While they were at Hanley Police Station I sent a detective, Detective-Sergeant Godfrey, to their lodgings, to see whether any clue existed there. He returned and reported 'nothing doing' but he mentioned that their room was very untidy, and there was a lot of rubbish in the fireplace. I sent him back to get that 'rubbish'. It contained a most valuable clue, which, with other evidence, was sufficient to prove their guilt. At Quarter Sessions, they got 20 months imprisonment, and, later, the factor got his money back.

It is true that certain people find it amusing to read of crimes in which the criminals concerned get away. But I think that the majority of people are becoming alarmed and disturbed; and some have found cause to say harsh things which cast doubt on the efficiency of the Police service. Personally, I am of the opinion that there is not sufficient co-operation within the Police Service. In forces where the C.I.D. and the Uniform branch are regarded as entirely separate from each other,

having nothing in common, and where C.I.D. personnel
consider themselves as superior beings not requiring
help from those who wear uniform, there is not the
co-operation there should be.   The C.I.D. of any
Police Force cannot be entirely successful without
co-operation from other people.   And this fact is borne
out, especially in Murder cases, when C.I.D's ask for
assistance from the public, and where failure by
detectives is attributed to lack of such co-operation.
One would think that a detective should be pleased to
acknowledge the receipt of useful information from a
member of the Uniform Branch, some of them do this,
but there are others who prefer success on their part
to be regarded as a case of 'Alone, I did it'.

SMUDGES ON THE ESCUTCHEON

During the 1960's a great tragedy fell on the
reputation of the Metropolitan Police, as the result -
it seems - of lack of discipline and supervision.
Without going into the wretched details, which required
a full book to describe, a small number of Police Officers
of low rank who needed supervision by Officers of higher
rank, produced false Exhibits to corroborate their own
Perjury; a procedure resulting in the wrongful conviction
of a number of men and boys.   When the awful facts
became known, Members of Parliament immediately took
action and asked questions of the then Home Secretary
(Mr. Brooke) and demanded a public inquiry.   The Home
Secretary was sorely troubled, for many serious
allegations of false arrests, which had resulted in
wrongful conviction and imprisonment of innocent persons,
were made and substantiated.   And the affair became a
scandal so great, that it detrimentally affected the
reputation of the whole Police Service of Britain.
The Home Secretary considered it necessary to convene
two separate Inquiries.   The report of one Inquiry which
was made by a Detective-Superintendent of the Metropolitan
Police to the Director of Public Prosecutions (though
not made public) caused the prosecution of a Detective-
Sergeant and three Constables, the Sergeant's aides in
some of the cases in which he and they were alleged to
have been concerned.   The Detective-Sergeant was found
'Unfit to plead', but the Constables were found Guilty
and sent to prison.
In sentencing the Constables, the Trial-Judge said:
"Honest Police Officers are the buttress of society.
But dishonest, perjured officers are like an infernal

machine ticking away to the destruction of us all.
As intelligent young men you must appreciate that a
crime of this gravity must be punished, and the
punishment must be such as show the revulsion of this
Court at your conduct and to warn any other Police
Officer who might be misguided enough to do what you
did of the danger he is running".

The offence of Perjury - arising from The Lord's
Commandment 'Thou shalt not bear false witness .....'
- which is a misdemeanour under The Perjury Act, 1911,
is regarded by all honest Police Officers as a very
serious crime, as it undoubtedly is, rendering an
adult person who commits it, liable to a maximum
punishment of seven years' imprisonment.   But where
a perjurer produces false Exhibits (weapons, implements,
etc.), and states on Oath that they were found on the
person he accuses or when he 'turned out his pockets',
when in fact the perjurer had 'planted' the exhibit
to give 'colour' to his false testimony, the perjurer
should, I think, be regarded by the Law as a criminal
of the worst kind, and should be liable to a special
form of punishment which should be compulsorily
awarded.

In the interests of the Police Service, its reputation as a Public Service, and for the purpose of
pleading for better relations between Police Departments,
which I think would make for greater success in bringing
about an improvement in the percentage of detections,
so far as hi-jackers and other highway robbers are
concerned, I would recommend that more Police Officers
in uniform be seen on the streets of our cities and
towns, and villages in which various industries are
carried on.

Members of the community - except of course, those
who prey on the public dishonestly - like to see Police
Officers in uniform; the sight of such Officers and
their availability, gives them confidence.   The public
miss the welcome sight of Sergeants and Inspectors
giving supervision and assistance to Constables on the
Beat.   Such Officers are still policemen.   Their
promotion did not indicate that their 'Bobbying days'
were over.   Promotion meant, in fact, they were
entrusted with and expected to carry out the important
and necessary duty of giving proper and adequate supervision.

Please permit me to say, once more, Police Forces
can be too large, and can have jurisdiction over too
wide an area, for the maintenance of supervision and

appropriate discipline. The bigger the Police Force, or any other organisation of personnel for that matter, the bigger is the risk of attracting to it a number of undesirable persons, whose acts or omissions would be likely to contribute to the number of complaints and/or allegations made and received, with such frequency, that public confidence would deteriorate.

The most unfortunate cases in which Police Officers have been convicted of crime, the cause could be traced - almost invariably - to lack of supervision in one form or another.

During my long Police career, there have been many cases in which persons on trial for serious crimes have complained of having various implements, keys, weapons, etc., placed in their personal belongings so as to provide evidence against them when charged with an offence which they hadn't committed.

Like many other people, I used to think that such allegations as 'the tales of old lags' just as Judges did at the Old Bailey and other Courts in London, who preferred to believe that Police Officers were incapable of such dastardly behaviour as that alleged by prisoners with a record of previous convictions against them.

As it has been firmly established that 'planting' of evidence is performed by a certain type of Police Officer with intent to obtain the conviction of an innocent person, all law-abiding people will hope that Judges, Magistrates and others whose duty it is to dispense Justice, will give mind to the possibility that a prisoner's allegation <u>could be true.</u>

What is it that tempts an unscrupulous police witness to commit Perjury? There could be one or more reasons.

1. To make an unlawful arrest appear to be justifiable;
2. To curry favour as one who is keen on showing that he is doing his duty when, in fact, he is exceeding it;
3. To obtain 'commendation' leading to promotion.

Perjury defined:-

Perjury is committed by any person who, being lawfully sworn as a witness or as an interpreter in a judicial proceeding wilfully makes a statement material to that proceeding, which he knows to be false or does not believe to be true.

What is a Judicial Proceeding?

> Judicial proceedings include proceedings before any Court, Tribunal, or person having by Law power to hear, receive and examine evidence <u>on oath</u> and also where a statement made for the purpose of a judicial proceeding is not made before the tribunal itself, but is made <u>on oath</u> before a person authorised by Law to administer an oath to the person who makes the statement.

The seriousness of perjured evidence will be realised when people recognise the fact that, if accepted by a Court as being true, it could result in an innocent person being convicted of <u>any</u> crime in the Criminal Calendar. And, such being the case, it will be appreciated that the words spoken by the Trial-Judge in sentencing the Constables were necessary and appropriate.

The shame, is, that the reputation of the entire Police Service, was seriously injured.

The second Inquiry convened by the Home Secretary was for the purpose of investigating complaints made by persons who alleged that Officers in the Birmingham City Police Force had 'planted' evidence against them and that they had been convicted on perjured evidence.

The allegations were investigated, but the result was not published.

Why was it that neither of these important reports was published? Many questions have been asked and numerous guesses made. Rumour has it that Mr."Whitewash" was involved. But nobody knows his address. Besides, rumour is an inveterate liar on most occasions.

Can Crime and Criminals be Curbed by Computer?

It would be most encouraging and refreshing to law-abiding citizens if the installation of a Computer - no matter how costly - would or could possibly result in a curb on crime and professional criminals.

At first sight, the Computer, known to be of great utility in certain circumstances, gives hope that great expectations could materialise from its use; but upon giving thought and consideration to the machine and its capabilities, some doubts are bound to appear to those people who are aware of its requirements before it could act as an 'Informer' upon which reliance could be placed. They know that it must first be fed, and will wonder what it must be 'told' in order to be of use to the

Police Service as an offensive and Legal weapon in preventing, detecting and investigating crimes.

Without infringing the 'Official Secrets Act', I could disclose the 'bill of fare' necessary to give such a machine a satisfactory meal and cause it to belch; but I think it would be imprudent on my part to 'grass'.

Many Police Officers, ex-police Officers and others - including professional criminals, will be wondering who will be held responsible for 'feeding the beast' and keeping it up to date.

On television, on the night we were told that the computer was on its way to London, and that it wouldn't be long before it would be helping the 'man on the beat' to catch the motor-car thief and criminals in such vehicles, we, the public felt that routine had changed; for quite recently we were told from the same source, that the number of motor vehicles stolen in London each day had reached such proportions, that it had been decided by Scotland Yard, that the registration particulars would not be passed to men on the beat.

The gentleman giving the news of the coming of the computer said, in answering a question, that if a Constable had cause to think that a certain motor car had been stolen, all he had to do was to ring-up to where the computer was kept, and he would be told. How marvellous! How simple! The man at the computer, be he Civil Servant or Police Officer - would have to be an angel in order to refrain from saying rude words to each of the hundreds of disturbers of his peace.

When it is appreciated that most of the information relating to any particular member of the criminal fraternity has been available ever since the various types of telephone came into existence, people are entitled to doubt the efficacy of a computer for this particular purpose, and the wisdom in spending so much money on its purchase. Personally, I think somebody has been pulling somebody's leg.

Only Theorists who have never been real and practical Police Officers or who have never had actual experience in making inquiries and performing the actual work of investigating crime; or those who have never been called to give evidence in a Quarter Sessional Court or an Assize Court, or have not had to learn the Rules of Evidence, or have never been subjected to keen cross-examination, would imagine that a computer could possibly be of use in the much desired reduction, prevention, and detection of crime, or bringing criminals to justice.

One supposes that to 'Scotland Yard' - whoever or whatever is meant by those words - which is merely the headquarters of the Metropolitan Police, will be attributed the source of the idea to install the computer as an Informer or a 'coppers nark' in the fight against crime and criminals. But, if the right to express one's opinion or to ask a question is accepted, I think that to attribute blame for spending money unnecessarily or so dubiously, would be to insult the intelligence of any Detective working in London or elsewhere. The blame, if any, must be borne by the person or persons responsible for the error; a Civil Servant, it seems.

I wonder who will launch 'S.Y. Computer'? Courtesy suggests that the instrument should be regarded as feminine. So all law-abiding citizens will wish her success in the work she will be expected to do. If I were asked to suggest appropriate material and words at such an important function - I am not expecting an invitation - I would recommend Ginger Beer as the launching liquid, and the words: "I name this Vessel 'Computer', may she be successful in all she is asked to do against all professional criminals; may those who feed her be blessed, and may she never suffer the pangs of indigestion".

Having criticised certain of the efforts said to have been made for the purpose of placing a curb on criminals, I, in lighter vein, will tell you how incensed were men who had been convicted many times when, on re-conviction if they were not credited with the correct number of stars recording the number of convictions.

The stars were worn on the cap they wore. Five convictions entitled the convict to wear a star for each; so if his cap did not bear that number of stars, he would want to know the reason why.

Whether the convicts received special concessions according to the number of stars they wore, I do not know, but it is possible.

In the first decade of the 20th century, I heard a Comedian - dressed as Convict 99 - sing:-

> "I'm as 'appy as a dickie bird, singing
>   in the old oak tree,
> No more moochin' for me breakfast or me tea,
> No more payin' any rent, no more naggin'
>   from the wife,
> I've been 'ere a month, and I'm stayin' for
>   a year,
> I've never 'ad sich lodgins in me life".

Conditions in the 'Nicks' in those days were not so good as they are in these days of leniency and the Welfare State. Yet there are 'do gooders' who would recommend 'kindness' as a cure for hardened criminals.

Many dependents of convicts today, are much better off when the 'bread-winner' is in prison than when he is at home.

XIX

Keeping the Watch

Most people are aware that in all organisations, especially those in which the community is entitled to rely upon for efficiency and the maintenance of repute, there are occasions on which it is imperative that a Watch be kept in order to avert or prevent, prove or disprove, any suspicion or rumour which might appear detrimental to its character, unless properly investigated.

Speaking from my personal experiences over a period of twenty-five years as a chief constable of three separate provincial police forces and from my observations carefully and diligently kept during my retirement, it has become obvious to me, and probably to other members and ex-members of the police service, that a very particular pattern or design has been in process of being woven, at the instigation of a carefully selected number of persons within the 'Inner Circle', who, unfortunately, consider themselves to be the elite of the police service of Britain.

Needless to say, the rank and file of the service are not implicated.

To come straight to the point, I state without the slightest fear that the scheme of things is to make sure that the higher and highest ranks in the police service are filled by members of the 'Inner Circle' and nobody else.

The 'beauty of the scheme, pattern or design' being the fact that the 'Climbing of the Tree' is obviated. The performance of <u>actual police work</u> - such as working the Beat, making awkward inquiries, keeping a lookout for criminals, plus the 'nuisance' of having to appear in court to give Evidence or to undergo cross-examination, being considered <u>infra dig</u>.

This statement I am prepared to substantiate at any time, and at any Independent Inquiry, if there should be any doubt about its veracity.

The Watch must be kept! Figureheads are obsolete, their rightful place is in Limbo.

There must be many thousands of people now living, who have been forced to bear the burden thrust upon them by that bugbear Frustration; an obstacle made more burdensome because of its irremovability. So, being aware of the obstacle to the rank and file of the police service, those of the 'Inner Circle' have passed the 'sop to Cerberus' by creating phoney appointments, designations, etc., to pacify the lovers of fair play and justice in the police service, who, by force of circumstances, would be bound to feel the dreadful frustration by having to mark time instead of advancing 'by the right'.

In days of yore, and in my time when police officers were dedicated to their work as such in the prevention and detection of Crime and were struggling in a fair and legitimate manner for advancement, chief constables of Cities and Boroughs were known as the Players while the chief constables of Counties were known as the Gentlemen.

The County chief constables were considered, by themselves, as far superior to the chief constables of Cities and Towns. County chief constables had a Club in London. It was a Sanctum to which no chief constable of a City or Borough was ever allowed to become a member. So none of them ever tried. This state of affairs was, of course, before the word: 'APARTHEID' was coined. We Players merely shrugged our shoulders, and put it down to snobbishness practised by 'gentlemen'.

In those days, chief constables of Cities and Borough police forces were - almost without exception - police officers who had joined the police service as constables, many after serving in H.M. Forces. They.entered into competition with officers from other police forces, and in the majority of cases obtained their appointments by possessing better - and certificated - qualifications than their competitors. And in this way were compelled to 'climb the tree' a right and proper essential. And for the purpose of encouraging personnel to increase efficiency and fitness to hold higher rank in the police service it is surely imperative that police officers holding high rank have high police qualifications and the necessary courage and ability to carry the 'responsibleness' attached to their rank.

My chief fear arising from the possibility of a national police force and/or a national detective force materialising, is the very probable admission of persons - into either of the services - who would be 'Ineffectives', 'Figureheads' or 'Sinecurists', whose sole object would be to hold a 'jobless' appointment in which responsibleness and work is 'put out', for others to take and perform.

There is nothing more certain than the fact that a great increase in all kinds of Crime would follow the nationalisation of the police service. Crime would be regarded as one of those things to be endured whether we liked it or not.

In 1970, we hear that Criminologists are to be consulted in order that something can be done to reduce crime. What - for goodness sake - is a Criminologist? I find the question difficult to answer. Perhaps he or she who reads and talks of crimes and criminals. A good dictionary tells us that a criminologist is one 'who studies the science of crime'. Our prisons must be full of 'em. But it may well be that the criminologist is the student who arranges the crime and dodges the consequences. The posting of a number of 'Criminologists' to a nationalised police service would cause little surprise to police officers and ex-police officers who have taken interest in the changes which have been and are being made in police circles by the people being allowed to 'run the show'.

In recent times there have been suggestions in the Press throughout the country, that Panels of people - specially selected and presided over by local superintendents of police - should be formed for the purpose of passing along information considered useful to the police service in its very important and difficult work in reducing crime.

At last, it seems, that it is being admitted that without assistance from members of the community the police, - including detectives - no matter to which police force they belong, are almost entirely powerless combatants in the battle against professional criminals.

Exception has been taken by sensible and far-seeing people, who, though seeing the urgent need for a continuous reduction in crime, appreciate the dangers and risks likely to arise from the creation of QUISLINGS.

The suggestion respecting the formation of the Panels came from London, and when the suggestion reached the provinces, it appeared, not as a Request, but as a kind of Command, given in the shape of News.

Actually, I am aware of the identity of the person in London from whom the suggestion respecting the formation of the Panels came.

It is significant, to say the least, I think, that the modus operandi followed by professional criminals both in London and the provinces, so far as hi-jacking and raids on banks are concerned, is identical. And, also significant, is the fact that the Uniform Branch of

the Police Service in the Provinces, has, since the
re-organisation of the Police commenced in 1967, been
deployed in a manner similar to that in vogue in
London, where the Uniform Branch is expected to regard
crime and its detection as matters which it should
treat with 'Masterly Inactivity'.

While 'Masterly Inactivity' by the Uniform Branch
is essential in cases of Murder and Espionage, and other
serious crimes against the State in which Secrecy <u>must
be</u> IMPENETRABLE; I am of the opinion that a serious
mistake is made when uniformed Police Officers are
encouraged to believe that the detection of ALL CRIMINALS,
including hi-jackers, bank raiders and the like, is no
concern of theirs.   This attitude is clearly WRONG!
It is not conducive to a Constable's regard for devotion
to duty, nor to the rights of the law-abiding community
to his protection.

There can be no doubt that the presence of Police
Officers in uniform on the highways and by-ways prevents
numerous offences, especially among juveniles.   And I
have no cause to hesitate in mentioning the fact that
'do gooders' and others at large, who have been and still
are responsible for the absence of personnel of the
Uniform Branch on the streets, are also responsible for
the increase in Juvenile Delinquency and Vandalism.   But
it would be a mistake to think that all vandalism is
committed by juveniles.

I don't get out much these days, but I am continually
being asked: "Where, except at places where crowds
collect, are 'coppers' to be found these days?"   I am
not at all surprised by the question, but I am getting
rather tired of its necessity, for I know that there is
no shortage of Policemen in the district in which I am
living!

Why should I be asked what is going on in the Police
Service today, when fifteen years have passed since my
retirement?   Perhaps it is because some friends and
acquaintances of mine are so alarmed at what is happening
nowadays, that they consider me responsible and that I
should be required to give them a satisfactory explanation.

With the greatest respect to all people who advocate
the necessity for a National Police Service for Britain,
and acknowledging their undoubted right to express their
opinion on such an important matter, I am wondering
whether or not their main reason for their belief in the
desirability is in order to prevent that which is known
to be rife in other countries, namely, Bribery and
Corruption, brought about by collusion between profes-

sional criminals and unscrupulous Police Officers.

If the main reason is to prevent such crimes, it is most laudable; but whether prevention would materialise is extremely difficult if not impossible.

These crimes are extraordinarily difficult to prevent or prove. And the existence of this fact cannot be better appreciated than by the offenders themselves.

That there is collusion between unscrupulous Police Officers and criminals in London, the Hot-bed of crime, is not denied. In fact, its existence has been admitted by high-ranking Police Officers in Television programmes, seen by millions of people.

And the Commissioner of Police of the Metropolis since 1968, has made it clear that he is aware of such collusion and he has told the Press that he is giving strict attention to the matter.

But he knows the difficulties ahead of him. Circumstances being as they are, and the Law respecting such crimes, and the weight of evidence required to prove Guilt, being as it stands today, it would appear that a special new Law is necessary; such as a Court Martial procedure provides.

It may well be, of course, that a Court Martial System already exists in the Metropolitan Police Force and that it has existed for many years. If such is the case, it would explain why prosecutions are rare.

It must be obvious that the larger an organisation becomes, the more likely it becomes liable to embrace a larger number of undesirable persons within itself.

No matter how strongly a community wishes for Perfection, it must be regarded as unattainable. And the wider an area covered by the organisation happens to be, the greater must be the amount of supervision given in order to reduce irregularities of any kind to the minimum.

Would it not therefore be better to confine a particularly detrimental or noxious irregularity to one district, rather than spread it Nation-wide? Surely a malady confined to a small area is easier to control or arrest than when it becomes an Epidemic.

Known for a long time is the fact that a 'decontamination' squad has existed for the purpose of keeping watch for traces of collusion between criminals and unscrupulous Police Officers. And it must be appreciated that such a squad is, and has been, necessary.

Commonsense dictates, I imagine, that a national Police Service would require a much greater amount of supervision than was necessary before 'Re-organisation' commenced.

Personally, I have no doubt that in the event of a
National Police Force or National Detective Force
coming into being, the Police Service would be Devalued
and that its reputation would deteriorate.   Am I not
entitled to express an opinion?

I have every faith in the rank and file of the Police
Service if they have been properly 'screened' before
acceptance as to their antecedent history.   It is the
so-called 'Leaders' of whom I feel dubiousness.

As an elderly person who has never for a moment
considered himself 'on the scrap-heap', but rather as
one who has tried to uphold the good reputation and
deserved status of the Police Service, I feel that the
reinstatement of Britain's Police Forces and Police
Authorities to the position in which they stood in 1966,
is necessary, and would restore Public confidence.

And, judging from 'information received' and things
which I have seen, greater <u>contentment</u> would be felt by
the rank and file of the entire Police Service than had
ever existed since the Bow-street Runners went out of
existence, in 1829; if steps are taken to ensure that
all appointments in the Police Service of and above the
rank of Chief-Inspector shall be filled by <u>*Police Officers</u>
of proved ability as such, over a reasonable period in
which they have displayed devotion to duty in the
varying phases of police work and administration; and
they should have shown their possession of experience
enabling them to 'Lead by Example'.

* Note: The words 'Police Officers' are necessary
          because high rank in the Police Service in
          London have been known to be given to men straight
          from Civil Life and to ex-Army Officers who
          have had no Police experience.

Before bringing this book to a close, I feel it
incumbent upon myself to say that if any re-organisation
of the Police is necessary, it is certainly Not needed
in the Provincial Forces, as much as it is in London.

And it is with the greatest respect to the highest
Authority in Whitehall - whoever it be - that I submit
for his consideration the suggestion that any official
described as being or who is actually appointed to carry
responsibility for the good conduct of the Police Service
or of any Police Force within it, should be regarded as
answerable to or subordinate to a known Authority; and

he should be held to the terms of his Office, and know the consequence of failure.

GOD SAVE THE QUEEN